DIVINE AND POETIC FREEDOM

IN THE RENAISSANCE

DIVINE AND POETIC FREEDOM IN THE RENAISSANCE

NOMINALIST THEOLOGY AND LITERATURE IN FRANCE AND ITALY

Ullrich Langer

PRINCETON UNIVERSITY PRESS

PRINCETON, NEW JERSEY

PUBLISHED BY PRINCETON UNIVERSITY PRESS, 41 WILLIAM STREET,
PRINCETON, NEW JERSEY 08540
IN THE UNITED KINGDOM: PRINCETON UNIVERSITY PRESS, OXFORD

LIBRARY OF CONGRESS CATALOGING-IN-PUBLICATION DATA

LANGER, ULLRICH.

DIVINE AND POETIC FREEDOM IN THE RENAISSANCE : NOMINALIST THEOLOGY
AND LITERATURE IN FRANCE AND ITALY / ULLRICH LANGER.

P. CM.

INCLUDES BIBLIOGRAPHICAL REFERENCES.

ISBN 0-691-06853-4 (ALK. PAPER)

1. FRENCH LITERATURE—16TH CENTURY—HISTORY AND CRITICISM.

2. ITALIAN LITERATURE—16TH CENTURY—HISTORY AND CRITICISM.

3. ITALIAN LITERATURE—15TH CENTURY—HISTORY AND CRITICISM.

4. FRENCH LITERATURE—TO 1500—HISTORY AND CRITICISM. 5. FREE WILL
AND DETERMINISM IN LITERATURE. 6. FRANCE—INTELLECTUAL LIFE—16TH
CENTURY. 7. ITALY—INTELLECTUAL LIFE—1268–1559. 8. NOMINALISM IN
LITERATURE. 9. THEOLOGY IN LITERATURE. 10. RENAISSANCE.

I. TITLE.

PQ239.L36   1990   840.9'003—DC20   90-31203

THIS BOOK HAS BEEN COMPOSED IN LINOTRON GALLIARD

PRINCETON UNIVERSITY PRESS BOOKS ARE PRINTED
ON ACID-FREE PAPER, AND MEET THE GUIDELINES FOR
PERMANENCE AND DURABILITY OF THE COMMITTEE ON
PRODUCTION GUIDELINES FOR BOOK LONGEVITY
OF THE COUNCIL ON LIBRARY RESOURCES

PRINTED IN THE UNITED STATES OF AMERICA BY
PRINCETON UNIVERSITY PRESS, PRINCETON, NEW JERSEY

1   3   5   7   9   10   8   6   4   2

For Susan

CONTENTS

ACKNOWLEDGMENTS

THIS BOOK would not have been possible without the excellent scholarship of recent and contemporary intellectual and religious historians of the European Middle Ages and Renaissance who have been providing modern critical editions of scholastic philosophy and theology, and who have thus rendered these precious sources more accessible to readers such as myself. My bibliography is insufficient witness to their labors. I am further indebted to the National Endowment for the Humanities for a summer stipend that launched me into the study of scholastic theology, and to the American Council of Learned Societies and the Institute for Research in the Humanities at the University of Wisconsin, Madison, for financial support that allowed me to devote a full year to the writing of the book. The Graduate School Research Committee at the University of Wisconsin was also generous in supporting summer research and research travel, especially to the Bibliothèque nationale in Paris and the Newberry Library in Chicago. The first two chapters of the book have appeared in shorter form in *MLN* 102 (1987, Italian Issue): 55–75, and *Renaissance Quarterly* 41 (1988): 218–41, respectively. I am grateful to Johns Hopkins University Press and the Renaissance Society of America for permission to reprint these articles here. Various friends and colleagues have given their time, either through invaluable advice or through readings and comments on many parts of the manuscript. In particular, I wish to thank Albert Russell Ascoli, François Cornilliat, William J. Courtenay, Susan J. Erickson, George Hoffmann, C. Stephen Jaeger, Douglas Kelly, William Klein, Christopher Kleinhenz, Jan Miernowski, David Quint, Robert J. Rodini, Marian Rothstein, Joshua Scodel, and Jane Tylus. John B. Dillon and John A. Tedeschi of the University of Wisconsin Memorial Library have been equally helpful. Any errors and infelicities that remain are entirely of my own doing. Finally, my thanks go also to two anonymous readers and to editor Robert E. Brown and Annette Theuring of Princeton University Press.

DIVINE AND POETIC FREEDOM

IN THE RENAISSANCE

INTRODUCTION

MAN is conceived as possibility without limits, as opening without confines." Thus Eugenio Garin characterizes the new sense of man's value and power in the Italian Renaissance.[1] If Garin's words are most appropriately used to illuminate Florentine thought of the late fifteenth century, the idea of limits and its complement, freedom from limits, are immensely productive in understanding some basic impulses of the French and Italian Renaissance in general. My study is a meditation on constraint, and on "absoluteness," in the sense of "being absolved of," or "being prior to," in French and Italian literature of the sixteenth century. This meditation is not grounded in Florentine Neoplatonism and hermeticism—a traditional departure point for studies of Renaissance literature and philosophy—but instead proceeds through a terrain that has been relatively unexplored by literary critics, namely, late scholastic, nominalist theology.[2] I will return often to the reasons for this choice; it will become apparent that the use of nominalist theological distinctions allows for readings of literary texts that focus on what we tend to find "modern" in this literature. In this sense mine is a heuristic as well as a historical thesis, and I believe it derives its strength from that interplay. Late scholasticism was in fact a remarkably rich and productive tradition parallel to humanism; it contained the most systematic reflection on the relationship between a free God and a free creature. The late scholastics' investment in God's absolute priority lays a conceptual groundwork for the

[1] "[L]'uomo [è] concepito come possibilità senza limiti, come apertura senza confini" (Eugenio Garin, *La cultura filosofica del rinascimento italiano* [Florence: Sansoni, 1961; repr. 1979], p. 137), referring especially to Giannozzo Manetti, Giovanni Pico della Mirandola, and Marsilio Ficino. Although the philosophical basis is not comparably worked out, Jacob Burckhardt's political and cultural analysis of the Italian city-states affirms a similar value and definition of the "individual," in *The Civilization of the Renaissance in Italy*, trans. S.G.C. Middlemore, 2 vols. (New York: Harper and Row, 1958), 1:143–74. Singularization and lack of inherent constraints to behavior go hand in hand.

[2] For a general orientation in the relationship between humanism and scholasticism, I am indebted to the work of Heiko A. Oberman, Charles Trinkaus, and Salvatore I. Camporeale. Throughout this introduction I will be referring to specific ways in which their studies of late scholasticism have been helpful. Although there has been some work in intellectual history linking humanist texts to scholastic problems, Renaissance literature has not been looked at systematically in this way. The most useful work in literary criticism has centered on Rabelais (Florence M. Weinberg, A. J. Krailsheimer, and the commentary of Etienne Gilson), although there has been a recent foray into Ockham and Montaigne, on the problem of universals, by Antoine Compagnon.

imagining of "absoluteness" in the human sphere. In many cases the late scholastics thought about God in a way specifically pertinent to literary texts, that is, to the imagining of worlds. This pertinence is usually not thematic or even topical. Rather, it is properly structural—that is, nominalist problems and distinctions help one understand premises of literary representation.

In the most interesting texts, the imagining of a fictional world involves the following problems, all of which arise in some form in nominalist theology. If the creator of a world is all-powerful, yet creates a world of contingency, how can contingency be represented? Is not the relationship between creator and creation a necessary one? How, in addition, is the reader's status defined within such a contingent created world? This is the subject of the first chapter. When the absolutely free God becomes the prince or the king, on what basis can the less powerful enter into a relationship with their sovereign? Can the less powerful be worthy of any reward from the absolutely powerful? The Renaissance court and its fictional representation is the subject of the second chapter. In the third chapter, the focus shifts to the author as creator, that is, as an absolute first cause. Late medieval conceptions of divine causality reaffirm the principle of divine causation, but the hierarchical chain of mediated causes and effects is undermined by the possibility of immediate causation by God, by his unforeseeable intervention. The affirmation of the author-creator, on the one hand, and the undoing of a temporal causal chain, on the other, are apparent as literary texts begin to authorize themselves in the Renaissance. The fourth chapter examines an aspect of this absolute authority in terms of will and decision: How do represented characters choose? The distinctions governing divine will are a model for the way in which literary characters come to a decision in the novels of Rabelais. Finally, the implicit analogy between a nominalist God and the secular sovereign is worked out in the fifth chapter, which contains the most extended discussion of "absoluteness" underlying the early modern understanding of sovereignty. What is the relationship between an entirely *prior* God, king, or poet, and the order that he[3] has set down? This relationship involves a promise or obligation

---

[3] Throughout this book, I have opted for the use of masculine pronouns referring to God, the poet, the reader, and so on. Similarly, I have chosen to use "man" as a generic term. The reason for this is simple. In the theological discussions, I have tried to stay as close as possible to the way in which medieval and Renaissance theologians and nontheologians would have talked about God. To use the pronoun "she" would imply that there is a God distinct from the kind of God these theologians talked about. Obviously I leave that question for the reader to answer. Other instances of masculine pronoun use, and of the generic "man" for "human beings," are for reasons of historical accuracy, for most authors, poets, and probably even readers were male, so the use of female pronouns would introduce a distinction not relevant to the historical argument. I beg the reader for her and his indulgence.

to oneself that is codified through gestures reenacted by the figure of the satiric poet. In the concluding analysis, Montaigne's essay on friendship demonstrates the self-binding of a sovereign self.[4]

The chapters contained in this book are concerned with different aspects of scholasticism, but they are all connected to each other by a common thread: the notion of God's absolute priority or freedom in late medieval nominalist theology. My literary concerns precede, of course, my forays into theology, and my analyses of literary texts occupy a privileged place in this study. This is, then, a double movement between the disciplines, with literature constituting both the *terminus a quo* and the *terminus ad quem*. However, the project of which this book represents one aspect needs more specific explaining, if not justifying. Several questions come to mind, at least for literary historians, concerning any study of nominalist theology and its relationship to Renaissance fiction. Briefly, they are the following:

—What is nominalist theology?
—Were not Renaissance writers hostile to scholastic theology? If so, how fruitfully can one speak of literature *and* scholasticism?
—What does it mean to analyze literature through the use of theological terms, especially when Renaissance literature usually does not treat theological issues?
—Finally, why should a literary critic pursue questions that assume a lack of boundaries between literature and other cultural discourses, such as theology? Should it not be the literary critic's task to demonstrate literature's specificity, its separate nature as an object of study?

Providing brief answers to these questions will serve to introduce the central problems of my study.

---

[4] Many of my literary analyses center on the radical contingency of the world represented through the literary text, and in this my interpretations come close to the interpretations of those who have taken a more purely literary approach. In particular I am thinking of the excellent work of David Quint. The notion of originality, as the historicization of literary authority, is relevant to the sort of problems I discuss throughout the book: as poet you do not begin *because of* something prior and greater, absolutely speaking; rather, you just begin, which means that what you produce has as its only order your own will to give it order. Commenting on Erasmus's *Praise of Folly*, Quint formulates this contingency: "When perceived from a strictly historicist viewpoint as the autonomous creation of human individuals, culture turns into a series of idols of the self. To be *original* in this context, the human creator is apt to set himself apart not only from the historically prior traditions of culture, but from an absolutely prior, authorizing origin" (*Origin and Originality in Renaissance Literature: Versions of the Source* [New Haven: Yale Univ. Press, 1983], p. 20). Rather than see this as a move *out* of the theological, as an alternative to the theological, I would argue that the theological, in its nominalist form, provides the basis for contingent creation.

Nominalist Theology?

We can first distinguish between "nominalism" and "nominalist theology." By "nominalism" one usually means one side of the debate over universals and particulars, namely, the position that universals are not actual entities in the real world in which individuals participate, but instead are names applied to similar objects by the human mind.[5] Although this debate may provide an interesting and useful subject for literary theory, and certainly preoccupied medieval philosophers, it is marginal to the issues I will be dealing with. These issues are more properly theological; they arise out of the late medieval discourse on God's power. Before I turn to them, however, there is another problem of definition.

My use of the term "nominalist theology" assumes a coherence of theological discourse from the fourteenth to the early sixteenth centuries. Unfortunately, such a coherence is far from given. Recent studies of the theology of the Middle Ages make this clear. In fact, the dominant tendency seems to be to emphasize the pluralism of doctrine and opinion found on the eve of the Reformation.[6] Not only is there reluctance on the part of many scholars to identify schools of theology, but one finds great disagreement about how to interpret central features and figures of late medieval thought itself. Since I will be concerned with some of those features in my own study, a brief explanatory digression seems appropriate.

Much has been made of the "nominalist" emphasis on the dialectic between the two aspects of God's power, absolute and ordained, referred to as *potentia dei absoluta* and *potentia dei ordinata*. This distinction is between all the possibilities open to God, absolutely and hypothetically speaking, and those that he has chosen (particularly in the order of creation and sal-

---

[5] See Meyrick Carré, *Nominalists and Realists* (Oxford: Oxford Univ. Press, 1946), for a brief summary of the medieval debate. For a study of Ockham's nominalist logic and literature (focusing exclusively on Montaigne's *Essais*), see Antoine Compagnon, *Nous, Michel de Montaigne* (Paris: Seuil, 1980). The debate over universals is also the point of departure for an analysis of "conjecture" in the writings of Nicholas Cusanus, as laying the basis for "creative action," in Ronald Levao, *Renaissance Minds and Their Fictions: Cusanus, Sidney, Shakespeare* (Berkeley: Univ. of California Press, 1985), pp. 57–66.

[6] Such as in Jaroslav Pelikan, *The Christian Tradition: A History of the Development of Doctrine*, vol. 4, *Reformation of Church and Dogma (1300–1700)* (Chicago: Univ. of Chicago Press, 1983), esp. pp. 10–68. See also William J. Courtenay, "Nominalism and Late Medieval Religion," in *The Pursuit of Holiness in Late Medieval and Renaissance Religion*, ed. Charles Trinkaus and Heiko A. Oberman (Leiden: E. J. Brill, 1974), pp. 26–59, and "Late Medieval Nominalism Revisited: 1972–1982," *Journal of the History of Ideas* (1983): 159–64. Courtenay suggests that one should approach the period "nominalistically," that is, by considering each theologian individually, rather than in terms of schools of thought.

vation).[7] Absolutely speaking, he could have chosen to create a different world, or to incarnate himself as an ass or a stone. He could also choose to save a man who in no way merits salvation, or to damn someone possessing the habit of grace. The only limitation to this power is the principle of noncontradiction—that is, God cannot do something logically contradictory. Of course, God has promised us that he will follow his own chosen order, so in fact God will not exercise his absolute power. The hypothetical possibility of God's exercise of his absolute power is a tool for speculation that was taken advantage of increasingly by the late scholastics, such as Nicolas d'Autrecourt, William of Ockham, Gregory of Rimini, and Pierre d'Ailly. Sometimes seemingly scurrilous questions were entertained: Can God restore a fallen woman's virginity—that is, can God undo the past?[8] This question arose already in the eleventh century. According to Peter Damian, in his *De divina omnipotentia*, the answer was yes, absolutely speaking, as God is not within time and can, by virtue of his omnipotence, undo whatever has been done.[9] Certain late scholastics made more frequent or at least decisive use of the distinction. Thus Ockham used argumentation *de potentia dei absoluta* (that is, from the perspective of God's absolute power) to show that certain propositions concerning causality cannot be established with complete certainty.[10] For example, we cannot prove absolutely that there is a first cause and not an infinite causal chain.

This sort of speculation has given rise to a great variety of interpretations of late scholasticism. Especially outside the field of historians of theology, the dominant view is probably still that of Etienne Gilson, whose admiration for Aquinas and the high scholastic synthesis of reason and faith was matched by his disappointment with Duns Scotus and especially with Ockham. The successors of Aquinas were, according to Gilson, dismantlers of the medieval worldview, *de potentia absoluta* argumentation was emblematic of the corrosiveness of nominalist theology. By emphasizing God's power and freedom the late scholastics were burning the bridges to God, thus making way for a secular, empiricist, and skeptical Renaissance and Enlightenment.[11] Gilson's assessment is most recently echoed (in a radical

---

[7] See below, Chapter Five, "God's Sovereignty," for a fuller discussion of this distinction, which informs much of my own analysis.

[8] See Francis Oakley, *Omnipotence, Covenant, and Order: An Excursion in the History of Ideas from Abelard to Leibniz* (Ithaca: Cornell Univ. Press, 1984), pp. 41–65; William J. Courtenay, "John of Mirecourt and Gregory of Rimini on Whether God Can Undo the Past," *Recherches de théologie ancienne et médiévale* 39 (1972): 224–56 and 40 (1973): 147–74.

[9] See *Pierre Damien: Lettre sur la toute-puissance divine*, ed. and trans. André Cantin (Paris: Editions du Cerf, 1972), pp. 386, 404–10, 418–32.

[10] See below, Chapter Three.

[11] See Etienne Gilson, *La philosophie au moyen âge: Des origines patristiques à la fin du XIVe siècle*, 2d ed. (Paris: Payot, 1962), pp. 638–87. For an account of Gilson's interpretation of

way) in a broadly synthetic work on the modern age by Hans Blumenberg, for whom the theology of omnipotence is a way of separating "theological assertions about God and theoretical assertions about nature."[12] Once God's freedom and autonomy are emphasized, God becomes hidden to man's reason: "The modern age began, not indeed as the epoch of the death of God, but as the epoch of the hidden God, the *deus absconditus*—and a hidden God is *pragmatically* as good as dead. The nominalist theology induces a human relation to the world whose implicit content could have been formulated in the postulate that man had to behave as though God were dead. This induces a restless taking stock of the world, which can be designated as the motive power of the age of science."[13] God's absolute power is seen, then, as the possibility of an essentially arbitrary intervention in the natural order. God becomes willful and unpredictable. Blumenberg, and the negative view of nominalist theology in general, understand the late scholastics' concept of God's absolute power as applying to inexplicable actual transgressions of the natural laws that are part of God's ordained power, that is, his order of salvation. Blumenberg does not emphasize the largely hypothetical nature of this concept. In that sense the nominalist God, absolutely speaking, is *unreliable* from the creature's point of view. He cannot be held to any laws he has set down, or rather, he can decide at any point to transgress them.[14]

Another view of fourteenth- and fifteenth-century scholastic theology, represented by scholars such as Paul Vignaux, Heiko A. Oberman, Phi-

---

late medieval theology and its impact on recent scholars of the period such as Gordon Leff, see Steven Ozment, *The Age of Reform (1250–1550): An Intellectual and Religious History of Late Medieval and Renaissance Europe* (New Haven: Yale Univ. Press, 1980), pp. 9–17. An example of this "negative" interpretation in literary analysis is Britton J. Harwood, "*Piers Plowman*: Fourteenth-Century Skepticism and the Theology of Suffering," *Bucknell Review* 19 (1971): 119–36.

[12] Hans Blumenberg, *The Legitimacy of the Modern Age*, trans. Robert M. Wallace (Cambridge, Mass.: MIT Press, 1983), p. 328.

[13] Ibid., p. 346. See also his judgment of Ockham: "William of Ockham (ca. 1300–1349) takes it as an elementary stipulation that reason is hardly sufficient to provide what is needed for salvation. That could easily be reinterpreted as implying that the theological impotence of reason by no means excludes its theoretical potency when directed at the world. Raising theology to its maximal pretension over against reason had the unintended result of reducing theology's role in explaining the world to a minimum, and thus preparing the competence of reason as the organ of a new kind of science that would liberate itself from tradition" (p. 347).

[14] This interpretation of divine *potentia absoluta* has obvious political parallels with absolutist theory. See below, Chapter Five ("God's Sovereignty") and Oakley, *Omnipotence*, pp. 93–118. The *de facto/de iure* distinction is also relevant here. Absolute power was thought of by Scotus as equivalent to what God can do *de facto*, and ordained power *de iure*, although when God does act outside of previous law, it is immediately in view of a (new) order, so he actually acts *ordinate*. See Jürgen Miethke, *Ockhams Weg zur Sozialphilosophie* (Berlin: Walter de Gruyter, 1969), pp. 145–49.

lotheus Boehner, and William J. Courtenay, maintains quite the opposite. According to these scholars, late scholastics see God's absolute power as demonstrating both the contingency and the *reliability* of the established order. If God does use his absolute power to transgress laws occasionally, his absolute power shows that the current order is a choice of God, not a necessity outside of God. Courtenay formulates it this way: "Even in the later 'nominalists' the distinction [between *potentia ordinata* and *potentia absoluta*] excludes the idea of a capricious, arbitrary God who might change his mind and reverse the established laws that obtain in the orders of nature and salvation. God has committed himself to maintain the order that he has created, and when he occasionally acts contrary to certain principles or laws that normally operate within that order, it is for reasons that are in keeping with the broader design of his established will."[15] The dialectic between the two aspects of God's power, then, is secondary to his covenant with mankind—a free, self-imposed promise to maintain the order of salvation set down by his revealed will. Late scholastic speculation does not remove theology entirely from man's present state; rather, it strengthens the sense of God's commitment to the (contingent) established order.

What should one make of these disagreements? Clearly, several different historiographical principles are at work here; these diverse interpretations of late scholastic theology are not simply contradictory, but tend to focus on different levels of historical explanation and understanding. Scholars such as Oberman and Courtenay, who have been revising Gilson's negative assessment of late scholasticism, tend to attempt to understand individual theologians on their own terms: How do these scholastics think of themselves? On this level, it is perhaps difficult to see them as corrosive critics of the high scholastic synthesis and as prophets of the skeptical-empiricist modern age. Their conscious use of the absolute-ordained power distinction tends to be less generalized and more conservative than has been believed. On another level, the moderate but continued negative view of fourteenth-century nominalist theology defended by scholars such as Gordon Leff and, to a certain extent, Francis Oakley tends to see features of late scholastic thought not only in the terms the individual thinkers would have accepted themselves, but as part of late medieval and early modern culture: in this case, misunderstandings or loose applications are just as important as the conscious functioning of an element in the entire thought of an individual theologian. Oakley, for example, draws parallels between

---

[15] Courtenay, "Nominalism and Late Medieval Religion," p. 43. See also Berndt Hamm, *Promissio, Pactum, Ordinatio: Freiheit und Selbstbindung Gottes in der scholastischen Gnadenlehre* (Tübingen: Mohr, 1977); and, most recently, Alister E. McGrath, *Iustitia Dei: A History of the Christian Doctrine of Justification*, vol. 1, *From the Beginnings to 1500* (Cambridge: Cambridge Univ. Press, 1986), pp. 119–28, for similar views.

the absolute-ordained power distinction and conceptions of the monarch's power in England that obviously blur certain aspects of the theological distinction, but that are nevertheless valid on a level of generality that exceeds the individual theologian.[16] On an even less individualistic level, philosophical syntheses of early modern culture tend to see nominalist theology not only in relation to the scholastic precedents but in terms of what came after, and in this sense the value given consciously to features of a theology by its proponents is hardly important at all. This seems to be the case with a historian such as Blumenberg.

Clearly, any study of theology in relation to other cultural discourses, or rather, the study of literary texts through theological distinctions, will be concerned only peripherally with a faithful reconstruction of how an individual theologian wanted to use these distinctions. The more general questions are the more interesting ones, especially since literature hardly ever reproduces any detailed conceptual system, or concerns itself particularly with accurate depictions of individual thinkers or schools. To some extent, then, the disputes about the interpretation of individual theologians become less relevant: what is important is the formulation within theology of certain concepts and issues that have literary analogues. Whether one evaluates negatively or positively the absolute-ordained power distinction is less pertinent than the features of the distinction and the basic view of God they entail. The contingency of the established order, the absence of prior constraints in God, the priority of his will: these are fundamental concepts repeated in various forms among late scholastics such as Scotus, Ockham, d'Ailly, Gregory of Rimini, Gabriel Biel, and John Major.

The term "nominalist" has also provoked debates as to its usefulness. Often the epistemological and theological views of diverse "nominalists" do not coincide, and it is even difficult to group late scholastics into schools, although there seems to be some agreement in distinguishing the *via moderna* (Ockham, Buridan, Oresme, Marsilius of Inghen, d'Ailly, and Biel) and the *schola augustina moderna* (Gregory of Rimini, Hugolino of Orvieto, and Thomas Bradwardine)[17] from more conservative Thomists and followers of Giles of Rome, and mystical currents represented by Eckhart, (Pseudo-)Dionysius, Cusanus, and Tauler. If one is seeking to establish the *influence* of, say, John Major on early sixteenth century French literature, through his teaching and that of his "school," problems of classification are important and in the end unresolvable. Yet an emphasis on certain concepts, rather than on the impact of an individual's or a school's entire thought, seems heuristically more valid and more faithful to what

---

[16] See Oakley, *Omnipotence*; for a critique see the review by William J. Courtenay in *Speculum* 60 (1985): 1006–9.

[17] I am relying here on Alister E. McGrath, *The Intellectual Origins of the European Reformation* (London: Basil Blackwell, 1987), pp. 75–93.

literature is about. A literary text does not attempt to represent truthfully contemporary figures or their thought, but reworks key attitudes, experiences, sensations, and concepts into an imaginative whole that is in a sense incommensurable with the initial givens (though not unrelated to them). This does not mean, however, that the Renaissance literary text is *opposed* to "rational" discourse. Writers of this period tend not to be hostile to reasoning or logical argumentation as in some way antiliterary. To the extent that theological argumentation contributes to what is most sophisticated in the way in which Renaissance culture justified and structured itself, theological argumentation is fertile ground for the development of conceptual paradigms in other cultural realms as well.

In my own study, I have decided to focus on the complex surrounding the basic intuition of God's freedom, which is especially developed in the Franciscan tradition and in the so-called *via moderna*. The centrality of God's freedom I take to be what defines nominalist theology, and it is in this sense that I will be using the term.

Combining the notion of divine freedom with the nominalist emphasis on the will and on conventional, rather than inherent, relations, Steven Ozment has suggestively and pertinently summarized nominalist theology: "In the final analysis, words are the connecting link between the mind and reality and between the soul and God. Man must come to grips with the world around him through 'signs voluntarily instituted'; and he must work out his salvation on the basis of 'laws voluntarily and contingently established' by God. In the final analysis, all he has is willed verbal relations."[18]

The Renaissance against Scholasticism?

Any detailed study of the relationship between the scholastic tradition and humanism, or the scholastic tradition and the Reformation, is entirely outside the scope of this book.[19] However, it is important to address some general assumptions regarding this relationship. The received impression is that both the Reformation and humanism grew out of a wholesale rejection of the scholastics, especially of the late scholastics (the *recentes*, or *theo-*

[18] Steven Ozment, "Mysticism, Nominalism and Dissent," in *The Pursuit of Holiness*, ed. Trinkaus and Oberman, p. 80.

[19] For the most recent attempt, see McGrath, *Intellectual Origins*, pp. 69–121. On the triumph of humanism over scholasticism in the field of education, see Anthony Grafton and Lisa Jardine, *From Humanism to the Humanities: Education and the Liberal Arts in Fifteenth- and Sixteenth-Century Europe* (Cambridge, Mass.: Harvard Univ. Press, 1986), especially the introduction, in which the authors claim (rightly so) that scholasticism was in fact a viable intellectual system. Precisely why it was viable is a question this study is at least in part addressing.

logastres), who, in the eyes of the humanists and Reformers, were more interested in subtle arguments and definitions than in the truth. Moreover, the Latin of the late scholastics was indeed far removed from the eloquence of Cicero, and they hardly possessed the philological skills sufficient for their exegesis of the Bible. Nevertheless, criticism of theologians shows an acute awareness, on the part of the humanists, of scholastic argumentation. The scholastic tradition of disputation and its complex logical metalanguage provoked detailed humanist attacks.[20] Academic rivalries masked, however, a more profound dependence on forms of late scholastic thought. Indeed, the pragmatic-ethical impulse of humanism is not incompatible with the theoretical emphasis on convention, will, and freedom found among nominalist theologians.

An example of the humanist philological critique is the work of Lorenzo Valla, who condemns the "recent theologians saturated with old Aristotelian precepts" for their ignorance of Greek and their poor Latin: they are, according to Valla, more preoccupied with Aristotle than with the truth.[21] A sample of Valla's own exegetical skills is his critique of the traditional choice of *fides* as a translation of the Greek πίστις—it should have been *persuasio*, as *fides* in Latin has more of the sense of *probatio*. Of course, *persuasio* is connected to rhetorical skill, whereas *fides/probatio* is a logical-deductive term. Thus theological inquiry is perhaps based on an overly rational view of Christian practice.[22] Valla's dialogue *De libero arbitrio* (composed ca. 1439, ed. 1483) affirms in a more systematic way the non-rational nature of theological truth, and it displays knowledge of the scholastic debates surrounding the question of God's omniscience and future contingent events. In the end, Valla does not save man's free will, and in this he goes farther than the late scholastics. The latter, however, had already problematized the relationship between man's will and God's absolutely prior will, going beyond the arguments and solutions of Boethius and Augustine. Valla radicalized the incompatibility that a late scholastic

[20] See Alan Perreiah, "Humanistic Critiques of Scholastic Dialectic," *The Sixteenth Century Journal* 13 (1982): 3–22.

[21] Valla summarizes what was to be a commonplace humanist attack on the late scholastics: "Quare illis contemptis ac spretis, si qua sunt, quae in Aristotele melius dici potuissent, ea temptabo ipse pro mea virili melius dicere; non hominis, quod absit, insimulandi gratia, sed honorandae veritatis, quae ut inquit Plato, potius est honoranda quam vir. Idque cum ob alia, tum vero ne recentes theologi aristotelicis praeceptis imbuti veteribus insultent atque illudant." These theologians are "graecarum litterarum imperiti" and "latinae linguae parum periti" (from the proem to the first book of the *Dialecticae disputationes*, 3d ed., composed after 1453, quoted by Salvatore I. Camporeale, *Lorenzo Valla: Umanesimo e teologia* [Florence: Istituto nazionale di Studi sul Rinascimento, 1972], p. 229).

[22] Lorenzo Valla, *Elegantiae* 5.30 (in *Opera* [Basel: H. Petrus, 1540; repr. Torino: Bottega d'Erasmo, 1962], vol. 1). See the discussion of this point in Camporeale, *Lorenzo Valla*, pp. 231–33.

such as Ockham saw between divine and human will.[23] Far from ignoring the conceptual issues in scholasticism, Valla's rejection of the *recentes theologi* is one that is conscious of the issues central to their work.

We also find an awareness of scholastic argumentation in the writings of Erasmus, who possessed works of scholastic theology in his library, including editions of Lombard's *Sentences*.[24] Even before the *De libero arbitrio diatribe seu collatio* (1524), in which Erasmus displays a knowledge of scholastic distinctions concerning merit and God's revealed will and good pleasure,[25] he refers to the "idle" disputes of scholastic theologians in his translation and annotation of the New Testament. Commenting on 1 Tim. 1:6–7 ("A quibus quod aberrarunt quidam, deflexerunt ad vaniloquium, volentes esse legis doctores, non intelligentes quae loquuntur, neque de quibus asseverant [There are some people who have gone off the straight course and taken a road that leads to empty speculation; they claim to be doctors of the Law but they understand neither the arguments they are using nor the opinions they are upholding; Jerusalem Bible]"), in the note to *vaniloquium*, he playfully associates the sound of the Greek ματαιολογία with *theologia* ("Quantum ad pronunciationem attinet, *mataeologia* non multum abest a *Theologia*, cum res inter se plurimum discrepent [As far as the pronunciation is concerned, *mataeologia* is not very different from *Theologia*, although the things signified differ greatly]").[26] We should not, Erasmus says, spend our time disputing about worthless things, lest theology become *mataeologia*, that is, idle or arrogant speculation. Erasmus

[23] See the translation and annotation of this text in Paul Oskar Kristeller, Ernst Cassirer, and John Herman Randall, Jr., eds., *The Renaissance Philosophy of Man* (Chicago: Univ. of Chicago Press, 1948), pp. 155–82, and the discussion in Charles Trinkaus, *In Our Image and Likeness: Humanity and Divinity in Italian Humanist Thought* (London: Constable, 1970), 1:166–68.

[24] See Jean-Claude Margolin, "Duns Scot et Erasme," in *Regnum hominis et regnum Dei*, ed. Camille Bérubé (Rome: Societas Internationalis Scotistica, 1978), pp. 89–112.

[25] See Desiderius Erasmus, *De libero arbitrio diatribe seu collatio*, in *Luther and Erasmus: Free Will and Salvation*, ed. and trans. E. Gordon Rupp et al. (Philadelphia: Westminster, 1969), p. 51 (on *meritum de congruo* and *de condigno*) and pp. 67–68 (on *voluntas signi* and *beneplaciti*). On Erasmus's use of nominalist distinctions in his writings on free will (including merit and the absolute power of God), see Charles Trinkaus, *The Scope of Renaissance Humanism* (Ann Arbor: Univ. of Michigan Press, 1983), pp. 274–301, esp. p. 282. Trinkaus sees Erasmus as unconsciously using many nominalist theological concepts.

[26] Desiderius Erasmus, *Opera omnia* (Loudun: P. Vander Aa, 1705), 6:926D n. 13. Unless indicated otherwise, all translations are my own. The pun on *mataeologia* is also used by Rabelais to characterize the scholastic theologians of old times who attempt to educate the young Gargantua: "Voyons, si bon vous semble, quelle différence y a entre le sçavoir de voz resveurs mateologiens du temps jadis et les jeunes gens de maintenant" (*Gargantua* 14, ed. Ruth Calder and M. A. Screech [Geneva: Droz, 1970], p. 100). See also Craig R. Thompson, "Better Teachers than Scotus or Aquinas," in *Medieval and Renaissance Studies* ed. John L. Lievsay (Durham, N.C.: Duke Univ. Press, 1968), 2:114–45. Thompson translates Erasmus's note ridiculing scholastic theology (pp. 141–45 n. 58).

goes on to list examples of worthless disputes that keep us from imitating Christ and making ourselves worthy of salvation. These vain questions concern such matters as created and uncreated grace and the distinction between the Father, the Son, and the Holy Spirit. The list of the scholastics' scurrilous disputes, their *quaestiunculae*, covers over 150 lines of the note. Many of these questions concern the power of God, and several of them are questions through which theologians distinguished between God's absolute and ordained power, such as whether God can command anything evil, even command man to hate him, and prohibit all good, even love and adoration of God; whether God was able to make this world even from eternity better than he did; whether God could make what is done undone, and so make a virgin out of a prostitute; and whether the proposition "God is a beetle, or a gourd" is as possible as the proposition "God is man."[27] The resolution of these questions involved a distinction between what it is possible for God to do, absolutely speaking, and what he has in fact chosen to do.[28] Moreover, the questions point to the issue of God's essential freedom. So although Erasmus considers them to be a waste of time, these *quaestiunculae* were part of what a humanist would have been aware of in scholastic theology of the early Renaissance.

Erasmus opposes to this *vaniloquium* what a Christian must know to lead a Christian life: what the Apostles have transmitted, namely, how we can exercise charity through a pure heart, a good conscience, and true faith (quoting 1 Tim. 1:5).[29] The Pauline ethical alternative to idle speculation is typical also of the French evangelical humanists. In Jacques Lefèvre d'Etaples's *Epistres et evangiles pour les cinquante et deux dimenches de l'an*, the author similarly condemns the "phantasie et presumption de noz intelligences et conceptions." We must believe God's word simply, according to his spirit, and not according to our own, and we must not "adjouster noz intelligences et en faire folles opinions [add our own intelligences and arrive at mad opinions]."[30] However, the evangelical critique of theological

---

[27] "An Deus possit quodvis malum, etiam odium sui praecipere, & omne bonum prohibere, etiam amorem & cultum sui. . . . An potuerit hunc mundum etiam ab aeterno meliorem facere quam fecit. . . . An possit ex facto facere infectum: ac per hoc ex meretrice facere virginem. . . . An haec propositio, Deus est scarabeus, aut cucurbita, tam possibilis sit, quam haec, Deus est homo" (Erasmus, *Opera omnia* 6:927B–D).

[28] See McGrath, *Iustitia Dei*, 1:126; Courtenay, "John of Mirecourt"; and Oakley, *Omnipotence*, pp. 41–65, on these questions in scholastic theology.

[29] "Breve tempus est, & arduum est negotium agere vere Christianum. Quin igitur omissis rebus supervacaneis, ea potissimum spectamus, quae Christus nos scire voluit, quae prodiderunt Apostoli, quae proprie ad charitatem faciunt, de corde puro, & conscientia bona, & fide non ficta, quam unam Paulus appellat finem & perfectionem totius Legis" (Erasmus, *Opera omnia* 6:927F).

[30] Jacques Lefèvre d'Etaples, *Epistres et evangiles pour les cinquante et deux dimenches de l'an*, text of the edition of Pierre de Vingle (1531–1532), ed. Guy Bedouelle and Franco Giacone

speculation and exegesis is not so much a disagreement with the content
or principles of late scholastic theology as it is a rejection of theological
speculation as such, in favor of a return to the Scriptures, faith, and charity.
This explicit rejection in no way precludes the use of concepts fundamental
to theology; in fact, the turn to the individual and ethical is not itself incompatible with the emphasis on God's freedom and covenantal relationship to man that characterizes nominalist theology.[31] Evangelical humanism, and, for that matter, rhetorical humanism, do not offer a truly
substantive and systematic alternative to the theology of the time. Humanism did not conceive of itself as being in the same category.[32]

The role of late scholastic theology in Renaissance Aristotelianism is another matter. In spite of the ostentatious Neoplatonism of Marsilio Ficino
and the syncretism of Giovanni Pico della Mirandola, Aristotle remained
the dominant classical philosophical influence in the Renaissance.[33] Scholasticism represented a long and vibrant university tradition of interpretation of Aristotle.[34] Renaissance philosophers such as Pietro Pomponazzi

---

(Leiden: E. J. Brill, 1976), p. 37. The Sorbonne censured these propositions: "Haec propositio innuens expositiones Sanctorum in Sacra Scriptura esse praesumptiones contemnendas,
neque veram esse intelligentiam Scripturae, maxime temeraria est et impia" (ibid.).

[31] This is the argument made by Heiko A. Oberman in "Some Notes on the Theology of
Nominalism with Attention to Its Relation to the Renaissance," *Harvard Theological Review*
53 (1960): 47–76. See also the concluding remarks in Margolin, "Duns Scot et Erasme," pp.
106–12. Finally, see, most recently, two general syntheses on the relationship between scholastic (including nominalist) theology and humanism: Charles Trinkaus, "Italian Humanism
and Scholastic Theology," and John F. D'Amico, "Humanism and Pre-Reformation Theology," in *Renaissance Humanism: Foundations, Forms, and Legacy*, ed. Albert Rabil, Jr. (Philadelphia: Univ. of Pennsylvania Press, 1988), 3:327–48 and 349–79, respectively, esp. pp.
353–55. Both Trinkaus and D'Amico provide extensive bibliographical notes.

[32] On the refusal of theory by the humanists, see Victoria Kahn, "Humanism and the Resistance to Theory," in *Literary Theory/Renaissance Texts*, ed. Patricia Parker and David Quint
(Baltimore: Johns Hopkins Univ. Press, 1986), pp. 373–96, esp. 374–78.

[33] On Ficino's connections to scholasticism, however, see Paul Oskar Kristeller, *Studies in
Renaissance Thought and Letters* (Rome: Edizioni di Storia e Letteratura, 1956), pp. 35–55.
Pico defended the scholastics (in particular, Scotus) against humanist charges of barbarous
style by saying that wisdom and truth do not need the disguises of eloquence, in his letter to
Ermolao Barbaro (see the translation in Quirinus Breen, "Giovanni Pico della Mirandola on
the Conflict of Philosophy and Rhetoric," *Journal of the History of Ideas* 13 (1952): 384–412);
Pico furthermore uses the figure of the Sileni of Alcibiades to describe scholastic philosophy:
uninviting on the outside, but jewels of truth on the inside (see Breen, p. 398). See the
discussion of this letter in Quint, *Origin and Originality*, pp. 7–8, 224 n. 18. Among his
various essays devoted to scholasticism and Renaissance culture, see, for a good overview,
Paul Oskar Kristeller, "Humanism and Scholasticism in the Italian Renaissance," in his *Renaissance Thought and Letters*, pp. 553–83.

[34] For an overview of Renaissance Aristotelianism, and a careful distinction between scholasticism and Aristotelianism, see Charles B. Schmitt, "Towards a Reassessment of Renaissance Aristotelianism," reprinted in his *Studies in Renaissance Philosophy and Science* (London:
Variorum Reprints, 1981), pp. 159–93.

crystallized their own thought through a critique of Aristotle and were very aware of scholastic attempts to reconcile Aristotle and Christianity. Their emphasis on human dignity and individuality is not exclusively the result of a reading of the Ancients. Rather, that emphasis must be seen in a wider contemporary cultural context that includes late scholastic theology, for one of the basic tenets of "nominalist" theology is the preservation of both human and divine freedom. The argumentation using God's absolute power has, as I will argue, the more or less unintended result of enhancing possibilities for human power, and gives human power a code through which to imagine its own extreme forms.

An example of the proximity of Italian Renaissance philosophy to late scholasticism is the "school of Padua"[35] and its most notable representative, Pietro Pomponazzi. His radicalization of the disjunction between the tenets of faith and rational truth uses arguments that derive from late scholasticism (although they go beyond those theologians' intentions).[36] His *De fato* (1520) offers a troubling juxtaposition of Stoic determinism, especially in the first book, and a Christian affirmation of divine and human freedom, in the third through the fifth books. Interpretations of this incoherence vary,[37] but whatever Pomponazzi's deep intentions, the working out of his own "Christian" solution uses conceptual channels that parallel late scholastic thinking about the powers of God. The problem, in very simplified terms, is the following: If God is both omniscient and omnipotent, and the first cause of all things, how can there be future events that are not foreknown and thus caused by God? If indeed there are no future contingent events (i.e., events that could be or not be), how can the human will freely choose anything? After rehearsing various solutions to the problem that either limit God's power or eliminate human free will, Pomponazzi offers his own solution: God foreknows a future event precisely as a contingent event, that is, as one that can happen or not happen, and the final outcome is not known beforehand by God in a determined way. Instead, God "separates" himself from the determination of either possible outcome ("Immo secundum istam considerationem, [Deus] abstrahit vel

[35] See Edward P. Mahoney, "Duns Scotus and the School of Padua around 1500," in *Regnum hominis et regnum Dei*, ed. Camille Bérubé (Rome: Societas Internationalis Scotistica, 1978), pp. 215–27. This volume is devoted to links between Scotus and Venetian and Paduan Renaissance thought.

[36] See Martin L. Pine, "Pietro Pomponazzi and the Medieval Tradition of God's Foreknowledge," in *Philosophy and Humanism: Renaissance Essays in Honor of Paul Oskar Kristeller*, ed. Edward P. Mahoney (New York: Columbia Univ. Press, 1976), pp. 100–15, on Pomponazzi's use of Ockham.

[37] See Giovanni Di Napoli, "Libertà e fato in Pietro Pomponazzi," in *Studi in onore di Antonio Corsano* (Manduria: Lacaita, 1970), pp. 175–220, and the more general overview of Pomponazzi criticism in Martin L. Pine, *Pietro Pomponazzi: Radical Philosopher of the Renaissance* (Padua: Antenore, 1986), pp. 3–39.

potius praescindit a determinatione partis").[38] In other words, human freedom is preserved through a voluntary limitation God imposes on his own power. This solution, in spite of its apparent originality, reflects the scholastic distinction between what is absolutely possible for God and what he actually chooses to do: God decides freely to limit himself to a certain temporal order.[39] In as "secular" a thinker as Pomponazzi we find, then, a radical insistence on God's power and freedom (seen from a Christian perspective) alongside a Stoic-Averroist determinism. Moreover, we find a use of the distinctions concerning God's power that we encounter among the late scholastics. Pomponazzi's use of scholastic distinctions was probably unintentional, but it is a measure of their explanatory power and natural appropriateness for the early modern period.

Another, more substantial alternative to scholasticism is, of course, the Reformation. The French and Italian writers I will be dealing with have, with the exception of Agrippa d'Aubigné, much less connection to Luther, Calvin, Zwingli, and Théodore de Bèze than to humanism and evangelism, so in a sense the Reformation's dialogue with scholasticism is less important to the argument. Luther clearly knew late scholasticism, especially as represented by Gabriel Biel, quite well, and in his *Disputatio contra scholasticam theologiam* (1517) he proposes theses that specifically treat the questions central to nominalist theology. One of those problems, the distinction between absolute and hypothetical necessity, is attacked in thesis 32: "Nihil quoque efficitur per illud dictum: praedestinatio est necessaria necessitate consequentiae, sed non consequentis [Also nothing is achieved by this sentence: predestination is necessary through necessity of the consequence, but not by necessity of the thing consequent]."[40] Briefly, absolute necessity is the necessary relation of God's all-powerful will and creation, whereas hypothetical necessity is the relation between God's will and creation that preserves contingency. Man's free will hinges upon the distinction between these types of necessity, according to the late scholastics.[41] In thesis 56 Luther implicitly attacks the distinction between the absolute and ordained powers of God: "Non potest deus acceptare hominem sine gratia dei iustificante. Contra Occam [God cannot accept man without God's jus-

---

[38] Pietro Pomponazzi, *Libri quinque de fato, de libero arbitrio et de praedestinatione*, ed. Richard Lemay (Lungano: Thesaurus Mundi, 1957), 2.6.5 (p. 184). On this solution of divine self-limitation, see Pine, *Pietro Pomponazzi*, pp. 315–17, 332. Pine argues for the novelty of Pomponazzi's solution.

[39] See, on the problem of future contingents, below, Chapter Four, and, on the problem of God's self-binding, Chapter Five.

[40] Martin Luther, *Werke. Kritische Gesammtausgabe* (Weimar: H. Böhlau, 1883), 1:225. On Luther's debate with scholasticism here, see Leif Grane, *Contra Gabrielem: Luthers Auseinandersetzung mit Gabriel Biel in der Disputatio contra Scholasticam Theologiam* (Copenhagen: Gyldendal, 1962), pp. 9–42.

[41] See below, Chapter One.

tifying grace. Against Ockham]."[42] Saving a man without justifying grace is one of the test cases of what God can do, absolutely speaking. In Luther's debate with Erasmus over free will, the distinctions concerning merit and necessity resurface.

Philip Melanchthon, in his *Loci communes* (1521), also refers frequently to important scholastic distinctions, among them the distinction between congruous and condign merit, which he attacks as granting too much to man's natural efforts.[43] This distinction, as we will see, serves to reconcile man's merit and God's freedom from any contractual constraint. In the expanded *Loci praecipui theologici* (1559) we find an explanation of the distinction between absolute and hypothetical necessity, and Melanchthon allows himself to praise it cautiously.[44]

Although Calvin studied in Paris and echoes some nominalist theological tenets in his emphasis on God's priority, the degree to which he was influenced by and aware of contemporary scholastic theologians such as John Major is far from certain.[45] He did, however, explicitly attack the distinction between the absolute and ordained powers of God.[46]

In the final analysis, the least one can say about the status of nominalist theology in humanist and Reformer circles is that major humanists and Reformers were aware of key questions or distinctions relating to divine

---

[42] Luther, *Werke* 1:227. On this thesis see Grane, *Contra Gabrielem*, p. 373.

[43] "Iam quae prodidere sophistae de merito congrui, scilicet quod ex operibus moralibus, id est, quae viribus naturae nostrae facimus de congruo, sic loquuntur, mereamur gratiam, ipse, lector, intelligis blasphemias esse iniuriam gratiae dei ementitas" (Philip Melanchthon, *Werke*, ed. Hans Engelland and Robert Stupperich, 2d ed. [Gütersloh: G. Mohn, 1978], vol. 2, pt. 1, pp. 47–48). See my discussion in Chapter Two.

[44] "Postremo et illud addendum est recte dici necessitatem esse duplicem. Alia necessitas nuncupatur absoluta, cum videlicet res aut propositio simpliciter necessaria est, ac poni oppositum prorsus impossibile est et destructio omnium rerum, ut hae propositiones sunt necessariae necessitate absoluta: Deus est, Deus est essentia. . . . Sed alia est necessitas consequentiae, quae est earum rerum aut propositionum, quae possent se natura sua aliter habere, sed fiunt necessariae vel propter praecedentes causas vel quia determinatae sunt. Et in his magna sunt discrimina. . . . Sic fit necessaria: Pharao persequetur Israelitas; haec non est sua natura necessaria, sed revera contingens. Ac fieri oppositum non esset impossibile, sed quia sic evenit, dicitur necessaria necessitate consequentiae. Haec puerilis distinctio non est inutilis et saepe traditur in scholis. . . ." (Melanchthon, *Werke*, vol. 2, pt. 1, p. 260). See my discussion in Chapter One.

[45] This is the "Reuter hypothesis": Karl Reuter proposed in 1963 that John Major taught Calvin in Paris and introduced him to the writings of Scotus, Bradwardine, and Gregory of Rimini. Reuter pointed to similarities in their doctrines of justification. See the discussion in McGrath, *Intellectual Origins*, pp. 99–106. For the relationship between Zwingli and scholasticism, see pp. 93–94; McGrath sees Zwingli as much more influenced by humanism than by late medieval scholasticism.

[46] See David C. Steinmetz, "Calvin and the Absolute Power of God," *Journal of Medieval and Renaissance Studies* 18 (1988): 65–79. Steinmetz also usefully discusses the various aspects of the distinction before Calvin.

freedom, whether or not they approved of them, and in many cases these distinctions consciously or unconsciously determined their own argumentation.[47] It is in fact much more likely that a "fragmentary" understanding of late medieval theology was the rule, rather than a profound absorption of the whole of an individual theologian's thought. This fragmentary understanding is often mediated through the *distinctiones* and *quaestiones* in scholastic commentaries on Peter Lombard's *Sentences*, which were a prevalent pedagogical tool in the universities.[48]

It is primarily through these commentaries on the *Sentences* that late scholastic thought survives, and they are a convenient way of isolating characteristic concepts or distinctions. As we have seen, Renaissance humanists and Reformers such as Erasmus, Melanchthon, and Luther often isolated distinctions or questions of the scholastics, usually for polemical or satiric purposes. My own procedure resembles, at least in that respect, the fragmentary approach of those external to scholastic theological circles. The distinctions I have found most fruitful in analyzing Renaissance literary practice are:

—hypothetical versus absolute necessity
—condign versus congruous merit
—immediate versus mediated causation
—revealed will versus divine "good pleasure"
—absolute versus ordained power

Most of these distinctions appear in the very cursory glimpse I have just given of the humanist and Reformation reaction to late scholasticism. In spite of their seemingly arcane nature, distinctions such as these were commonplaces in theological discourse, even if (and perhaps especially if) they were argued against or overtly dismissed.[49]

[47] For a recent synthesis of nominalist theological influence on Erasmus, Luther, Zwingli, and Calvin, see Heiko A. Oberman, "*Via antiqua* and *via moderna*: Late Medieval Prolegomena to Early Reformation Thought," in *From Ockham to Wyclif*, ed. Anne Hudson and Michael Wilks (Oxford: Basil Blackwell, 1987), pp. 445–63.

[48] See, for example, James K. Farge, *Orthodoxy and Reform in Early Reformation France: The Faculty of Theology of Paris, 1500–1543* (Leiden: E. J. Brill, 1985), pp. 13–28, on the use of the *Sentences* in the Faculty of Theology curriculum.

[49] A good example of the accessibility of these concepts as *loci communes* is the dictionary by Johannes Altensteig, *Vocabularius theologie* ([Hagenau]: Henricus Gran, 1517), which underwent several editions during the sixteenth century and is still a valuable introductory guide to nominalist theology. Undoubtedly part of scholasticism's problem is the fact that we as moderns tend to participate happily in its rejection by the humanists. Especially literature is often seen as serenely separate from the rebarbative labyrinth of scholasticism: we like to see literature as the realm of unadulterated pleasure and "creativity," or as the realm of individual ethical choices resistant to the constraints of any system. This alleged separateness of literature is, however, anachronistic to the Renaissance, which was not at all as exclusive in its categories of cultural discourses as, say, the Enlightenment and what followed it.

Theology and Literary Analysis

It would not be appropriate to claim that the contacts between scholastic, humanist, and literary cultures were such that authors were *influenced* by their reading of, say, this or that commentary on the *Sentences*. No such argument can be made for most of the writers I am dealing with; the only author with extensive contact with scholasticism is Rabelais, who was trained by the Franciscans. The others had more or less contact with humanist culture, and sometimes direct contact with evangelism, as in the case of Marguerite de Navarre and her circle. For some, theological issues as such were unimportant, or, when they came up, were sometimes treated satirically (as in Ariosto). So even if it is granted that fragments of scholastic discourse were important parts of intellectual culture in the Renaissance, that does not prove any real influence on the content of the literary texts of the period.

If theological analysis of literature is conceived of as allegorical hermeneutics, as the uncovering of intentional allegories of Christian dogma, then the fact that the literature of the Renaissance with which I am dealing was little influenced by scholasticism is an all-important obstacle. Moreover, literary works such as Ariosto's *Orlando furioso*, Castiglione's *Libro del cortegiano*, Rabelais's novels, and Marguerite de Navarre's *Heptaméron* are much too open-ended to present a consistent *scholastic* position or argument, even if they treat theological themes. Often, evangelical messages seem to be woven into the literary material, but these references to basic Christian topics, when they are explicit, are by nature unsystematic and rhetorical, rather than representations of intricately argued positions in the schools.

Allegorical or even topical analyses seem to be excluded by the very nature of scholastic theological discourse itself, which lacks the mythic-symbolic appeal of Neoplatonism and the ethical-rhetorical impetus of evangelical-humanist writings. But scholastic theology formulated in a systematic way some essential issues of early modern culture: the contingency of creation, the freedom of God, and the absoluteness of God's power. The value of theological analysis lies less in the demonstration that this or that writer believed this or that dogma than in our ability to illuminate Renaissance writing. Theology of the period provides us with codes that enable us to look fruitfully at the way in which fictional worlds are constructed in early modern France and Italy. Theology, then, becomes a way of defining elements of a larger picture of which literature is a part.

I would argue furthermore that theology, conceived of as a particularly sophisticated cultural discourse, is not an attempt to talk about "the Other." Seen as the conceptualizing of *human* problems, it is less the definition of what is different from man than the definition of what man is capable of defining, for himself.[50] From this perspective, the definition of God is a limit concept in human culture. Theological discourse inevitably participates in the formulation of human problems: for example, God's relationship to creation is never far from the sovereign's relationship to his subjects. God's attributes are a logical limit of what man is.

My structural use of theology as a cultural discourse assumes, then, a secularization of theological knowledge, in the sense that theology is part of human culture and conveys knowledge that has analogues in human society in general. Interestingly, my secular use of scholastic theology is consonant with the dangers contemporary reformers saw in it. In talking about God we run the risk of making God into something that can be talked about, that is, into one of us. The evangelical reaction against scholastic theology is partially aware of the humanization of God, and vice versa, through theological inquiry. Evangelical condemnation of "curiosity" and "sophistic" argument reflects an emphasis on the otherness of God, on his imperviousness to human reasoning. The violence of sixteenth-century theological debates should make theological analysis valuable precisely for this period, as theology was felt by many to be of urgent and universal concern.

My use of theology is structural, rather than topical or allegorical. Certain distinctions characteristic of late scholasticism are used to illuminate the way certain Renaissance writers put together their fictional worlds, whether this happened consciously or not. These distinctions all concern God's freedom, or priority, and have to do with the effect of divine freedom on God's relation to creation. I am interested specifically in the analogy between the divine creative act and human "creation" of literary fiction. On the surface, at least, this is a highly problematic analogy, and in the chapters that follow I will refer frequently to its difficulties. Briefly, there is relatively little explicit evidence of literary "creation" being conceived of as anything like creation ex nihilo, either in the literary works themselves or in theological discussions of creation.[51] Late medieval and

---

[50] In this sense I am taking the underlying existential perspective of Kenneth Burke, in *The Rhetoric of Religion: Studies in Logology*: "This investigation does not require us to make any decisions about the validity of theology *qua* theology. Our purpose is simply to ask how theological principles can be shown to have secular analogues that throw light upon the nature of language" (Boston: Beacon Press, 1961; repr. [Berkeley: Univ. of California Press, 1970], p. 2). Theology is always also a discourse that is a product of human historical exigencies.

[51] See below, Chapter Three. For a discussion of the status of literary authorship in the Middle Ages, see Alistair J. Minnis, *Medieval Theory of Authorship: Scholastic Literary Attitudes in the Later Middle Ages* (Philadelphia: Univ. of Pennsylvania Press, 1987). For the Italian Renaissance, see Robert Durling, *The Figure of the Poet in Renaissance Epic* (Cambridge, Mass.: Harvard Univ. Press, 1965); Durling makes more of the divine analogy. For the

Renaissance authors perceived their work largely as the disposition of preexistent material, not as the free creation of something out of nothing. The author[52] augmented and fashioned a continuous stream of literary activity, and saw himself as working with previous limits or elements furnished by a generic tradition. Constraint by prior material was in many cases perceived as enabling, rather than disabling, for the fictional world was thought of as a celebration of the *survival* of culture, not its reinvention by the individual. In theological terms, the human author was an *artifex* rather than a *creator*, and was caused to write by conditions outside of himself. Human imagination was not the freeing of the mind from the constraints of this world, but an ability to reproduce images and spiritual constructs that were already contained in the fabric of the world itself. The imagination allowed man to uncover the similitudes in the vast network of signs around him, not to produce an alternative to that work. Imagination, then, in a sense, belonged partly to the objects contemplated, partly to the person contemplating them.

The persistence of this tradition can hardly be overemphasized, but it should not obscure the fact that in *practice* alternatives to it emerged in the Renaissance. Although, for example, the Renaissance poet may continue to invoke the Muses', the patron's, God's, or a previous writer's authority, there is an increasing sense that the individual author is largely free to do whatever pleases him. The most obvious instances are found in the Italian romance or mock epic tradition, in writers such as Luigi Pulci and Ludovico Ariosto. But on the French side we find a similar, if less explicit, sense of freedom from generic and narrative constraints. Freedom from such constraints has become a value at least in practice. My argument is not that this freedom represents a turning away from the theological, that is, a secular-empirical tendency—although that is not excluded—but rather that late medieval theology already contained within itself similar elements in its definition of God. It is not enough to say that the writer becomes God, for which God is one speaking of? The Aristotelian-Averroist God? the Thomist God? the mystics' God? the nominalist God? My contention is that specifically nominalist features of God can be seen in the way certain Renaissance authors construct their fictional worlds, and that these features often point to the most interesting aspects of those fictional worlds: the feeling of contingency, the feeling that things could easily be otherwise, and that they are dependent on an only partially motivated *decision* of their author.

In many cases there are precedents in the literary tradition for the fictive

---

French Renaissance, see Grahame Castor, *Pléiade Poetics: A Study in Sixteenth-Century Thought and Terminology* (Cambridge: Cambridge Univ. Press, 1964).

[52] For etymologies and definitions of "author," see M.-D. Chenu, "Auctor, actor, autor," *Bulletin Du Cange (ALMA)* 3 (1927): 81–86.

contingency I will be looking at; however, the confluence of theological concerns with God's freedom, the political-theoretical tendencies toward absolutism, and the despotic structure of the court shows that the literary is part of a larger cultural phenomenon and is more usefully understood in this intellectual context. The view of the literary text as something serenely separate belongs to the very phenomenon of freedom I am describing; to hold that this autonomy somehow expresses the permanent nature of all literature is a profound anachronism. The recourse to purely literary antecedents to elucidate a certain feature of a literary text reflects a partial, estheticist understanding of literature. This understanding, in turn, is a product of cultural conditions that define the literary as the site of the autonomous pleasure of great poets, for reasons that are often determined by nonliterary considerations and interests.[53]

My own study is an attempt to practice a more or less structural history of ideas, with a focus on close readings of literary texts. I am not, for the most part, attempting new interpretations of these texts. Rather, I wish to insert them into a broader cultural complex, part of which still determines our own understanding of literature today. For the freedom of God, the freedom of the sovereign, and the implicit freedom of the poet are features of what we take to be the individual. In this sense my study is remotely connected to a very old view of the Renaissance as a period during which the notion of the individual was born, a view that, in spite of numerous shortcomings, is not entirely off the mark.[54]

The question of necessity and its relationship to the construction of the fictional world is the subject of the first chapter, in which I use the poet-God/reader-creature analogy as a point of departure. The second chapter is centered on the court, on the analogy between the courtier's service and

[53] For an incisive critique of such literature-as-object-of-pleasure approaches, see Terry Eagleton, *Literary Theory: An Introduction* (Minneapolis: Univ. of Minnesota Press, 1983), esp. "The Rise of English," pp. 17–53.

[54] See the *locus classicus*, Jacob Burckhardt, *Civilization of the Renaissance in Italy* 1:143–74, for a political-cultural perspective on the emergence of the "individual"; for a socioeconomic perspective, see Alfred von Martin, *Soziologie der Renaissance* (1932; repr. Munich: C. H. Beck, 1974); see also Ernst Cassirer, *The Individual and the Cosmos in Renaissance Philosophy*, trans. Mario Domandi (New York, Barnes and Noble, 1963), esp. "The Subject-Object Problem in the Philosophy of the Renaissance," pp. 123–91. Although I think that his claim for the importance of the theological-mystical writings of Cusanus for the Renaissance are exaggerated, many of his insights and formulations on self-consciousness remain pertinent. For a recent look at Cusanus from a literary perspective, including a discussion of possible nominalist interpretations of Cusanus's use of "conjecture," see Ronald Levao, *Renaissance Minds*, pp. 3–96. A study that appeared too late for me to include its findings in this book is William Kerrigan and Gordon Braden, *The Idea of the Renaissance* (Baltimore: Johns Hopkins Univ. Press, 1989); the authors discuss both Burckhardt's and Cassirer's interpretations of the Renaissance, offer a confirmation of their importance in shaping views of that period, and carefully endorse their vision.

the creature's merit, and on literature written in a courtly context. Causality and its *mise en question* by the late scholastics inform my analysis of medieval, but especially Renaissance, models of literary authority and creation in the third chapter. The final two chapters are concerned with more purely theological concepts: God's will(s) and God's freedom or sovereignty. These concepts are seen, respectively, in relation to the creature's will in a literary text on the one hand, and to the problem of sovereignty in political discourse and literary satire on the other.[55]

[55] Although the chapters deal with facets of the same underlying issue, they are written to be read more or less independently of each other. There is, therefore, a certain amount of repetition, especially in clarifications of scholastic distinctions, which are in any case fairly unfamiliar to the nonspecialist reader. In referring to commentaries on the *Sentences*, I have used the following abbreviations: a = article, c = chapter (*capitulum*), cor = corollarium, d = distinction, n = note, p = part, q = question (q unica = only question).

ONE

THE FREE READER: HYPOTHETICAL NECESSITY

IN FICTION

T HE FIGURE of the poet and the role of the reader in Renaissance fiction have been the focus of critical attention: Robert Durling's classic analysis of the poet in epic and Terence Cave's recent essay on the reader and reading are two emblematic cases.[1] Elizabeth L. Eisenstein, in her recent *summa* on the cultural effect of printing, rightly characterizes the reading public as "more atomistic and individualistic than a hearing one."[2] The poet and the reader are roughly the two poles of the communicative situation, and the emergence of strong poet and reader figures is a sign of the increased insistence on the process of communication in the early modern period. Increased rhetorical self-consciousness also makes problematic that communicative process, and one may consequently argue for the emergence of epistemological issues in the literature of the fifteenth and sixteenth centuries. Self-conscious narrative and the predominant questions of interpretation and knowledge constitute the ground of early modern fiction, or at the very least those elements that will be developed in postmedieval fiction. The point of this study is not to once again demonstrate these "epistemic" conditions. Neither is it my intention to show their inapplicability or their origin in an earlier period. Rather, I am interested in the way in which a specific self presentation of the poet projects or implies a certain ontological status of the reader. What kind of com-

---

[1] See Durling, *Figure of the Poet*; in the introduction, Durling argues convincingly that in the Renaissance the poet figure was both increasingly revealed as the inventor of fiction and revealed as being *only* an inventor, that is, not an inspired epic poet (pp. 8–10). For his discussion of the analogy between God and the poet as creators in Ariosto, see pp. 123–32. My study is intended to elaborate some of the poet's highly complicated ways of "defining and keeping before the reader the nature of the poem in comparison with the real world" (p. 130), especially in his ending gestures. For the reader's importance, see Terence Cave, "The Mimesis of Reading in the Renaissance," in *Mimesis: From Mirror to Method*, ed. John D. Lyons and Stephen G. Nichols, Jr. (Hanover, N.H.: Univ. Presses of New England, 1982), pp. 149–65, and Cathleen M. Bauschatz, "Montaigne's Conception of Reading in the Context of Renaissance Poetics," in *The Reader in the Text*, ed. Susan R. Suleiman and Inge Crosman (Princeton: Princeton Univ. Press, 1980), pp. 264–92. See also the critique by Victoria Kahn, "The Figure of the Reader in Petrarch's *Secretum*," *PMLA* 100 (1985): 154–66.

[2] Elizabeth L. Eisenstein, *The Printing Press as an Agent of Change: Communication and Cultural Transformations in Early-Modern Europe*, 2 vols. (Cambridge: Cambridge Univ. Press, 1979), 1:132. See her somewhat sketchy discussion on pp. 129–36.

municative process is put into question by the self-conscious rhetoric of the poet? What kind of reader does that process project?

One of the most striking instances of the poet's self-presentation is the analogy Durling sees in Ariosto's *Orlando furioso* of the poet as God and the text as his creation. The constitution of the fictional text as a second creation in imitation, or in parody, of the creation of the world, is significant mainly because of its intellectual context: from late scholasticism on, the relationship between God and man is felt to be highly problematic—the interminable debates and conflicts over this question are manifestations of its invested nature.

The violence of the confrontations seems to contrast with the complexity of the question that is articulated through a series of distinctions concerning God's grace, man's merit, and man's free will. The abolition of certain conceptual distinctions is associated with the Reformers' logical radicalization of Augustinian doctrine, whereas the maintaining of late medieval scholastic distinctions characterizes the orthodox attempt to preserve a synthesis between man's reason and free will, and God's will. In this chapter I will look at the relationship of one of those distinctions concerning necessity to certain narrative strategies in Luigi Pulci's *Morgante*, Ludovico Ariosto's *Orlando furioso*, the novels of François Rabelais, and finally, as a counterpoint, in Torquato Tasso's *Gerusalemme liberata* and in Agrippa d'Aubigné's *Les tragiques*.

Absolute versus Hypothetical Necessity

In 1517 Johannes Altensteig published a compendium of scholastic theological terms first called *Vocabularius theologie*, and in later editions *Lexicon theologicum*.[3] This theological dictionary was reprinted frequently throughout the sixteenth and early seventeenth centuries, and constitutes an accessible sourcebook for scholastic definitions that had become commonplace in the intellectual atmosphere of the Reformation.[4] Under the entry "ne-

[3] In a cursory check I have found references to editions published in Paris, Antwerp, and Venice in 1567, 1576, 1579, 1580, and 1582. The 1567 edition is in fact an abridged version, with only lapidary definitions without references to sources. Beginning with the 1576 edition the source material from the first edition is restored. For the sake of convenience I quote from the currently available facsimile reprint of the 1617 Cologne edition (entitled *Lexicon theologicum*), revised by Johannes Tytz (Hildesheim: G. Olms, 1974). In no case have the initial definitions of the terms I examine been modified in later editions.

[4] For example, scholastic distinctions concerning necessity were a specific issue in the Luther-Erasmus debate on free will; Erasmus alludes to the different types of necessity, and Luther dismisses them as "Sophist delusion" (cf. the *De servo arbitrio* [1525], in *Luther and Erasmus: Free Will and Salvation; Erasmus: De libero arbitrio; Luther. De servo arbitrio*, ed. and trans. E. Gordon Rupp et al. [Philadelphia: Westminster, 1969], pp. 120–22). Similarly, in

cessitas" we find a distinction culled most directly from Gabriel Biel between "necessitas absoluta vel simpliciter" and "necessitas ex suppositione
vel ex conditione." A couple of pages further, there is an equivalent distinction between "necessitas consequentis" and "necessitas consequentiae."
The usual English translation is absolute versus hypothetical necessity and
necessity of the thing consequent versus necessity of consequence.[5]

Something is absolutely necessary if its opposite entails a contradiction.[6]
The examples given are "homo est risibilis, Deus est [man is capable of
laughter, God exists]." Hypothetical necessity is said to characterize only
the relationship between the antecedent and the consequent of an implication: for example, if Peter is predestined, then Peter will be saved. However, both the antecedent and the consequent can be contingent events,
that is, not determined by any necessity external to the sequence itself.[7]
Peter's predestination is not necessary, but contingent upon God's free

Pietro Pomponazzi's *De fato* (4.3.20–24) the distinction between *necessitas consequentiae* and
necessitas consequentis is not thought sufficient to solve the problem of God's foreknowledge
and human free will (pp. 342–44). However, Pomponazzi's own solution relies, it seems to
me, on another scholastic distinction. See my discussion in the Introduction.

[5] For the scholastic source, cf. Saint Thomas Aquinas, *Summa theologia*, vol. 1, *Summa
contra gentiles* I.81–85. See also Boethius, *Boethii consolationis philosophiae libri quinque*, ed.
and trans. Ernst Gegenschatz and Olaf Gigon, 3d ed. (Zürich: Artemis, 1981; Darmstadt:
Wissenschaftliche Buchgesellschaft, 1984), 5 prosa 6, and Gabriel Biel, *Collectorium super IV
libros sententiarum* (Tübingen: Johann Otmar, 1501), IV d 1 q 2 a 1 n 1A. The most recent
treatment of this distinction is Jaroslav Pelikan, *The Christian Tradition*, vol. 4, *Reformation
of Church and Dogma (1300–1700)* (Chicago: Univ. of Chicago Press, 1983), pp. 29–30 (on
Duns Scotus). I am less interested in various complex readings of the distinction than in a
more accessible, common definition, such as the one found in Altensteig.

[6] "Necessitas absoluta vel simpliciter dicta est quando aliquid est simpliciter necessarium,
ita quod eius oppositum includit contradictionem" (Altensteig, *Vocabularius theologie*, p.
582). The definition of necessity is taken up in William of Ockham, *Quodlibet* VI q 2 a 1:
"Dico quod duplex est necessitas: scilicet absoluta et ex suppositione. Necessitas absoluta est
quando aliquid simpliciter est necessarium, ita quod eius oppositum esse verum includit contradictionem. Et sic haec est absolute necessaria 'homo est risibilis,' 'Deus est' et huiusmodi,
quia contradictio est quod haec sint falsa et eorum opposita sint vera. Necessitas ex suppositione est quando aliqua condicionalis est necessaria, quamvis tam antecedens quam consequens sit contingens. Sicut haec est necessaria 'si Petrus est praedestinatus Petrus salvabitur,'
et tamen tam antecedens quam consequens est contingens. Vel quando aliqua talis conse-
quentia est necessaria, tunc dicitur necessitas ex suppositione," in *Opera philosophica et theologica (Opera theologica)*, ed. Joseph C. Wey, c.s.b., et al., 10 vols. (St. Bonaventure, N.Y.:
Franciscan Institute, 1980), 9:590. See the discussion in Gordon Leff, *William of Ockham:
The Metamorphosis of Scholastic Discourse* (Manchester: Manchester Univ. Press, 1975), pp.
455–56.

[7] "Necessitas ex suppositione vel ex conditione est quando aliqua conditionalis est necessaria, quamvis tam antecedens quam consequens sit contingens" (Altensteig, *Vocabularius
theologie*, p. 582). See note 6, above, on hypothetical necessity in Ockham. Charles Trinkaus
discusses hypothetical necessity in the works of Coluccio Salutati in *In Our Image and Likeness*
1:76–88.

choice to predestine him. Of course, these events can also be necessary, in theory, but in fact all events linking God's will to his creation are contingent events, according to scholastic definitions.

God's relationship to creation is precisely one of hypothetical necessity. If God wills an event, then it will necessarily take place. The necessity resides in the relationship between his will and the fact of the willed event taking place. This necessity must be distinguished from that conveyed in the following statement: It is necessary that God wills an event, and that event will take place necessarily. Necessity is not outside of or prior to God, but is found only, according to the scholastics, in the connection between his will and the willed event. This is emphasized repeatedly by phrases such as "Deus nihil agit ad extra de necessitate [God never acts towards the outside of necessity]" and "Deus ad extra non nisi contingenter agit [God acts to the outside only contingently]."[8]

The contingency of God's relationship to his creation preserves his free will and his power, for if God were to will an event because he was determined to do so by an external necessity, his power would be limited. A demonstration of God's free will and his concurrent power is provided by the contingency of the events he wills, through hypothetical necessity. God can will an event to take place *contingently*, that is, as determined by man's will, by his natural effort ("facere quod in se est"). That event will take place. God then *foresees* the event's taking place; he does not will it to necessarily take place. The difference between the foreknowledge of a contingent event and the willing of a necessary event defines the space of man's free will. Man can will a contingent event even though God has foreseen it to take place. Hypothetical necessity, or the necessity of consequence, includes both God's foreknowledge and man's free will.[9]

To put it in somewhat simpler terms, man's free will is preserved through the distinction between foreknowledge (hypothetical necessity) and cause (absolute necessity). An event *foreseen* by God can be not *caused* by him, but is caused by his creature's choice. Moreover, in order to maintain God's omnipotence, one must posit the creation of *contingency* as one

---

[8] Altensteig, *Vocabularius theologie*, pp. 583, 585. For a more elaborate logical distinction between the different types of necessity, see Linwood Urban, "Was Luther a Thoroughgoing Determinist?" *Journal of Theological Studies*, n.s., 22 (1971): 117–33. Unless indicated otherwise, all translations are my own.

[9] "Sic in praescito . . . non est necessitas absoluta, sed solum consequentiae, quia necessario sequitur: Deus praescit hoc, ergo erit, & c" (Altensteig, *Vocabularis theologie*, p. 584). See again Boethius, 5, prosa 6, and Saint Augustine, *City of God* 5, 10, for a synthesis between God's foreknowledge and man's free will. For the first humanist critique of the synthesis, see Lorenzo Valla, *On Free Will* [*De libero arbitrio*] (1483), trans. Charles Trinkaus, in *The Renaissance Philosophy of Man*, ed. Paul Oskar Kristeller, Ernst Cassirer, and John Herman Randall, Jr. (Chicago: Univ. of Chicago Press, 1948), pp. 155–82. Valla criticizes specifically the passage in Boethius.

of God's possible acts. In other words, there must be a principle of the *unnecessary* in what is otherwise a totally necessary structure, for only the unnecessary is a guarantee of God's power. It is tempting to say further that in the Augustinian tradition, and in the scholastic elaborations of that tradition, the necessary structure of God and his universe must maintain at its very origin a principle of the arbitrary, for it is precisely the arbitrary that manifests his power, and it is also the arbitrary that defines the space of man's free will.[10] Finally, one should underline the distinction between a system determined from the outside by (absolute) necessity and a system that stages a causal chain within itself, as hypothetical necessity.

The commonplace distinction between absolute and hypothetical necessity in scholastic theology is one of the paradigms by means of which the late Middle Ages and the early Renaissance conceive of the relationship between a creating consciousness and its creation. Especially in the case of allegory, the connection between poetic creation and the order of the cosmos has been frequently noted, and analogies between the human creative act and divine creation are similarly common.[11] This study is concerned less with any specific representation of these analogies than with a reproduction, in early Renaissance fiction, of the conceptual paradigm of necessity. Whether or not the respective authors were actually conscious of their use of hypothetical necessity is a secondary question: the intentional or unintentional use of conceptual paradigms is less interesting than, simply, their presence in the texts. It is in the communicative status of fiction that the issue of necessity can be raised: How does the textual universe represent its own perimeter, and the outside world reacting to it? How does the authorial consciousness represent something, or rather someone, outside of its creation, that is, the reader? This chapter began with the reiteration of recent observations of the increased role of the reader in Renaissance texts; it will be shown that hypothetically necessary fiction, in representing the reader as a free agent reacting (favorably) to the book, actually projects the real reader as an ontologically distinct entity. This essential distinction, brought on by the gesture of the reader's inclusion, is the ground of a modern notion of fiction as representing reality and, by the very nature of representation, as cut off from that reality.

[10] "Arbitrary" should be taken to mean "nonnecessary," and in certain circumstances "unpredictable." In some contexts this unnecessariness comes close to whimsicalness; the scholastics would maintain that God always has his order, even if it is not immediately understandable to man. This order is, however, not outside of God, constraining him, but is more an inner *ratio*. The line between whim and contingency is sometimes difficult to perceive, especially in *de potentia absoluta* speculation. Protestant reaffirmations of the anti-Pelagian position (grace is in essence unmerited) only confirm this tendency.

[11] See Durling, *Figure of the Poet*, pp. 130–32.

Pulci, Ariosto, Rabelais: Hypothetical Worlds

Pulci's *Morgante* (1478 and 1483) blithely posits itself as an imitation of God's creation through the Word. The poem's beginning, as linguistic creation, is identical to the beginning of the gospel of John, which defines all beginning as the Word:

> In principio era il Verbo appresso a Dio,
> ed era Iddio 'l Verbo e il Verbo Lui:
> questo era nel principio, al parer mio,
> e nulla si può far sanza Costui.
>
> (1.1.1–4)[12]

[In the beginning was the Word with God, and God was the Word and the Word was God; this was in the beginning, it seems to me, and nothing can be done without him.]

This well-known self-conscious exordium points to the analogy between poetic creation and divine creation as a secondary, playful parody. For all its serenity, the parody is, of course, not without uncertainty as to the connection between the poet and God ("al parer mio"); however, this beginning is a surface manifestation of what is an implicit analogy between poem and creation in the articulation of the poem's ending, or in the various prologues to the ending, in the final canto of the poem. Pulci repeats a traditional nautical metaphor for the book[13] and elaborates on the connection between book and reader:

> Io me n'andrò con la barchetta mia
> quanto l'acqua comporta un piccol legno,
> e ciò ch'io penso con la fantasia,
> di piacere a ognuno è il mio disegno:
> convien che varie cose al mondo sia,
> come son varii volti e vario ingegno,
> e piace all'uno il bianco, all'altro il perso,
> o diverse materie in prosa o in verso.
>
> (28.140)

---

[12] All quotations from Pulci are from the *Morgante*, ed. Franca Ageno (Milan: Ricciardo Ricciardi, 1955). On this exordium, see David Quint, *Origin and Originality*, p. 81.

[13] See Ernst Robert Curtius, *European Literature and the Latin Middle Ages*, trans. Willard Trask (Princeton: Princeton Univ. Press, 1953), pp. 128–30. The "little boat" is possibly a self-deprecatory allusion to Dante's exordium to the second book of the *Paradiso*: "O voi che siete in picrioletta barca, / desiderosi d'ascoltar, seguiti / dietro al mio legno che cantando varca" (2.1–3).

[I will go forward with my little boat, as much as the water will support a small skiff, and it is my design to please everyone with that which I think with my imagination: I agree that there are diverse things in the world, as there are diverse faces and diverse minds, and white pleases one, blue another, or diverse things in prose or in verse.]

As the ending of the *Morgante* is in sight, the poet reflects on the possible reaction to his book. He makes a distinction between *fantasia, disegno* (according to which he would like to please everyone), and *mondo* (where there is diversity, and where presumably not everyone will like the poem). This distinction is, however, not essential, as the poet does not simply leave the world to itself and thereby exclude it from his poem. Rather, Pulci's poet figure is setting up the reaction to his book as a *contingent* event, one that will depend on varying taste, as there are various faces and various *ingegni*. The poet is not predetermining reaction to his book as a necessary event, but is allowing for its immediate causation by various conditions in the *mondo*.[14]

Contingent events "outside" the book are once again foreseen, and this time specific reactions to the book are listed, in the following stanza:

> Forse coloro ancor che leggeranno,
> di questa tanto piccola favilla
> la mente, con poca esca, accenderanno
> de' monti o di Parnaso o di Sibilla;
> e de' miei fior come ape piglieranno
> i dotti, s'alcun dolce ne distilla;
> il resto a molti pur darà diletto,
> e l'aüttore ancor fia benedetto.

(20.141)

[Perhaps those who will read will, with this so small spark, light, with little kindling, the spirit of the Parnassus or the Sybil's mountain; and the learned will gather from my flowers like bees, if any nectar can be distilled from them; the rest of the poem will, however, give pleasure to many, and the author will, in addition, be blessed.]

The future tense of the verbs (*leggeranno, accenderanno, piglieranno, darà diletto, fia benedetto*) indicates the poet's certainty that diverse reactions *will* take place, although the series of clauses originates in *Forse*. The hesitating beginning seems to contradict the assurance of the following statements. Nevertheless, the very accumulation of confident pronouncements, culmi-

---

[14] The rhetorical procedure of *captatio benevolentiae* (cf. Aristotle, *Rhetoric* 1415a 25–1416a 1; [Cicero], *Ad herennium* 1, 4–7, etc.) often includes direct addresses to the reader or listener; what interests me is the specific elaboration in the texts that represent favor as *already* having been "seized."

nating in "e l'aüttore ancor fia benedetto," confirms the emergence of actual *foreknowledge* of the reaction to his book, underlined by the religious resonance of the final *benedetto*.

The foreknown reaction to the poem is further detailed when the poet enumerates several readers who will have a favorable reaction to his book (Bernardo Bellincioni, Antonio di Guido, and Poliziano [28.143–47]), although there will also be "detrattori, o spiriti maligni" (28.144.8). In summary, the *Morgante* determines its reading to be a contingent event but foresees the event anyway. Pulci's fiction stages its communication as hypothetical necessity.

Where does this leave the *real* reader? In a sense, the text appears to foreclose any reaction to itself other than the one foreseen. If one is not a detractor or evil-wisher, one cannot but find pleasure in the poem and praise its author. In a more profound sense, this staging of foreknowledge forces the reader to realize his ontological difference, as a being whose substance cannot be captured by *any* text. Even if Poliziano does like the *Morgante* and will voice a favorable opinion of it, he has done so not *because of* the foreknowledge of his reaction, but because of his choice to praise a good poem. His favorable opinion represented in the text that he then chooses to praise only demonstrates his distinctness as a being precisely not determined by the text. There is Poliziano$_1$, the real person, and Poliziano$_2$, the represented person, and it is the presence of Poliziano$_2$ that forces Poliziano$_1$ to realize his difference, even if in fact he acts just the way he was foreseen to act, as Poliziano$_2$. The real gesture of reaction is made to be felt as irrecoverable by the fact that the text represents it. So the apparent all-inclusiveness of the fictional world is at the same time an essential demarcation between itself and the "real" world of freely choosing subjects. This silent demarcation is simultaneously a projection of ontological difference.

In the ending of Pulci's poem, the inclusiveness and foreknowledge demonstrated by the figure of the poet is combined, as we have seen, with contingency, with variety, with the *forse*. It is the defining of events as contingent events which guarantees, in the theological model, man's free will, as contingency is that feature of God's relationship to creation which distinguishes foreknowledge from causation. Contingency is also that feature of God's actions which manifests his omnipotence, for God is not governed by a necessity outside himself ("Deus ad extra non nisi contingenter agit").

Similarly, the presence and exhibition of contingency in Pulci's fiction ("Forse . . . ," "come son varii volti e vario ingegno") can be understood paradoxically as a denial of any *external* necessity. The text itself produces necessity as a relationship between events that could have been otherwise—the text decides what will follow what among a variety of possibilities. Nothing outside has dictated this choice; however, once the choice is made, all is foreknown and all is included in the textual universe. This textual imperialism in its denial of exteriority produces the essentially distinct real reader who is characterized by privative freedom,[15] inaccessible to the text because denied by it. Fiction and the real reader have become absolute Others.

The denial of absolute, external necessity is evident in the *Morgante*'s ending, as it is in the final canto of Ariosto's *Orlando furioso*. A work's *ending* is an implicit admission of exteriority, of the work's limits and limitations, of a real, other world beyond its perimeter. If, analogously, there is any external necessity determining human life, it is certainly death, life's end.[16] In Altensteig's theological dictionary we find, between the entries "Necessitas absoluta" and "Necessitas consequentiae," the entry "Necessitas . . . moriendi."[17] Death and the limits of the textual world are linked in suggestive ways by Pulci in the poem's last canto: his benefactress Lucrezia Tornabuoni had unexpectedly died before the completion of the work. The poet affirms that "ma non pensai che innanzi al fin morisse [but I did not think she would die before the end]" (28.131.4). The timing of her death is thought of in terms of the poem itself ("innanzi al fin"), as if she had little right to die until after its completion. What is most radically external to the poet's control is strangely subsumed by the construction of the textual world. What is most radically other to the poem is assimilated to the poem ("innanzi al fin" is, moreover, ambiguous, and could also read "before her [expected, rightful] death"). Of course, the gesture of death's integration points to the *impossibility* of controlling real death.

The unexpected death of Lucrezia Tornabuoni is a haunting realization of a much earlier invocation of another guiding star, the Virgin Mary. As is customary in his poem, Pulci begins and closes his cantos with somewhat whimsical apostrophes to Christ, God, or the Virgin. The exordium to the thirteenth canto is particularly relevant:

[15] The distinction between privative freedom and freedom of possibility, or freedom *to* do something, has been applied with varying success by Erich Fromm, *Escape from Freedom* (New York: Holt, Rinehart and Winston, 1941), to the transition from the Middle Ages to the Renaissance (see pp. 56–122).

[16] This connection has been discussed in the classic work on closure, Frank Kermode's *The Sense of an Ending: Studies in the Theory of Fiction* (Oxford: Oxford Univ. Press, 1966); his chapter "Literary Fiction and Reality" contains a subtle meditation on the relationship between the order of fiction and the disorder of reality, based on a reading of Sartre's *La nausée*. See, for a fine discussion of the function of death in ending the "error" of Ariosto's romance, Patricia A. Parker, *Inescapable Romance: Studies in the Poetics of a Mode* (Princeton: Princeton Univ. Press, 1979), pp. 36–38.

[17] Altensteig, *Vocabularius theologie*, p. 583.

Virgine sacra, d'ogni bontà piena,
madre di Quel per cui si canta osanna,
Virgine pura, Virgine serena,
dammi la tua cotidïana manna;
colla tua mano insino al fin mi mena
di questa storia, ché 'l tempo c'inganna,
e la vita e la morte e 'l mondo cieco,
sì ch'io faccia ascoltar ciascun con meco.

(13.1)

[Holy Virgin, full of all goodness, mother of the one for whom we sing hosanna, pure and serene Virgin, give me your daily bread, with your hand lead me to the end of this story (for time deceives us, and so does life and death and the blind world), so that I can make everyone listen with me.]

The Virgin Mary guides the poet to the end, "insino al fin." It is only the next line that resolves the possible confusion inherent in the "end," making clear that the word means the end of the poem, not the end of the poet's life—"di questa storia." The poet needs the Virgin's help, "for time and life and death and the blind world deceive us." Apparently the poem is admitting the imposition of external necessity; only through the Virgin's hand can the poet overcome outside obstacles to the finishing of his poem. However, the distinction between poem and world is identified here as the distinction between sincerity and deception, as time, life, and death *deceive us*. It is not the poet who, through his fictions, deceives the real world; rather, the real world is a source of illusion. In this sense the poem has a more substantial ontological value than life, death, and time. The end of the poem becomes more important than the end of life. Rather than accepting the existence of external necessity, Pulci's fiction tends to trivialize whatever is outside itself, to the (impossible) extent of rendering death a deluding obstacle to the end of the poem. The textual world of the poem includes and deforms external necessity, just as the poet includes all those around him ("ciascun con meco"). This inclusiveness denies *real* death; this denial, however, is a tacit admission of death's complete otherness. Real death is entirely outside of the textual world; it is literally incomprehensible.

Death is also one of the a priori intertextual constraints of the *Morgante*. Orlando's death at Roncesvalle is a given necessity external to Pulci's poetic universe, and the introduction of this "prior" event into what is largely a whimsical *rifacimento* of popular epic, at the end of canto 23, is another example of the text's implicit denial of exteriority. Rinaldo and Fuligatto have just eaten well (a hermit has supplied them with plenty of fish), and they lie down to sleep:

Lasciàgli come il bruco in su le frasche,
Rinaldo e Fuligatto, insino al giorno,
ch'a questo modo smaltiran le lasche
e il mosto e ciò che la sera mangiorno;
perch'altra fantasia par che mi nasche:
sento di lungi chiamarmi col corno,
e suona quel che chiama, quanto puote,
ché qui comincian le dolenti note.

(23.48)

[He left them like a caterpillar on leafy twigs, Rinaldo and Fuligatto, until day, so that they would digest the mullets and the wine and that which they ate during the evening; for another idea seems to be coming to me: I hear from afar that someone is calling me with his horn, and he who calls is sounding (it) as much as he can, since here begin the notes of mourning.]

The "corno" calling the poet is obviously Orlando, who is calling his king, and who dies as he blows the horn (in a rewriting of Dante's "le dolenti note"). Instead of calling Charlemagne, he calls the poet ("chiamar*mi*"), who is on the same diegetic plane as the other epic characters. The poet seems, then, to be yielding to external necessity, as he is called upon by his intertext, or his historical *sujet*, to represent the death of his hero, Orlando.

However, the external death of Orlando is presented in a highly ambivalent fashion. The decision to leave Rinaldo and Fuligatto alone for a while, that is, the decision to turn to other, more pressing material, is motivated in two ways: first, so that Rinaldo and Fuligatto may digest their food ("ch'a questo modo smaltiran le lasche / e il mosto . . ."), and only then (but more importantly) because another *fantasia* appears to be emerging in the poet. *Fantasia* refers to the *idea* of a new subject matter, Orlando's death, which is presented as born in the poet's mind (cf. "ciò ch'io penso con la fantasia" [28.140.3]). Yet in the following lines the origin of the *fantasia* is determined to be the sound of the horn, something external to the poet. Thus, internal and external, invention and prior constraint, are mixed in such a way as to suggest that there is *no* exteriority, that all prior intertextual material is a consequence of the *dispositio* and the *fantasia* of Pulci's poetic universe. Perhaps the successive recounting of Rinaldo's digestion and the idea of Orlando's death is a consequence: *because* Pulci wanted to let Rinaldo digest his fish and wine he is turning to Orlando's death, as if it were not external, prior to his own free disposing of his material.

The following lines confirm this paradoxical denial of all a priori material, while the poet seems to superficially acknowledge external constraints:

O Ricciardetto, ove t'ho io lasciato?
Tu non sai, lasso, del futuro ancora.
Omè, ch'io veggo il mondo avvilupato!

(23.49.1–3)

[Oh Ricciardetto, where have I left you? You do not know, poor man, your
future yet. Alas, how confused do I see the world!]

Although Pulci's characters are part of a prior textual tradition, it is the
decision of the poet to leave Ricciardetto far away ("ove t'ho *io* lasciato").
The implication is that the poet could have decided to do otherwise, to
place him, say, at Roncesvalle. The prior material of the epic is thus re-
modeled into a contingent *dispositio* of the poet-creator who foresees future
events: "io veggo" punctuates the concluding stanzas of the canto. The
status of these events is one of hypothetical necessity—they are both foreseen by the poet and presented as contingent events, in spite of the exteriority, the priority, of Orlando's death. In this way the problem of the real
reader is mirrored in the treatment of the poetic material itself.

Whereas Pulci describes the reader's reaction to the ending of his nautical voyage as an event that will take place after he has returned, Ariosto, in
a brilliant development of this topos, includes various friends' reactions to
his return *as* he is returning to port. In canto 46 of the *Orlando furioso*
(1516, 1521, 1532), before relating the final events of the diegetic plane,
culminating in Ruggiero's killing Rodomonte, the poet sees the end of his
journey approaching:

Or, se mi mostra la mia carta il vero,
non è lontano a discoprirsi il porto;
sí che nel lito i voti sciToglier spero
a chi nel mar per tanta via m'ha scorto;
ove, o di non tornar col legno intero,
o d'errar sempre, ebbi già il viso smorto.
Ma mi par di veder, ma veggo certo,
veggo la terra, e veggo il lito aperto.

(46.1)[18]

[Now, if my map shows me the truth, the harbor will be discovered not far
from here; so that I hope to fulfill my promises on the shore to the person
who has escorted me on the ocean over such a long route; I was already afraid
of not returning with an undamaged boat, or of wandering about forever. But
it seems to me that I see, yes, I see certainly, I see land, and see the open shore.]

---

[18] Ludovico Ariosto, *Orlando furioso*, ed. Lanfranco Caretti (Turin: Einaudi, 1966). On
this stanza, see also the perceptive analyses in Parker, *Inescapable Romance*, pp. 16–17, and
Albert Russell Ascoli, *Ariosto's Bitter Harmony: Crisis and Evasion in the Italian Renaissance*
(Princeton: Princeton Univ. Press, 1987), pp. 20–21.

The beginning of the end is a gradual focusing and verification of objects seen.[19] The first perceptions are hesitant and unclear, both in theory and in practice ("*se* mi mostra la mia carta il vero"; "Ma mi *par* di veder . . ."), but eventually visual acuity is achieved ("veggo certo") as correctness is attained (as opposed to the "errar sempre")[20] and as the text is completed (the poet can in fact return "col legno intero"). The movement from indistinctness to distinctness represents, one may argue, the incompleteness of the subjective vision of the poet figure; on the other hand, the objects seen are the perimeters of his own text, that is, its end. This movement is thus not a gradual perception of things *outside* the poet's vision, but a seeing-through of his own creation: a temporal *perspicuitas* of his textual world. Similarly, the poet suggests that he is obeying an external necessity in finishing (he is guided by "la mia carta"); however, this map is nothing but the diegetic plane that the poet has so flippantly manipulated in the past ("seguitiamo," "torniamo," etc.).

Not only does the poet see the poem's ending, but he can begin to discern individuals as he approaches the shore, just as Pulci names specific readers after having referred to the reader in general ("coloro che leggeranno"):

> Or comincio a discernere chi sono
> questi che empion del porto ambe le sponde.
> Par che tutti s'allegrino ch'io sia
> venuto a fin di così lunga via.

> (46.2.5–8)

[Now I begin to discern who are those who fill both shores of the port. All seem to be happy that I have come to the end of such a long journey.]

Then follows a long list of friends who are anxiously awaiting his return. Visual terminology dominates this list: *veggo, veggio, riconosco*, and the deictic *ecco* punctuate the enumeration. Although these terms are part of the rhetorical procedure of *evidentia* or *enargeia*,[21] their specific function here

[19] Compare the beginning of the "Prologue de l'autheur . . . aux lecteurs benevoles" of Rabelais's *Quart livre* (1552): "Gens de bien, Dieu vous saulve et guard! Où estez vous? Je ne vous peuz veoir. Attendez que je chausse mes lunettes! Ha, ha! . . . Je vous voy" (ed. Robert Marichal [Geneva: Droz, 1947], p. 11).

[20] On the importance and various senses of "error" in Ariosto, see Parker, *Inescapable Romance*, pp. 16–53. Parker's reading is insightful, and in many instances comes close to my own (especially her remarks on authority and contingency), but it remains in the end a formal, literary reflection on the vicissitudes of romance and poetic language, although the introduction announces a concern for historical difference (pp. 4–5). See also Ascoli, *Ariosto's Bitter Harmony*, p. 21 n. 41.

[21] Cf. Terence Cave, *The Cornucopian Text: Problems of Writing in the French Renaissance* (Oxford: Clarendon, 1979), pp. 27–31, on these concepts in Erasmus.

is to underline the poet's *seeing* of the readers' reactions; the readers thus are the metaphorical representation of his foresight or foreknowledge.

But what, exactly, does the poet foresee? He literally sees the joy on his friends' faces as they see him return. Why they are joyous is not perfectly clear:

> Par che tutti s'allegrino ch'io sia
> venuto a fin di così lunga via.
>
> (46.2.7–8)

[All seem to be happy that I have come to the end of such a long journey.]

> Oh di ch'amici, a chi in eterno deggio
> per la letizia c'han del mio ritorno!
>
> (46.3.3–4)

[Oh what friends, to whom I am in eternal debt, because of the happiness they have over my return!]

> . . . e ciascun d'essi noto (o ch'io vaneggio)
> al viso e ai gesti rallegrarsi tanto
> del mio ritorno, che non facil parmi
> ch'io possa mai di tanto obligo trarmi.
>
> (46.11.5–8)

[And I notice that each one of them (or else I am dreaming) is in his face and gestures so happy about my return, that it does not appear easy for me to do justice to so many obligations.]

The poet's friends are happy to see the poet end his journey. It is unclear whether they are happy to see the end because the journey has been tedious or whether they are happy to see him finish so they may read the finished product. Presumably they did not accompany the poet (they are distinct from "chi nel mar . . . m'ha scorto"), but since they, as real friends, are actual readers of the poem, the reason for their joy is unclear, and Ariosto does not provide any further explanation for their rejoicing. So this reaction to the poem is either one of boredom or one of pleasure—both interpretations are possible, given the confused ontological status of Ariosto's "friends": they are apparently both inside and outside the book.

The ambivalent joy of Ariosto's readers corresponds to the hesitant foreseeing of the poem's end: "*par* che tutti s'allegrino," "mi *par* di veder," "o ch'io *vaneggio*." The poet's hesitation has a function similar to Pulci's *forse*, for Ariosto has also set up reaction to his book as a contingent event, as something perceived first indistinctly, then as a perfectly ambivalent emotion on the faces of his represented readers. Neither a negative nor a positive reaction is predetermined by the poem.

The contingent reaction of Ariosto's friends is, however, slyly foreseen by the poet, as he announces his own reaction to their reaction by his sense of debt or obligation ("in eterno deggio" [46.3.3], "tanto obligo" [46.11.8]) caused by their favorable reaction to the ending of the book. If their joyous reaction to the ending were motivated by boredom, the poet would be under no obligation or, a fortiori, under no *debt* to them, as they have given him nothing positive. The debt, fulfilled by the book's pleasing ending, is, then, a knowledge of the reader's reaction, before this reaction has taken place.[22]

So Ariosto, like Pulci, has it both ways: the book determines the reaction to itself to be a contingent event (as a product of factors other than itself, such as the reader's free will), and then foresees that event. The free reader chooses to like the book, which will then reward this choice with a pleasing ending. The obligation or debt of the poet is a reward for a foreseen and represented reaction of the reader, as God rewards freely accomplished good works that he himself has foreseen and in fact laid all the necessary ground for. The representation of hypothetical necessity in the *Orlando furioso* is again a demonstration of the real reader's essential distinctness by this attempt to completely assimilate him; in the apparent all-inclusiveness of the textual universe we find a silent projection of an absolutely free reader.[23] Foreknowledge of the reader's reaction is distinct from *causing* this reaction: even if the real reader reacts the way he was foreseen and represented to react, that real action is inaccessible to its representation, for

[22] We find a similar ending to the poem-voyage in Joachim Du Bellay's *Regrets* (1558). The poet-narrator is returning home from his "exile" in Rome and sees his friends waiting for him on the shore of France (it is probable that Du Bellay in fact took a land route). The visual terminology recalls Ariosto's text, and Du Bellay also displays confidence in his friends' reaction to his return: "Ja vers le front du port je commence à ramer, / Et voy ja tant d'amis, que ne les puis nommer, / Tendant les bras vers moy, sur le bord faire feste. / Je voy mon grand Ronsard, je le cognois d'ici, / Je voy mon cher Morel, & mon Dorat aussi, / Je voy mon Delahaie, & mon Paschal encore: / Et voy un peu plus loing (si je ne suis deceu) / Mon divin Mauleon, duquel, sans l'avoir veu, / La grace, le sçavoir & la vertu j'adore" (ed. Jean Jolliffe and M. A. Screech [Geneva: Droz, 1966], 129.6–14). The last three lines are puzzling, as Du Bellay introduces the characteristic hesitancy ("si je ne suis deceu"), but then also emphasizes that he has never seen Mauleon [Michel-Pierre de Mauléon]. Either he is debunking the poetic convention, and underlining the difference between real seeing and conventional poetic language, or he is not sure that he is seeing Mauléon because he has never seen him before, and he is standing a bit farther back. This confusion is not resolved; it is a product of the uncertainty surrounding the distinction between the fictional and the real worlds. Du Bellay is here not as whimsically imperialistic about his fiction as Ariosto, perhaps owing to the fact that underlying the sonnet is a *real* return to France.

[23] The inclusive and expansive text is treated suggestively by David Quint in "Astolfo's Voyage to the Moon," *Yale Italian Studies* 1 (1977): 398–408; my discussion is indebted to his analysis. For further study of intricate rhetorical techniques in the *Furioso* cf. William J. Kennedy, *Rhetorical Norms in Renaissance Literature* (New Haven: Yale Univ. Press, 1978), pp. 136–51. Kennedy, however, gives rather short shrift to Pulci's no less interesting devices.

the real reader knows that he could have chosen otherwise. *Causing* the reader's reaction would have meant, in this situation, not representing it.

In Rabelais's novels the traditional nautical metaphors of textual limits are replaced by a great variety of metaphors for the book and by multiple representations of the reader: the bone and the dog, the barrel of Diogenes, the boxes with deceivingly grotesque exterior decoration, Socrates the person, and so forth. Whereas Pulci and Ariosto thematize favorable or unfavorable reaction to their poems, Rabelais adds to the representation of mere like or dislike the problem of allegorical interpretation. Although interpretive themes are not absent from the Italian poems, the insistence on the possibility of a hidden meaning (especially from the *Gargantua* prologue on) seems to distinguish Rabelaisian fiction and its communicative situation. However, the shift from the reader as someone who praises or blames to the reader as someone who interprets is only a shift in the content ascribed to the reader's reaction, not a change in the way this reaction is projected by the text.

All of Rabelais's novels contain gestures toward the reader; these gestures either praise or vilify in *Pantagruel*, praise, vilify, include, and exclude in *Gargantua* and the following books. According to this differing characterization, the reader will like or dislike the novels. The text thus claims to determine reaction to itself, especially in that those excluded will dislike the novel and those included will like it.

Yet the projection of the reader is more subtle than the preceding lines suggest. In the prologue to the *Tiers livre* (1546), after a long comparison of the writer to Diogenes and his barrel, the narrator wonders if this book will not displease rather than please:

> Cestuy exemple [of Ptolemy I, whose showing of a camel produced an effect opposite to the one intended] me faict entre espoir et craincte varier, doubtant que pour contentement propensé je rencontre ce que je abhorre, mon thesaur soit charbons, pour Venus advieigne Barbet le chien, en lieu de les servir je les fasche, en lieu de les esbaudir, je les offense, en lieu de leurs complaire, je desplaise. (pp. 17–18)[24]

> [This example makes me vary between hope and fear, as I fear that instead of intended satisfaction I meet what I am afraid of, my treasure should be coals, instead of Venus should come Barbet the dog, instead of serving them, I annoy them, instead of making them gay, I offend them, instead of pleasing, I displease.]

The oscillation between fear and hope admits the contingency of reaction to the book and corresponds to the "perhaps" at the beginning of textual

[24] François Rabelais, *Le tiers livre*, ed. M. A. Screech (Geneva: Droz, 1974). All references are to this edition.

considerations of what is external to itself. This uncertainty nevertheless quickly gives way to "recognition" of certain qualities in the reader that guarantee a favorable reaction: "Je recongnois en eulx tous une forme specificque et propriété individuale, laquelle nos majeurs nommoient Pantagruelisme, moienant laquelle jamais en maulvaise partie ne prendront choses quelconques ilz congnoistront sourdre de bon, franc et loyal couraige [I recognize in all of them a specific form and individual property, which our ancestors called Pantagruelism, through which they will never take badly what they know to come from a good, free, and loyal heart]" (p. 18). The reaction of Rabelais's readers is foreseen, after all, because of the author's knowledge of his readers, who, being in the author's image (that is, "bon, franc, et loyal") will choose to accept his text. Once again the contingent event is foreseen to take place, and this time there is a more explicit connection between the creation of the text and the creation of a certain kind of reader. The reaction foreseen by the creator is determined to be a contingent event by the uncertainty and admission of variety that constitute the beginning of reflection on the limits of the textual world.

The initial admission of variety is developed by Rabelais a few lines later, when the narrator returns to his "tonneau" and enjoins the reader to read, or rather to drink, with him: "Enfans, beuvez à pleins guodetz. Si bon ne vous semble, laissez le. Je ne suys de ces importuns Lifrelofres, qui par force, par oultraige et violence, contraignent les Lans et compaignons trinquer, voire caros et alluz, qui pis est [Children, drink as much as you can. If it doesn't appear good to you, leave it. I am not among those inopportune guzzlers who by force, outrage, and violence make the soldiers and companions drink, and empty their glasses, which is worse]" (pp. 18–19).[25] Here it is less an issue of liking or disliking than of reading or not reading. The freedom of the reader is defined as the freedom to *not* read, as the possibility of being free *from* the text. This should be distinguished from all readers' freedom to like or dislike. As we have seen, Rabelais includes as readers all those who resemble himself and like his book; he excludes from the status of reader all those who dislike the book. Thus he can foresee all readers' reactions.[26]

The narrator's predetermination of the act of reading goes beyond the foreknowledge of different readers' reactions in Pulci and Ariosto. Rabelais

[25] A similar defense of his fiction is used by Pierre de Ronsard in the "Elegie à Loïs des Masures Tournisien" (1560): "Je ne contraincts personne à mon vers poeticque" (in *Oeuvres complètes*, ed. Paul Laumonier, Isidore Silver, and Raymond Lebègue [Paris: Droz, 1939], 10:363, 30).

[26] This inclusionary and exclusionary strategy is theologically overdetermined, as it were: the gospel's reception works in a similar way. God does not force people to receive his calling: in fact he sometimes forces them to *not* receive his calling (see the hardening of the Pharaoh's heart).

has redefined textual limits in terms of readers and nonreaders, and has in addition defined their freedom as privative, as a freedom from constraint. Yet it is this privative freedom that all along has been implicit in the radical distinction between the fictional world, including its represented readers, and the "real" reader. The ontological distinction between represented reader and "real" reader means that the latter is inherently *inaccessible* to his representation. This inaccessibility is recast by certain moments in Rabelaisian fiction as freedom from the constraint of reading, or rather, from the constraint *to* read.

Tasso, d'Aubigné: Return to Absolute Necessity

In counterpoint to the preceding examples of hypothetical necessity and privative freedom in Pulci, Ariosto, and Rabelais are two examples of literary works that attempt to retrieve an absolute determination of the fictional world. Torquato Tasso's *Gerusalemme liberata* (1580) is a work that was intentionally composed against the fictive play of Ariostesque romance, and that appears to stage a relation between poet and reader that is fundamentally contrary to Ariosto. The poet figure is deliberately reduced to the pre-Pulci and pre-Ariosto epic narrator who is relating something true and whose explicit responses to the diegetic events are usually emotional invitations to admire examples of virtuous behavior. Similarly, there are no extradiegetic discussions of the ending and possible reception of the book. There is only one exception to this lack of gestures to the represented reader, in the opening stanzas of the first canto. The poet addresses his patron, Alfonso II d'Este:

> Tu, magnanimo Alfonso, il qual ritogli
> al furor di fortuna e guidi in porto
> me peregrino errante, e fra gli scogli
> e fra l'onde agitato e quasi absorto,
> queste mie carte in lieta fronte accogli,
> che quasi in voto a te sacrate i' porto.
> Forse un dí fia che la presaga penna
> osi scriver di te quel ch'or n'accenna.
> E ben ragion, s'egli avverrà ch'in pace
> il buon popol di Cristo unqua si veda,
> e con navi e cavalli al fero [T]race
> cerchi ritôr la grande ingiusta preda,
> ch'a te lo scettro in terra, o, se ti piace,
> l'alto imperio de' mari a te conceda.

Emulo di Goffredo, i nostri carmi
in tanto ascolta, e t'apparecchia a l'armi.

(1.4–5)[27]

[You, magnanimous Alfonso, who protect me, wandering pilgrim, from the furors of fortune, who guide me to port, between the cliffs and the agitated water, almost sunk, and who receive these pages of mine with a serene face, pages which I bring almost like an offering to you. Perhaps a day will come when the prophetic pen will dare write about you that which it now only suggests. It is just that, if ever it will happen that the people of Christ sees itself at peace, and with boats and horses seeks to take back the great unjustly acquired prey from the savage Turk, the command of the land army, or, if you like, the naval forces, be conceded to you. Emulator of Goffredo, listen to our songs, and prepare yourself for the arms.]

These two stanzas can be seen as written against Ariostesque fiction, both in their textual echoes of Pulci and Ariosto and in the reformulation of the reader's function. The nautical metaphor is the most obvious link. As in the earlier poems, the patron is conceived as a guide (cf. the probable reference of "chi nel mar per tanta via m'ha scorto," *Orlando furioso* 46.1.4) to a safe port. Ariosto's "mia carta" (ibid.) becomes "queste mie carte." The joyful reaction of waiting friends ("la letizia c'han del mio ritorno," 46.3.4) becomes the "lieta fronte" of Alfonso, and the reaction in Tasso seems rather less ambiguous than in Ariosto's poem.

However, a fundamentally different reading is projected here, for Tasso insists on the imitation or emulation of Goffredo by Alfonso. The positive reception of the book is taken for granted, or is indifferent to its basic intention. The poem is thought of as causing its reader to act; the poem leads to action, enables action, and is not essentially separate from the real world of readers. The hortatory, confident tone of the final two lines, distinct in their syntactic simplicity from the preceding sentences, underlines the cause-effect relationship between book and real action.

The homogeneity of poem and world is manifest in other ways. The poet essentially performs the same actions as his represented heroes, and as the reader Alfonso d'Este. The final line of the stanzas quoted exhorts Alfonso to take up arms ("t'apparecchia a l'armi"), which recalls what the poet is doing ("Canto l'arme pietose [I sing of pious arms]," 1.1.1). In addition, the offering of the poem ("queste mie carte . . . in voto a te sacrate i' porto") is not a gratuitous gift, but also entails a promise of return on the part of the receiver. "Voto" is ambivalent here, meaning both offering and promise, as the final line of Tasso's poem implies: "[Goffredo] il gran Sepolcro adora, e *scioglie il voto* [Goffredo adores the grand sepulchre

[27] Torquato Tasso, *Gerusalemme liberata*, ed. Luigi de Vendittis (Turin: Einaudi, 1961).

and fulfills the promise]" (italics mine). Goffredo has kept his promise; the poet has kept his promise to Alfonso; now it is up to Alfonso to keep *his* promise and to conquer the Holy Land. The poem stages its relationship to the reader as homogeneity ("i nostri carmi"), as causation, and as providing conditions *to* act. In this sense the reader is free *to* take up arms in defense of Christendom, but not free *from* his textual representation. Not only is the real reader submitted to the necessity of emulation, but the poem, too, is a product of anterior, external causes. The fact that Goffredo kept his promise obliges the poet to keep his promise. The poet is subject to his representation, which is subject to external, real events. In this aspect also Tasso is writing against the hypothetical, internally necessary universe of the Ariostesque poet-God.

Yet Tasso's impossible attempt to situate himself *before* Ariosto is undercut by its very concentration *on* Ariosto. Intertextuality seems to condemn even the Christian poet to the hypothetical. The poem is only a collection of pages "*quasi* in voto a te sacrate"; although the obvious meaning of this hesitation is Tasso's refusal of idolatry, he cannot avoid introducing uncertainty concerning the book's reception, given the previous hesitating perceptions of textual limits in Pulci and Ariosto. Similarly, the prophecy concerning Alfonso's future actions is undercut by an initial admission of contingency ("*Forse* un dí fia"), which in turn is reinforced by the conditional exhortation to Alfonso ("*s'egli averrà ch'*in pace . . .") (italics mine). The reappearance of these gestures of hesitation points to the paradoxical situation of the early modern poet who necessarily writes in the absence of external necessity, who will always be irrecoverable by his representation. Tasso recasts the poet figure as the "peregrino," but cannot avoid adding the ambiguous "errante," which not only is a depiction of Christian life as a *peregrinatio* between birth and death but also recalls Ariosto's "errar sempre" (46.1.6) and reintroduces all the epistemological problems it was so important to exclude.

Whereas in the *Gerusalemme liberata* the poet figure is extremely reduced, so as to let the imperatives of Christian life seem more universal, in Agrippa d'Aubigné's *Les tragiques* (composed ca. 1577–1589, published 1616), the poet is at the same time actor, witness, and intermediary between God and man.[28] The poem commemorates the struggle of the Huguenots, satirizes the Catholic monarchy, and calls for action, on the part of God and on the part of the readers. The exordium makes clear the sameness of fictional world and real world:

[28] For an analysis of the rhetorical situation in *Les tragiques*, see Kennedy, *Rhetorical Norms*, pp. 151–66, and my *Rhétorique et intersubjectivité: 'Les tragiques' d'Agrippa d'Aubigné* (Tübingen: Papers on French Seventeenth-Century Literature, 1983). See also Frank Lestringant, "L'ouverture des 'Tragiques': D'Aubigné, César, et Moïse," *Bulletin de la Société de l'histoire du protestantisme français* 133 (1987): 5–22.

Puisqu'il faut s'attaquer aux legions de Rome,
Aux monstres d'Italie, il faudra faire comme
Hannibal, qui par feux d'aigre humeur arrosez
Se fendit un passage aux Alpes embrasez.
Mon courage de feu, mon humeur aigre et forte
Au travers des sept monts faict breche au lieu de porte.

("Misères," 1–6)[29]

[Since one must attack the legions of Rome, the Italian monsters, one must
do like Hannibal, who by fires of acid liquid cut for himself a passage through
the blazing Alps. My heart of fire, my acrid and strong temper across the seven
hills makes a breach, not a door.]

The opening line is the conclusion of an argument or deliberation. What
has preceded the poem, and is outside of the poet, is projected as being of
the same material as the poem itself. There is no variety outside the poem:
the "hors-texte" directs the poem's teleology as a unified, simple force.[30]
This force not only arises from the miserable circumstances of the religious
wars, but can be found in history (Hannibal), and imposes imperatives for
the future ("il faudra faire"). The poem is merely one of a necessary chain
of events; the poet displays his determination by these events. Among Renaissance epics this is probably the most single-minded invocation of absolute necessity. We have here a literal version of the rhetoric of *movere*:
everything is moved by forces outside, necessarily.

D'Aubigné addresses his readers at various points in the poem, and in
contrast to writers like Pulci, Ariosto, and Rabelais, he does not posit a
free reaction on the reader's part. The readers are as much determined as
he is himself, and the poem's world *is* their real world:

Vous qui avez donné ce subject à ma plume,
Vous-mesmes qui avez porté sur mon enclume
Ce foudre rougissant aceré de fureur,
Lisez-le: vous aurez horreur de vostre horreur!

("Princes," 9–12)

[You who have given this subject to my pen, you yourselves who have carried
onto my anvil this lightning reddening, sharpened by fury, read it! You will
be horrified by your own horrors!]

[29] All quotations are from Agrippa d'Aubigné, *Oeuvres*, ed. Henri Weber, Jacques Bailbé,
and Marguerite Soulié (Paris: Gallimard, 1969).

[30] These words of Montaigne can be applied to d'Aubigné ("mon humeur aigre et forte"):
"C'est toujours un'aigreur tyrannique de ne pouvoir souffrir une forme diverse à la sienne"
("De l'art de conferer," in Les *essais* III, 8, ed. Pierre Villey, revised by Verdun-L. Saulnier
[Paris: Presses univ. de France, 1965], p. 928).

The poem takes its horrible subject from the readers (Catholics, here) and gives it back to them: the reader is merely discovering his own horrors in the horrors depicted. The fictional world is not an alternative world, and in fact does not conceive of a distinction between itself and its context. Free will is simply irrelevant. The poem *causes* reactions on the outside, just as it is caused to come into being by outside events.

The poet does realize his own limitations: he has not *always* devoted his poetic talent to the Huguenot cause, and, in a gesture recalling Saint Augustine, he repudiates his youthful errors ("Misères," 55–58); the Calvinist leader Théodore de Bèze similarly proclaimed the sinfulness of his youthful poetry. But that wavering is now over. If the poem lacks in efficient causation of intended effects, it is not because of the inherently illusory nature of literary representation or any other epistemological doubts, it is because God has not conferred enough power to the poet. So the poet must invoke divine retributory power, and the poem will *be* that retribution:

> Je voi ce que je veux, et non ce que je puis,
> Je voi mon entreprise, et non ce que je suis:
> Preste-moi, verité, ta pastorale fonde,
> Que j'enfonce dedans la pierre la plus ronde
> Que je pourrai choisir, et que ce caillou rond
> Du vice-Goliath s'enchasse dans le front.
>
> ("Princes," 43–48)

[I see what I want, and not what I can. I see my enterprise, and not what I am: give me, Truth, your pastoral slingshot, so that I may place into it the roundest stone that I can choose, and so that this round stone may plant itself into the forehead of the vice-Goliath.]

The poem becomes the "caillou rond"; this stone will lodge itself in the head of the Catholic Goliath. The "voluntarism" of d'Aubigné is quite distinct from the whimsical construction of a fictional world by the poet's will; it is secondary to the truth, and is more a sign of election than of autonomy.

Election is also what the poet asks God to do, and what the poet would like the poem to do ("ce pacquet à malheurs ou de parfaicte joye [this package of sorrows or of perfect joy]," "Jugement," 22). Especially in the last two books of *Les tragiques*, the poet describes and exercises the selection of the elect and the designation of the reprobate. The poem places itself, then, *after* contingency. The poem is, as it were, the apodosis of a condition: "If you persecute the true Church, then you will be damned." The persecution *has* taken place, so damnation will necessarily follow. There is no more question of choice here, neither on man's nor on God's part. Any contingency has ended before the poem begins and is irrelevant to the poem. Events are now necessary.

D'Aubigné's epic is exceptional in its insistence on the sameness of fictional and real worlds, and in its rhetoric of divine causation. The absolutely involved author and the correspondingly determined reader strike us as somehow strange; critics have remarked on the singularity of *Les tragiques*, on its lack of generic "place."[31] This is certainly a measure of how familiar the model of hypothetical necessity has become, and how Ariosto, Rabelais, and Tasso (in his doubts) have come to determine our view of the fictional world. In d'Aubigné's poem we are dealing with literary representation that is vehemently beyond self-consciousness and that defies what we think of as an inherent limitation of the fictional world. We as readers are part of a divine plan, we are captured in our *essence* by our representation. Nothing could be more antagonistic to our sense of literature.

The conception of fiction as hypothetical necessity, as we have seen, is parallel to certain conceptions of both the authorial subject and the reader. The arbitrary self-generation of the godlike creator is a model for the inaccessible, ontologically distinct consciousness of the creating author, and concurrently projects the reader as a radically autonomous consciousness. Real author and real reader are posited as inaccessible by the text, which purports to communicate between them.

The conjoining of early modern fictional strategies and the divine analogy produces a kind of reader and a kind of author that should be familiar to post-Saussurean readers. The concept of author and reader as ineffable entities underlies, for example, narratology in its separation of the text-object from any real instance of enunciation and reception. A classic example of this separation is the distinction between the *sujet de l'énonciation* (the subject performing the act of enunciation) and the *sujet de l'énoncé* (the subject of the enunciated sentence, or the represented subject, in a phrase such as "I see a house"). Parallel to and implied by this distinction we find the *lecteur réel* and the *narrataire* or *lecteur virtuel* (the real reader versus the represented or implied reader). These distinctions are forcefully put forth in an early summary of structuralism in poetics by Tzvetan Todorov:

> Voir une maison, et dire "Je vois une maison" sont deux actes non seulement distincts mais opposés. Les événements ne peuvent jamais "se raconter eux-mêmes"; l'acte de verbalisation est irréductible. Sinon, on confondrait le "je" avec le véritable sujet de l'énonciation, qui raconte le livre. Dès que le sujet de

---

[31] See, for example, Marguerite Soulié, *L'inspiration biblique dans la poésie religieuse d'Agrippa d'Aubigné* (Paris: Klincksieck, 1977); she sees it as profoundly biblical, prophetic, and hardly "literary."

l'énonciation devient sujet de l'énoncé, ce n'est plus le même sujet qui énonce. Parler de soi-même signifie ne plus être le même "soi-même." L'auteur est innommable: si on veut lui donner un nom, il nous laisse le nom mais ne se trouve pas derrière lui; il se réfugie éternellement dans l'anonymat.[32]

[Seeing a house and saying "I see a house" are two acts not only distinct but opposed. Events can never "recount themselves"; the act of verbalization is irreducible. If not, one would confuse the "I" with the real subject of the enunciation, who is recounting the book. As soon as the subject of the enunciation becomes the subject of the enunciated sentence, it is no longer the same subject that enunciates. Speaking about oneself signifies no longer being "oneself." The author is unnameable: if one wants to give him a name, he leaves us the name but never is behind the name; he eternally takes refuge in anonymity.]

It would be a lengthy project to examine the concept of "world" implied by this radical distinction between acts and speech representing those acts. In the light of the preceding analyses, a few remarks on the way in which this distinction is presented can be made here. Speech acts and "real" acts are thought of not only as different, but as *opposed*. The author is not only difficult to recapture through the language he uses, but is properly *unnameable*; he eternally vanishes and recedes before attempts to give him a name.[33] The analogy with God as a perfectly irreducible, perfectly ineffable, and perfectly autonomous being will not have escaped attention. God, and the author, can never be submitted to any necessity outside of themselves—concurrently the real reader is a creature ontologically distinct from the text that attempts to recuperate him.

In many ways the irrecoverable subject of the enunciation and the inviolable real reader are self-evident concepts underlying our understanding of the nature of fiction (and possibly also of language in general); however, the preceding examples have shown that in literature such concepts can be linked to a certain historical understanding of the textual universe and to a certain conception of freedom. Thus narratology is a child of early modern

[32] Tzvetan Todorov, *Qu'est-ce que le structuralisme?* vol. 2, *Poétique* (Paris: Seuil, 1973), p. 65. A similar distinction is urged by Durling, *Figure of the Poet*, pp. 1–3. An analogous rule covers the reader: "Le narrataire n'est pas le lecteur réel, pas plus que le narrateur n'est l'auteur: il ne faut pas confondre le rôle avec l'acteur qui l'assume. Cette apparition simultanéé n'est qu'une instance de la loi sémiotique générale selon laquelle 'je' et 'tu' (ou plutôt l'émetteur et le récepteur d'un énoncé) sont toujours solidaires" (p. 67). The standard study of the vicissitudes of the reader is Gerald Prince, "Introduction à l'étude du narrataire," *Poétique* 4 (1973): 178–96. Much work has since been done in this area. See W. Daniel Wilson, "Readers in Texts," *PMLA* 96 (1981): 848–63, for a lucid summary.

[33] Compare, in a different register, Michel Foucault, "What Is an Author?" trans. Josué Harari, in *The Foucault Reader*, ed. Paul Rabinow (New York: Pantheon, 1984): "In current usage, however, the notion of writing seems to transpose the empirical characteristics of the author into a transcendental anonymity" (p. 104).

fiction: the taxonomic and functional definitions of narrative set forth by the scientists of the text are pendants to the expansion of textual perimeters in early modern romances and novels. At the same time, the investment in the absolute inaccessibility of the "real" author and the "real" reader is produced by that very taxonomic and descriptive functional impulse. The reader is free *from* such constraints, just as the real reader in fiction is free *from* his textual representation.[34]

The privative freedom that characterizes the relationship between real authors, real readers, and texts that represent them is a link between a modern concept of fiction, exemplified by narratology, and the emergence of fiction as hypothetical necessity in the early Renaissance. The starting point for the examination of this emergence was a scholastic distinction between two kinds of necessity. This distinction involved the contingency of events foreseen by God: God can will an event to happen contingently, as a result of man's free choice, and foresee its happening. This foreknowledge is perceived as different from causation or determination of an event. It is when this difference is no longer felt to be significant (as in Lorenzo Valla, in Luther, and in the Reformers) that the scholastic synthesis between man's reasonable actions and God's will breaks down. The difference between foreknowledge and causation is insignificant precisely when freedom is not conceived of as freedom *to* determine an event, but freedom *from* any constraint, freedom from foreknowledge of the result of an action. Foreknowledge, then, resembles causation in the sense that an event foreknown by God and an event caused by God both could not have been otherwise, could not have *not* taken place. Once this becomes the criterion for freedom, man's free will is radically incompatible with God's power, and radically incommensurate with any plan of events.

The scholastic synthesis and inclusiveness depends in this case on a certain notion of freedom; fiction reproduces the schema of scholastic inclusiveness, but the notion of freedom essential to the sameness of real world

[34] In these pages I am assuming a different understanding of the textual world in the Middle Ages, although late scholastic emphasis on privative freedom contains within it the conceptual foundation of the phenomena I have been discussing. For examples of an earlier, different understanding of the textual world, see below, Chapter Three, on causality, esp. "Authority as Prior Cause." A typical example of the status of the reader is the (non)prologue of Chrétien de Troyes's *Chevalier au Lion (Yvain)*: "Artus, li boens rois de Bretaingne / la cui proesce nos enseigne / que nos soïens preu et cortois, / tint cort si riche come rois / a cele feste qui tant coste, / qu'an doit clamer la Pantecoste" (vol. 4 of *Les romans de Chrétien de Troyes*, ed. Mario Roques [Paris: Champion, 1971], ll. 1–6). Although the tone of the last two lines is ironic (with the pun on "Pantecoste"), the reader is included in the initial first person plural, without being specifically designated as distinct from the courtly community. The reading of *Yvain* will *enable* the reader to increase his own valor and courtesy, and thus feel a part of the textual world, which is not essentially distinct from the "real" world.

and textual world is no longer taken for granted, and as a result, the very gesture of inclusion becomes a projection of complete irretrievability of author and reader. The gesture of inclusion, then, masks a more fundamental exclusion, and it is this exclusion of the real by its representation that constitutes our notion of fiction.

TWO

FREE REWARD: MERIT IN COURTLY LITERATURE

Spesse volte mi viene un dubbio, s'è dato dal nascimento
(come nell'altre cose ancora) ch'i Principi siano propitii &
favorevoli verso questi, iniqui & crudeli verso quegli altri, o se
pure è posto nella industria nostra.
(Francesco Sansovino, *Propositioni in materia di cose di Stato*)[1]

ASTIGLIONE'S *Libro del cortegiano* (1528) and Renaissance courtesy literature in general chart an uneven course between the description of an illustrious courtly ideal never fully incarnate and the establishment of a set of rules enabling courtly practice and prescription. These two intentions, one roughly Platonic and the other roughly Aristotelian, are in the end contradictory, for the more substantial the ideal becomes, the less it can accommodate varying experience and therefore practice. The impulse to set forth an ideal as something outside of life's diversity through which experience is to be judged is incompatible with the production of that ideal through the experiential mean of varying extremes. Thus courtesy literature presents an unstable mixture of the specific and the universal; it constantly demands concise portraits of the ideal courtier but refuses to give definitive rules by which all aspiring courtiers might be able to become successful servants of the prince. That which courtly manuals are designed to teach precisely cannot be taught: "[è] quasi in proverbio che la grazia non s'impari [it is almost proverbial that grace is not learned]."[2] The subsequent solution, the imitation of living successful courtiers (1.26), is of course in itself an imitation of Cicero's and Quintilian's advice to rhetoricians, but it hardly resolves the epistemological problem endemic to the uneasy combination of Neoplatonic ideals and Aristotelian practice.[3]

---

[1] "Often a doubt comes to me, if it is given from birth (as in other things) that princes are favorable to some, unjust and cruel to others, or if this lies in our own work." Unless indicated otherwise, all translations are my own.

[2] Baldassarre Castiglione, *Il cortegiano del conte Baldesar Castiglione*, ed. Vittorio Cian (Florence: Sansoni, 1894), 1.25. All quotations are from this edition. Translations are from *The Book of the Courtier*, trans. Charles S. Singleton (New York: Anchor, 1959). On the difficulties of the *Cortegiano*'s dual insistence on the technical and the ideal, and its "discursive" consequences, see Roberto Esposito, *Ordine e conflitto: Machiavelli e la letteratura politica del rinascimento italiano* (Naples: Liguori, 1984), pp. 97–108.

[3] See Cicero, *De oratore* 1.22, 3.21; Quintilian, *Institutio oratoria* 10.2. On the difference

If the preceding problem is suggested by the sources of courtesy literature in antiquity, it seems necessary to relocate these esthetic and ethical dilemmas in the intellectual context of the early Renaissance. For example, the civic virtues of the Ciceronian orator must be seen in the light of a more or less despotic court.[4] Similarly, the esthetic discussion of *grazia*, of service, dignity, merit, and their rewards, can be seen in analogy to theological models of grace, merit, and works. The structural homology between esthetic grace and divine grace is implicit, but conceptually powerful, as it is exactly Christian culture that distinguishes Castiglione from Cicero, in spite of the Renaissance's ostentatious attempts to retrieve a pure antiquity.[5] The contradictions delineated by courtesy literature between the esthetic and ethical realms can be conceived of as the progressive accommodation of a principle of the arbitrary, or, conversely, it is the arbitrary that dictates a certain esthetic or ethical problem. The refusal to render ideals accessible, and the refusal ultimately to guarantee the successful application of rules, result from an avowed original arbitrariness that takes the form of Fortune or the prince's whims.[6] Similarly, the principal conceptual distinction defining late medieval reasoning on the relationship between man's merit and God's grace can be seen as an attempt to accommodate God's incommensurability with the creature, or, from the creature's point of view, his arbitrariness.

Before reviewing late scholastic definitions of merit, a few remarks about the way theological analysis is used in this study are in order. The demonstrations of conceptual homologies in the realms of theology, courtly politics and esthetics, and literary narrative are intended to be attempts to illuminate the channels of thought through which early modern society conceived of arbitrary or at least unconstrained power in ethical and es-

---

between Cicero and Castiglione, see Daniel Javitch, *Poetry and Courtliness in Renaissance England* (Princeton: Princeton Univ. Press, 1978), pp. 21–49. On the influence of the *Nicomachean Ethics*, cf. Eduardo Saccone, "Grazia, Sprezzatura, Affettazione in the Courtier," in *Castiglione: The Ideal and the Real in Renaissance Culture*, ed. Robert W. Hanning and David Rosand (New Haven: Yale Univ. Press, 1983), pp. 45–67.

[4] See Daniel Javitch, "Il cortegiano and the Constraints of Despotism," in *Castiglione*, ed. Hanning and Rosand, pp. 17–28. Javitch usefully relates behavior of the courtier to the ever-present power of the sovereign; my own discussion is indebted to his reorientation of the study of the *Cortegiano*; I attempt to elaborate and deepen discussion of the relationship between esthetics and power through the use of contemporary nominalist distinctions concerning the gratuitousness of reward.

[5] Obviously Bembo's Neoplatonic rapture at the end of the *Cortegiano* represents a conflation of Christianity and Platonism; however, his speech hardly presents adequate solutions to the various problems indicated in the first three books, and is only one of several points of view.

[6] See, on this problem, the suggestive analysis in Frank Whigham, *Ambition and Privilege: The Social Tropes of Elizabethan Courtesy Theory* (Berkeley: Univ. of California Press, 1984), pp. 33–35.

thetic realms of culture. These "channels" do not form a coherent model, but instead show an interference or conflict between two visions of the relationship between Creator and creatures, between sovereign and subjects. This book does not intend to demonstrate the *influence* of one cultural domain on another, although that has been a concern of some studies of nominalist theology and humanism.[7] Rather, it is concerned more with *possibilities* of thought—that is, neither the explicit relationship of one idea to another nor actual historical contact between persons thinking various thoughts. The reason for according theology a certain privilege in elucidating a specific channel of thought is simple: there is no other intellectual domain as elaborately and brilliantly worked out in late medieval and Renaissance culture.

Condign versus Congruous Merit

Although early scholastics identify numerous types of merit,[8] by the late Middle Ages the primary discussion of merit revolves around the distinction between *meritum ex condigno* and *meritum de congruo*.[9] Condign merit is a pact of justice between equals, or at least between commensurable partners: man freely performs a charitable act and is rewarded necessarily by God with grace.[10] According to the scholastics, and in general according to medieval anti-Pelagian thought, condign merit is beyond natural man's capacities. Natural man's actions are never in proportion to the grace re-

[7] Heiko A. Oberman argues for at least a parallelism between the nominalist emphasis on the autonomy of man and Neoplatonic individualism, in "Some Notes on the Theology of Nominalism." See the critique of this study by Charles Trinkaus, in *In Our Image and Likeness* 1:59–60. In spite of Oberman's rather too brief treatment of humanist texts, the conceptual parallels are important and, I believe, even more pervasive and structural.

[8] See Artur Michael Landgraf, *Dogmengeschichte der Frühscholastik* (Regensburg: F. Pustet, 1952), vol. 1, pt. 1, pp. 249–80, on antecedents to condign and congruous merit. Peter Cantor names seven types of merit (pp. 269–70), for example.

[9] For discussions of this distinction, see Reinhold Seeberg, *Lehrbuch der Dogmengeschichte* (Darmstadt: Wissenschaftliche Buchgesellschaft, 1959), 3:459–62; Jaroslav Pelikan, *The Christian Tradition*, vol. 4, *Reformation of Church and Dogma (1300–1700)*, pp. 145–46; Steven Ozment, *The Age of Reform (1250–1550)*, pp. 233–36; finally, a succinct set of definitions is found in Johannes Altensteig, *Vocabularius theologie*. Luther criticizes this distinction: see Luther, *De servo arbitrio*, pp. 309–12, 321. Gabriel Biel nearly conflates the distinction (see Heiko A. Oberman, *The Harvest of Medieval Theology: Gabriel Biel and Late Medieval Nominalism* [Cambridge, Mass., Harvard Univ. Press, 1963], pp. 169–74).

[10] "Meritum ex condigno est meritum pro quo exigitur praemium ex debito. . . . Meritum condigni sive de condigno, est actus à voluntate elicitus vel libere procedens ad praemium alicui secundum debitum iustitiae retribuendum. Consistit autem iustitia illa in quadam proportione meriti ad praemium & aequalitate." (Altensteig, *Vocabularius theologie*, p. 546).

warded. Congruous merit, on the other hand, posits an essential incommensurability between man's actions and God's rewards; it is through God's initial *liberalitas*, a free and unrequired generosity, that he renders man capable of good actions and then rewards those actions with grace, although those actions are never inherently proportionate to their reward.[11] God can be more or less relied upon to reward charitable actions, for he has promised that he will do so: God keeps his own promise, his pact with himself.[12] The relationship between man and God is, then, still one of incommensurability, but by virtue of God's proportionality to himself he will reward charitable actions of natural man. The term *congruous* refers to this promise, and to the fittingness of actions performed to the best of natural man's capacities (*facere quod in se est*).[13] This double fittingness (*idoneitas*), which arises out of God's *liberalitas*, is a substitute for the pact of equal partners implied by the unacceptable condign merit.[14]

[11] "Meritum de congruo est actus libere elicitus, acceptatus ad aliquid retribuendum non ex debito iustitiae, sed ex sola acceptantis liberalitate. Et hoc meritum non coexigit aequalitatem dignitatis cum retributo neque in operante, nec in opere, nec in retribuente" (Altensteig, *Vocabularius theologie*, p. 547).

[12] This promise is his *potentia ordinata*, based on Zech. 1:3 ("Si converteris, convertam te"), as opposed to his *potentia absoluta*, which holds that all of God's actions are contingent upon his free will and he does nothing absolutely out of external necessity. See Altensteig, *Vocabularius theologie*, p. 547: "Et licet Deus nullius debitor esse possit ex natura rei, potest tamen se facere debitorem nostrum ex sua libera voluntate, nobis promittendo pro talibus actibus tantum praemium. Sicut homo gratis promittens alicui ex sua libertate donum, se debitorem illi constituit, tenetur enim secundum iustitiam servare promissum." For an extensive discussion of the distinction in God's powers see Francis Oakley, *Omnipotence*, pp. 48–59; on its relationship to salvation see pp. 62–64.

[13] See the lapidary definition of *facere quod in se est* in Johannes Altensteig, *Compendium vocabularii theologici scholastici anno 1517* . . . : "[Ratio] per quam potest comprehendere Deum esse, & invocare adiutorium Dei" (ed. F. Thomas Beauxamis [Paris: Guillaume Chaudiere, 1567], f. 41ʳ). In the other editions we find a more elaborate definition: "Si peccator avertit suum liberum arbitrium ab actu peccati, considerando divinam iustitiam damnantem reprobos, & convertit ipsum ad obediendum Deo, & diligendum Deum ex consideratione misericordiae, qua salvat electos, ex primo generatur timor, è secundo spes: hoc faciendo facit quod in se est" (Altensteig, *Vocabularius theologie*, p. 548). This concept of doing one's best under the circumstances also appears in Aristotle's discussion of friendship between unequals in the *Nicomachean Ethics*: "This then is also the way in which we should associate with unequals; the man who is benefited in respect of wealth or excellence must give honour in return, repaying what he can. For friendship asks a man to do what he can, not what is proportional to the merits of the case; since that cannot always be done, e.g. in honours paid to the gods or to parents; for no one could ever return to them the equivalent of what he gets, but the man who serves them to the utmost of his power is thought to be a good man" (1163b 12–18; trans. W. D. Ross and J. O. Urmson). See also 1159a 1–5, where Aristotle seems to question the possibility of friendship with God.

[14] On this double fittingness, Landgraf quotes Guillaume d'Auvergne (*De meritis*, c. 1): "Similiter et qui orat Deum, ut remittat sibi peccata, quod suum est vel potest lugendo, dolendo, penitendo, lacrimando, *congruit divinae bonituti*, ut misereatur ipsius, *congruit etiam cordi sic parato*, ut respiciatur a Deo eique gratiam suam infundat" (*Dogmengeschichte*, vol. 1, pt. 1, p. 274 n. 25; italics mine).

These scholastic definitions of the two most important types of merit are relevant to the problem of courtesy in that they constitute a conceptual backdrop in theology for two central issues in court life: the issue of power and favor, and the issue of esthetic grace. In the move from a contractual situation defined by the commensurability of the partners to a situation defined by the powerful sovereign's or God's generosity we see sketched out the transition from a feudal-contractual relationship between the king and his vassals to the preabsolutist court, where the courtiers are made to depend entirely on the favor of the prince.

This transition is undoubtedly most obvious in the definitions of the feudal lord's and the absolute king's powers: their contrast closely parallels the definition of God's powers in the merit distinction outlined above. On the one hand, the proportionate, reciprocal relationship characteristic of feudal *homage* is summarized clearly in the thirteenth century by Philippe de Remy in his *Coutume de comté de Clermont en Beauvaisis*: "Nous disons et voirs est selonc nostre coustume, que pour autant comme li hons doit a son seigneur de foi et de loiauté par la reson de son homage, tout autant li sires en doit a son homme [We say and it is true according to our custom that inasmuch as the vassal owes his lord faith and loyalty in virtue of his homage, the lord owes these to his vassal as well]."[15] The feudal relationship is, then, at least in principle (and often in practice), one of mutual dependence, even if the powers of the lord are acknowledged as being greater. In fact, the common measurability of power is what is important here. Similarly, in the quasi-Pelagian relationship of condignity, man's right to salvation through good works assumes an inherent quality in works that is measurable in relationship to the grace God has to offer.

On the other hand, the absolutist concentration of power tends to deny precisely a measure outside of the sovereign in relation to which sovereign and subject can both be evaluated. The king becomes the *lex animata*, that is, his actions *are* the law, rather than *conform* to a law. In this sense he possesses, as Jean Bodin formulates it, *summa legibus soluta potestas*.[16] Once

[15] Quoted in F. L. Ganshof, *Feudalism*, trans. P. Grierson (New York: Harper and Row, 1961), p. 94; see also pp. 94–97. For a standard summary of mutual obligations between lord and vassal, see Heinrich Mitteis, *Lehnrecht und Staatsgewalt: Untersuchungen zur mittelalterlichen Verfassungsgeschichte* (Weimar: H. Böhlaus, 1933), pp. 531–55 ("Die Rechte and Pflichten aus dem Lehnsverhältnis im allgemeinen"). Mitteis does point out that the feudal relationship is weighted in favor of the lord, and in this differs from Roman contract.

[16] These are, of course, formulas derived from Roman law (for a more elaborate discussion of sovereignty in political theory, see Chapter Five). Although feudal mutual obligation does continue to play a role in the practice of royal power, the tendency is to generalize an absolute concentration of power. Thus court relations begin to supplant feudal relations of *homage*. This is especially true, in the period I am dealing with, of the French monarchy. See on this question the brief summary in R. J. Knecht, *Francis I* (Cambridge: Cambridge Univ. Press, 1982), pp. 89–98, and the discussion of absolutist theory (Claude de Seyssel and Guillaume Budé), pp. 19–23. I realize that there is much debate as to how truly absolutist or even

in place, the monarch's transcendent status is analogous to the nominalist God's *potentia absoluta*: there is nothing *prior* to God by which he may be constrained, although God tends to keep his promises to man.[17] This priority of God's free will and power can appear to the insufficient creature as a principle of capriciousness or the arbitrary.

The progressive supplanting of feudal relations between king and vassals by relations between sovereign and courtiers, or at least their increasing conflict, implies an esthetic cleavage: on the one hand, courtly literature is determined by the nostalgic desire for harmony between the inherent value of the courtier as artifact and his effect on the prince; on the other hand, the absolute priority of the prince's favor corresponds to a grace that is not inherent but fitting. Fittingness, *decorum*, *accommodazione*, and so on are terms that define the vague esthetic architecture of the court. The emphasis on relational qualities rather than inherent qualities is precisely a consequence of the prior arbitrariness perceived in courtly merit.

Favor and Merit in Castiglione's *Libro del cortegiano*

On a first reading, the *Cortegiano* conveys a powerful image of an ideal court constituted through relations of condign merit. The various yet or-

---

preabsolutist the French monarchy was in the early sixteenth century. For standard (but not very recent) studies of the development of absolutism in early modern Europe, see Walther Hubatsch, ed., *Absolutismus* (Darmstadt: Wissenschaftliche Buchgesellschaft, 1973), especially the articles of Reinhold Koser (pp. 1–44) and Leo Just (pp. 288–308). A fine work on the role of the court in seventeenth-century monarchy is Jürgen Freiherr von Krüdener, *Die Rolle des Hofes im Absolutismus* (Stuttgart: G. Fischer, 1973). Seen from the point of view of the courtier at a Renaissance court, what might objectively still be a fairly constitutional or feudal political system becomes rather more arbitrary and absolute. It is this point of view that is important to keep in mind.

[17] See note 12. This a priori limitlessness (except for the principle of noncontradiction) of God's power in nominalist argumentation *de potentia Dei absoluta* has been discussed by, among others, Paul Vignaux, in *Nominalisme au XIVe siècle* (Montreal: Institut d'études médiévales, 1948), esp. pp. 12–39. The theory of absolutism is similarly based on a positing of the absence of a priori limits to the monarch's power. For an abstract formulation of this idea, see Preston King, *The Ideology of Order: A Comparative Analysis of Jean Bodin and Thomas Hobbes* (London: Barnes and Noble, 1974): "Normative absolutism is most fully instanced in recommendations for unlimited concentrations of power. On one level it does not much matter whether power can or cannot in fact be unlimited. For even if we accept that it cannot be unlimited, we are not thereby accepting that the existing limits cannot be extended outwards, nor that there is some a priori way of stipulating an empirical point beyond which such outward extension ceases to be possible. Normative absolutism, defined as a recommendation for an unlimited concentration of power, can always be interpreted practically as a relentless a priori disposition to demand an increasing concentration of power for its own sake" (p. 45). See also Oakley, *Omnipotence*, pp. 93–118. See Chapter Five for a fuller discussion of unconstrained power.

dered polite society at Urbino ("une agitation sans désordre [restlessness without disorder]," in Madame de Lafayette's terms) seems to be the incarnation of inherent worthiness. In the introductory rhetoric of his book, Castiglione sets up a relationship between service and reward that may serve as a good introduction to its manifestation elsewhere. He frequently alludes to the dignity and praiseworthiness of the assembled courtiers and belittles his own capacity to express their value. Here, however, his courtly modesty only demonstrates the inherent merit of the book, and of the excellent society it describes:

> Così noi desideramo che tutti quelli, nelle cui mani verrà questa nostra fatica [this book], se pur mai sarà di tanto favor degna che da nobili cavalieri e valorose donne meriti esser veduta, presumano e per fermo tengano la Corte d'Urbino esser stata molto piú eccellente ed ornata d'omini singulari, che noi non potemo scrivendo esprimere. (3.1)

> [Even so, we hope that all those into whose hands this work of ours shall come (if indeed it prove so worthy of favor as to deserve to be seen by noble cavaliers and virtuous ladies) will suppose and firmly believe that the Court of Urbino was far more excellent and adorned with singular men than we can set down in writing.]

If noble, valorous men and women grant this book the favor of reading it, they will be assured of the value of the Urbino court, although this value can never be fully expressed. In other words, the book can be worthy ("degna"), can merit the favor of being read ("meriti esser veduta"). The rhetoric of *captatio benevolentiae* sets up an exchange between merit and favor that, interestingly, seems to lead to the transcendent value of the court represented in the main body of the work, for the reader will be convinced of the *inexpressible* nature of its excellence. The proportionality of service and favor, then, has allowed the representation of a disproportionately excellent society. The book will have succeeded in representing an ideal court that, by its ideal nature, is beyond the powers of writing! This rather intricate sentence in the *Cortegiano* implies a movement from an exchange of comparable service and rewards to the attainment of an ideal or transcendent good, a movement that is characteristic of the structure of condign merit, where works and reward are proportionate, and where the reward is salvation and infinite happiness. It is within the powers of the exchanging partners to produce an ideal society.[18]

---

[18] A comparable move from proportionate reward of merit to "adoration" can be noted in 4.33: "Appresso, come dovesse amare i propinqui di grado in grado, servando tra tutti in certe cose una pare equalità, come nella giustizia e nella libertà; ed in alcune altre una ragionevole inequalità, come nell'esser liberale, nel remunerare, nel distribuir gli onori e dignità secondo la inequalità dei meriti, li quali sempre debbono non avanzare ma esser avanzati dalle remunerazioni; e che in tal modo sarebbe nonché amato ma quasi adorato dai sudditi."

Similarly, the ideal courtiers at Urbino choose a "game" that will establish the qualities of the ideal courtier. Everyone purports not to be of sufficient merit to fit that description; such modesty is of course both an indication of the ideal and its proof, since ideal courtiers are modest. The relationship between the insufficient book and the ideal court is mirrored here, and we find in the description of the characters' project a similar structure of condign merit. The courtiers discussing the ideal courtier are worthy of the greatest praise ("omini degni di somma laude ed al cui giudicio in ogni cosa prestar si potea indubitata fede [men worthy of the highest praise, and in whose judgment on all things we may have unquestioned faith]," 1.1), as is the sovereign whose court attracts the ideal courtier: "Vegniamo adunque ormai a dar principio a quello che è nostro presuposto e, se possibil è, formiamo un Cortegian tale, che quel principe che sarà degno d'esser da lui servito, ancor che poco stato avesse, si possa però chiamar grandissimo signore [So let us now make a beginning of our subject, and, if that be possible, let us form such a Courtier that any prince worthy of being served by him, even though he have but small dominion, may still be called a very great lord]" (1.1). The ideal courtier takes to a logical extreme the relationship of proportionate reward inherent in condign merit; he is *so* worthy that the exchange is reversed, for it is the prince who must be worthy to be served by him. The contractual relationship of condignity implies precisely such a reversal, for if works are always rewarded in proportion to their merit, then the completion of a meritorious action *demands* the comparable reward. So the prince is in effect indebted to the courtier; he is dependent on him. If the courtier is ideal, then only an enormous reward will be comparable to his service, and only *worthy* sovereigns are capable of this reward.[19] From this initial positing of a proportionate exchange, we arrive at a disproportion: even if the sovereign has a small state, he will be known as a *grandissimo signore*.

The reversal of the dependency relationship announced in the choice of a game corresponds to the first part of the fourth book, in which the courtier educates the prince and is able to guide him to perfect justice and social

[19] For a study of the theological overtones of the sovereign's *dignitas* in medieval political theory, see Ernst H. Kantorowicz, *The King's Two Bodies: A Study in Medieval Political Theology* (Princeton: Princeton Univ. Press, 1957), pp. 383–409. In contrast to medieval kingship, Renaissance despotism tends to deemphasize the external, prior constraints to the office of the king or prince, at least as it is reflected in courtesy literature. Despotism implies that adherence to rules of justice is a (mostly pragmatic) *choice* of the sovereign, not something *given*. Machiavelli's manual for the prince presents his behavior as a set of alternatives among which the sovereign decides. "Dignity" becomes, then, a functional concept. See also Estienne de La Boëtie, *De la servitude volontaire*: "C'est un extreme malheur d'estre subject à un maistre duquel on ne peut jamais asseurer qu'il soit bon puis qu'il est tousjours en sa puissance d'estre mauvais *quand il voudra*" (ed. Malcolm Smith [Geneva: Droz, 1987], p. 33; italics mine).

harmony (4.5ff.). The absolute power of the prince in determining the lives of his subjects makes the educative function of the courtier all-important. The ideal situation is described by Ottaviano in the following terms:

> Essendo aiutato dagli ammaestramenti e dalla educazione ed arte del Cortegiano, formato da questi signori [the Urbino courtiers] tanto prudente e bono, [the prince] sarà giustissimo, continentissimo, temperatissimo, fortissimo e sapientissimo, pien di liberalità, magnificenzia, religione e clemenzia; in somma sarà gloriosissimo e carissimo agli omini ed a Dio, per la cui grazia acquisterà quella virtú eroica, che lo farà eccedere i termini della umanità e dir si potrà piú presto semideo che omo mortale. (4.22)

> [Being aided by the teachings and the training and skill of so prudent and good a Courtier as these gentlemen have devised, he will be very just, continent, temperate, strong, and wise, full of liberality, magnificence, religion, and clemency. In fine, he will be most glorious and dear to men and God, by Whose grace he will attain the heroic virtue that will bring him to surpass the limits of humanity and be called a demigod rather than a mortal man.]

The educative function of the courtier implies proportion and dependency, since the prince relies on his courtiers to "form" him, just as, incidentally, the ideal courtier is "formed" by the noble men and women at Urbino. This vision of condign partners, then, concludes with the supreme value of the prince, his divine grace. An excess or disproportion results once again, for the prince is elevated to the status of a half-god and transcends the limitations of humanity. This excess is, however, a product of initial proportion: without the rewarded service of the courtier the ideal would not have been attained.

Castiglione has thus reconciled man's reasonable work with infinite secular salvation, and has put forth their relationship as consequence. If man's actions have merit and are rewarded, then man will be able to perfect himself. Such perfection is analogous to the state of grace that is in excess of any other value, and yet attainable, if condign merit is granted to the creature. Castiglione's vision of a paradoxical conjoining of proportion and incommensurability is strengthened by its double representation through worthy men who "form" *the* worthy man.

However, the very incarnation of ideal courtly values seems to entail an unavoidable retreat from the reconciliation of proportion and salvation. Castiglione's treatment of the court at Urbino is simultaneously triumphant and melancholy: triumphant in the sense that the Italian courtiers are equal to the best men and women antiquity had to offer, melancholy in the sense that death has ravaged his illustrious group. Death and loss pervade the author's introductions to his books, and, in spite of an explicit refusal of nostalgia in the introduction to the third book, Castiglione writes with an acute awareness of the pastness of his ideal society.[20] The ideal courtier and the ideal conversants compose a past project that has become irrecoverable. The tone of the book is set by sentences that describe what *would have been*: "Questi [Gaspar Pallavicino, Cesare Gonzaga, Roberto da Bari] adunque *se vivuti fossero*, penso che sariano giunti a grado, che *ariano ad ognuno che conosciuti gli avesse potuto dimostrar* chiaro argomento, quanto la Corte d'Urbino fosse degna di laude e come di nobili cavalieri ornata [Thus, had these men lived, I think they would have attained such eminence that they would have been able to give to all who knew them clear proof of how praiseworthy the Court of Urbino was, and how adorned it was with noble cavaliers]" (4.2; italics mine). Castiglione's "se vivuti fossero" corresponds to the statements of the melancholic whose present is dominated by unfulfilled past projects ("had I only done this or that")[21] and who writes in a "non mediocre tristezza" (Preface). Condign merit ("degna di laude") is clearly not within the reach of actual courtiers; it is an unrealized project in an irretrievable past, although during their lifetimes other courtiers at Urbino did achieve fame and fortune. Castiglione writes about this illustrious circle in order to give examples to the living, but death and sickness have rendered these examples as remote as the examples of antiquity.

Yet death and time are excuses. The moments of condign merit, the paradoxical secular salvation envisaged in glimpses, are constantly undermined by another view of the courtier's situation organized not by proportion and ensuing grace, but by disproportion and the essential priority of grace. The courtly situation is already disproportionate from the beginning, for any affirmation of a discrepancy in power entails a disproportion between service and reward. Merit can at best be only congruous.

The *Cortegiano* does not simply begin with the dialogic description of the perfect courtier, but places itself before the principal conversational "game," so that the reader may witness the selection of the game. The elucidation of the premises of an argument is characteristic of this hypothetical courtly game, and characteristic also of the melancholy project: in a profound way courtly life is a development of an "If . . . then . . ." proposition. The signora Emilia Pia, given lieutenant powers by the duchess (who herself is a substitute for the ailing duke)[22] proposes a game in which

[20] On nostalgia in Castiglione, see also Wayne A. Rebhorn, *Courtly Performances: Masking and Festivity in Castiglione's Book of the Courtier* (Detroit: Wayne State Univ. Press, 1978), pp. 91–115.

[21] Compare Ludwig Binswanger, *Melancholie und Manie: Phänomenologische Studien* (Pfullingen: Neske, 1960), p. 27: "Hier aber [in the conditional phrases of the melancholic] zieht sich, was freie Möglichkeit ist, zurück in die Vergangenheit."

[22] The sick duke is no less powerful for being absent and represented by a substitute. Substitutability is at the same time an impoverishment of power and its measure; see, in a differ-

each courtier should describe another possible game: "e questo [gioco] sarà ch'ognun proponga secondo il parer suo un gioco non piú fatto; da poi si eleggerà quello che parerà esser piú degno di celebrarsi in questa compagnia [and this shall be that each propose some game after his own liking that we have never played; then we shall choose the one that seems the worthiest of being played in this company]" (1.6). The *worthiest* game will be selected, or rather, what seems to be the worthiest (the most fitting) game in this company. To whom? The reflexive construction in Emilia Pia's sentence allows of no specified agent. The reward for the worthiest proceeds initially from an unspecified though understood source.

Various games are proposed by the (male) courtiers, but none receives a response from the *locotenente* or from the duchess, although the company itself receives the proposals with ambivalent laughter. Emilia Pia passes from one to the other without displaying positive or negative reaction: "ma la signora Emilia gl'impose silenzio, e . . . fece segno all'Unico Aretino [but signora Emilia bade him keep quiet, and . . . made a sign to the Unico Aretino]" (1.9); "ma non facendone la signora Emilia altramente motto, messer Pietro Bembo . . . cosí disse [but, as signora Emilia said nothing about it, messer Pietro Bembo spoke as follows]" (1.11); "Attendeva ognun la risposta della signora Emilia; la qual non facendo altrimenti motto al Bembo, si volse e fece segno a messer Federico Fregoso [Everyone was awaiting signora Emilia's reply; but she, saying nothing more to Bembo, turned to messer Federico Fregoso]" (1.12).

When it is Federico Fregoso's turn, he proposes the description of the perfect courtier. Emilia interrupts him to announce that this will be the game of the evening, if it pleases the duchess, who says simply "Piacemi." The indifference shown to the other games and the abrupt, totally unmotivated choice of Fregoso's proposal are a demonstration of the lack of proportion between the courtiers' various acts of service and the reward offered. One game pleases, apparently arbitrarily, whereas the others evoke *no* reaction. There is no gradation of reaction, no sense in which some are worthier than others. The pleasing nature of Fregoso's game seems not inherent in the game itself, but rather determined by the generosity of the powerful duchess and her *locotenente*. Subsequently, of course, everyone

---

ent context, Theodor W. Adorno and Max Horkheimer, *Die Dialektik der Aufklärung* (1944; repr. Frankfurt: Suhrkamp, 1971): "Wie Vertretbarkeit das Maß von Herrschaft ist and jener der Mächtigste ist, der sich in den meisten Verrichtungen vertreten lassen kann, so ist Vertretbarkeit das Vehikel des Fortschritts und zugleich der Regression. Unter den gegebenen Verhältnissen bedeutet das Ausgenommensein von Arbeit, nicht bloß bei Arbeitslosen sondern selbst am sozialen Gegenpol, auch Verstümmelung. Die Oberen erfahren das Dasein, mit dem sie nicht mehr umzugehen brauchen, nur noch als Substrat und erstarren ganz zum kommandierenden Selbst" (p. 34). See also Whigham, *Ambition and Privilege*, p. 39: "Paradoxically, this evacuated authority had an infinite allure. . . ."

agrees that this is a wonderful choice: "Allor quasi tutti i circunstanti . . . cominciarono a dir che questo era il piú bel gioco che far si potesse [Where-upon nearly all of those present began to say . . . that this was the finest game that could possibly be played]" (1.12). The arbitrary gesture of the prince or duchess has a totally constraining effect: her very lack of moti-vation implies the absolutely binding nature of her order.[23]

So the choice of a game, to repeat Thomas Greene's formulation, reflects the congruity of merit characteristic of court life.[24] At the outset of the exchange implied by merit one must posit the arbitrary gesture endowing certain service with the capacity to please. This initial infusion of grace is not determined by a contract between the courtier and the prince, in the sense that certain actions are bound to be rewarded in certain ways, but instead depends on a promise of the sovereign to himself: the rules set up for courtly games are defined by the duchess and her substitute and ex-change is channeled through these provisional rules. Yet the final, and ini-tial, authorizing of pleasure is a product of power's generosity.

The initial arbitrariness of the prince's favor or disfavor is often pre-sented by Castiglione through the figure of Fortune, which determines the unpredictable whims of the sovereign. Fortune, however, is only an ele-ment in the functioning of despotic power; in fact, obversely, Fortune is a *product* of despotism, for the whimsicality of the prince is precisely a sign and a proof of his absolute power. "Fortune" is also polyvalent: it covers both disfavor and death in the *Cortegiano*. Thus a prince's whims are im-plicitly tied to the unpredictable death of many of Urbino's illustrious courtiers.

Inexplicable disfavor is the theme of a brief discussion by Fregoso in the second book. This unfortunate situation may arise at the very outset of one's career as a courtier:

> Ma perché par che la fortuna, come in molte altre cose, cosí ancor abbia gran-
> dissima forza nelle opinioni degli omini, vedesi talor che un gentilomo, per
> ben condizionato che egli sia e dotato di molte grazie, sarà poco grato ad un
> signore, e come si dice, no gli arà sangue; e questo senza cause alcuna che si
> possa comprendere. (2.32)

---

[23] See below, Chapter Five, especially "The Sovereign as the Unbound," for a discussion of the role of "pleasure" in the affirmation of royal sovereignty. I believe it is of the greatest importance that there be no need for *explicit* motivation of decision by the sovereign, al-though choice may in fact be motivated, in the sense that the sovereign may have his private reasons.

[24] Thomas Greene, "*Il cortegiano* and the Choice of a Game," in *Castiglione*, ed. Hanning and Rosand, pp. 1–15. Greene emphasizes the inappropriateness of the other games; that inappropriateness is, of course, never stated in the text, and the final granting of appropriate-ness is an *apparently* unmotivated choice by the duchess. It is this appearance that counts.

[But because it seems that, in this as in many other things, Fortune has great power over men's opinions, we sometimes see that a gentleman, no matter how good his character may be, and though endowed with many graces, will find little favor with the prince, and will, as we say, go against the grain; and this for no understandable reason.]

In spite of all wit, fine gestures, manners, and distinguished speech, if the courtier is not known prior to his arrival, and the prince shows any dislike of him, "da questo nascerà che gli altri subito s'accommodaranno alla voluntà del signore e ad ognun parerà che quel tale non vaglia [and thus it will come about that the others will immediately follow the prince's bent, and everyone will find the man to be of little worth]," for "tanto sono fermi ed ostinati gli omini nelle opinioni che nascono da' favori e disfavori de' signori [so are men set and obstinate in the opinions that are engendered by the favor and disfavor of princes]" (2.32). The acceptance of Fregoso's game by the immediately agreeing courtiers in the first book is mirrored in the rejection of anyone apparently displeasing to the prince, in spite of all inherent qualities the unfortunate courtier may possess. In fact, as Fregoso comments at length on this problem, *whatever* the courtier does or says will be displeasing—there are *no* inherent qualities.[25]

The solution offered concerns the courtier's prior experiences: if preceded by a good reputation, a courtier will have a much better chance of being initially agreeable at a new court. This solution is not really an answer to the difficulty, for it is exactly the *first* impression that will count in a courtier's career. That first impression is still absolutely dependent on a sovereign's whims. This problem is conceptually parallel to the acquisition of grace: how does one learn to be graceful when grace is that which cannot be learned? One imitates those who already are graceful. How does one become agreeable at a new court? One is agreeable at a previous one. Courtly esthetics *refuses* the question of ultimate origin or ultimate accessibility by rules. Such a refusal is indistinguishable from the supposition of an initial arbitrariness which, in turn, is indistinguishable from the priority of the prince's absolute power.

At the beginning of the fourth book Castiglione relocates the esthetic discussion of the perfect courtier onto an ethical plane: what are the re-

---

[25] The absolute effect of favor or disfavor is a commonplace in court manuals. See Antonio de Guevara, *Aviso de favoriti et dottrina de cortegiani*, trans. Vicenzo Bondi (Venice: [M. Tramezino], 1544), f. 16ᵛ: "Non è alcuno servigio che mai sia cattivo, quando a colui che si serve è grato, e non è alcuno che mai sia buono, quando non è accetto a colui che viene servito. Se quello che serve non si vede nella gratia di colui ch'egli ha da servire, si può bene affaticarsi e struggersi il corpo, ma non aspettare giamai guidardone nel servigio ch'egli fa." See also Pierre de Ronsard, "La promesse": "Les uns [among the courtiers] vont les premiers, les autres les derniers, / Selon le bon visage, & selon la caresse / Que leur fait en riant ceste brave Deesse" (in *Oeuvres complètes*, 13:5, 42–44).

sponsibilities of the courtier toward the prince? The courtier as pedagogue is intended to counteract the image of an infinitely servile and flexible Proteus, an image that is preponderant in medieval and Renaissance anticourtier literature.[26] The courtier's educative function is, however, always explicitly based on the premise of the prince's favor. Cesare Gonzaga develops his conception of the responsibilities of the courtier depending on two conditions: "Però s'io mi sentissi esser quell'eccellente Cortegiano che hanno formato questi signori [the other conversants] *ed aver la grazia del mio principe*, certo è ch'io non lo indurrei mai a cosa alcuna viziosa [Hence, if I felt that I was that excellent Courtier which these gentlemen have fashioned, and if I had the favor of my prince, I certainly would not lead him to anything vicious]" (4.36; italics mine). The duchess herself admits this initial condition, in posing the problem and in asking Ottaviano to respond: "Diteci ancora tutto quello che voi insegnareste al vostro principe, se egli avesse bisogno d'ammaestramenti, e presupponetevi d'avervi acquistato compitamente la grazia sua [Tell us also everything that you would teach your prince if he had need of instruction—and let us assume that you have won his favor completely]" (4.25). The duchess hedges her bet by leaving open how the need for improvement is determined, but her assumption of initial grace or favor is repeated by the courtiers, who explain their pedagogic functions. In this sense the ethical depends explicitly on the esthetic of agreeableness, the structure of which, in turn, is determined by the prince's whim.

Underlying the conflict between condign and congruous merit is the analogy between the sovereign and God. This connection is made expressly by Ottaviano in the fourth book. He prefers monarchies, for the reign of a single prince is similar to the reign of God, who alone governs the universe (4.19). In discussing the advantages and disadvantages of monarchies and republics, Ottaviano admits that the problem of single rule is its ambivalence: "Vero è che sono due modi di signoreggiare: l'uno imperioso e violento, come quello dei patroni ai schiavi, . . . l'altro piú mite e placido, come quello dei boni principi per via delle leggi ai cittadini [It is true that there are two modes of ruling: the one absolute and violent, like that of masters towards their slaves, . . . the other is more mild and gentle, like that of good princes over the citizens by means of laws]" (4.21). Both of these ways of governing are said to be analogous to relations between the faculties of the mind and the body, and both are useful. Of course, in the end, the second way is to be preferred.

The difference between the two ways of governing can be reformulated

---

[26] For a useful survey of this literature, see Pauline M. Smith, *The Anti-Courtier Trend in Sixteenth-Century French Literature* (Geneva: Droz, 1966); for a more analytical presentation, see Claus Uhlig, *Hofkritik im England des Mittelalters und der Renaissance: Studien zu einem Gemeinplatz der europäischen Moralistik* (Berlin: Walter de Gruyter, 1973).

in terms of the difference between God's *potentia absoluta* and his *potentia ordinata*. Absolutely speaking, God is not constrained by anything external to himself; nevertheless he will tend to keep his own promises and the laws he himself has set down. The theological distinction between the two types of divine power is reflected in an earlier discussion of evil sovereigns, whose power must be absolute in order to be perfect:

> Però alcuni [princes] hanno in odio la ragione e la giustizia, parendo loro ch'ella sia un certo freno ed un modo che lor potesse ridurre in servitú e diminuir loro quel bene e satisfazione che hanno di regnare, se volessero servarla; e che il loro dominio non fosse perfetto né integro, se essi fossero constretti ad obedire al debito ed all' onesto, perché pensano che chi obbedisce non sia veramente signore. (4.7)

> [Therefore some princes hate reason or justice, thinking it would be a kind of bridle and a way of reducing them to servitude, and of lessening the pleasure and satisfaction they have in ruling if they chose to follow it, and that their rule would be neither perfect nor complete if they were obliged to obey duty and honor, because they think that one who obeys is not a true ruler.]

This equation of perfect power and the absence of obligation or debt is precisely the condition out of which congruous merit arises. Condign merit implies an obligation on the part of God to reward meritorious works, yet the completeness or perfection of God's absolute power does not allow for any external obligation. Only, then, a generous infusion of grace can render actions by man worthy of reward; this reward is disproportionate to the action completed, in an absolute sense. The prince has an initial choice between an affirmation of his absolute power and that of his ordinate power, that is, his power to institute and follow laws governing his principality. The initial choice points to the priority of absolute power: it is a measure of his absolute power that he can decide to constrain himself by instituting laws. The prince governs through a pact with himself.

Ottaviano goes on to describe the prince who affirms his absolute power:

> Però andando drieto a questi principii, e lassandosi trapportar dalla persuasione di sé stessi, divengon superbi, e col volto imperioso e costumi austeri, con veste pompose, oro e gemme, e col non lassarsi quasi mai vedere in publico, credono acquistar autorità tra gli omini ed esser quasi tenuti Dei. (4.7)

> [Therefore, following these principles and allowing themselves to be transported by self-conceit, they become arrogant, and with imperious countenance and stern manner, with pompous dress, gold, and gems, and by letting themselves be seen almost never in public, they think to gain authority among men and to be held almost as gods.]

According to Ottaviano, these princes are similar to statues stuffed with straw and will necessarily ruin their principality. Yet the repeated emphasis on these problems indicates that they are quite real, especially in a political situation where there is no authorization of power external to itself. The analogy between the prince and God, or a godlike figure, is once again explicit ("quasi tenuti Dei"), and this time an absence of public visibility is connected to the prince's desire to be thought of as godlike.

The imperious look and the pompous dress of the bad prince are, of course, quite in contrast with the laughter of the Urbino court; in fact, laughter may be conceived as a guarantee against godlike absolute power. However, in another significant way the signs of absolute power are to be found in Urbino. The absence of the (sickly) duke, and the chain of sub-stitutions emanating from the sovereign (—Duchess—Emilia Pia) point to the distance of power's origin. Its *face* is indifferent, or neutral, except when decisions are made by the duchess or her *locotenente*. The decisions made by the powerful are based on the pleasingness of an activity or an alternative, not on its inherent value. In spite of the tendency to portray the Urbino court in terms that reflect the structure of condign merit, Ca-stiglione cannot exclude from his representation of worth an interference of the congruous, the fitting, and the arbitrary.

Castiglione's account of courtly civilization is a model for the fictional representation of merit in the Renaissance; it is poised between a utopian Pelagianism and a melancholy admission of man's reduced, congruous merit in the face of a remote God who is the paradigm of secular power.[27]

Complaining Courtiers: Marot and Ronsard

In counterpoint to the nostalgic symposium of the old courtier, the im-plicit treatment of merit by a young poet soliciting the king's favor and money reveals a pervasiveness of the courtier's problems. Clément Marot's oft-cited "Petite epistre au roy" (composed 1518–1519), which opens his *Adolescence Clementine* of 1532, presents a young courtier seeking a rela-tionship with François Ier that will enable him to write poetry and be com-pensated for it. The poem is addressed to the king, who is characterized as someone who is in no need of Marot's (or anyone's) poetry:

[27] For a study of the medieval connection between God's power and the king's power, see Kantorowicz, *The King's Two Bodies*. In courtesy manuals the most striking analogy I have found between God's inexplicable grace and the sovereign's inexplicable favor is in Claude Chappuis, *Discours de la court* (Paris: A. Roffet, 1543), [pp. 54–56]. This analogy is occa-sioned by the arbitrary gesture of the prince, another commonplace of courtesy literature. See, other than the *Cortegiano*, Antonio de Guevara, *Le favori de court*, trans. Jaques de Roche-more (Anvers: C. Plantin, 1557), f. 137.

En m'esbatant je faiz Rondeaux en rime,
Et en rimant bien souvent je m'enrime;
Brief, c'est pitié d'entre nous Rimailleurs,
Car vous trouvez assez de rime ailleurs,
Et quand vous plaist, mieulx que moy rimassez,
Des biens avez et de la rime assez.
Mais moy, à tout ma rime & ma rimaille,
Je ne soustiens (dont je suis marry) maille.[28]

[Enjoying myself I make Rondeaux in rhyme, and while rhyming I often catch a cold; briefly, we rhymesters are in a pitiful state, for you find enough rhyme elsewhere, and when it pleases you, you rhyme better than I do; goods and rhyme you have enough of; but I, with my rhyme and my rhyming, I don't own anything (about which I am upset).]

The transcendent status of the patron-king is emphasized, on the one hand, by an abundant supply of "Rimailleurs," and, on the other, by the presumably greater talent of the king. There is, then, no *reason* why, first of all, the king would choose Marot over another poet, and, second, the king would choose to reward poets at all. Any "reward" hinges on that little but all-important formula, "Et quand vous plaist," which is used to motivate the king's choice of writing poetry but which implicitly characterizes the absolute power of the monarch over the soliciting rhymester. The king has enough of everything ("Des biens avez et de la rime assez") and would never *gain* anything by receiving the poet's offering. Thus any contract between subject and king is excluded. The disproportion of the two sides is such that only the king's *arbitrary* generosity will furnish a ground for rewarding the poet's efforts. That arbitrary generosity is, of course, at the same time a confirmation of his transcendence, for if his decision to grant favor to the poet were motivated by the latter's *merit*, his own poetic merit would thus be lessened, or at least would be commensurable with the poet's.

The following lines seem to interfere, however, with this blatant assertion of the king's absolute power, by redirecting the discussion of poetry in such a way that Marot is justifying himself to a *commensurable* partner:

Or, ce me dist (ung jour) quelque Rimart:
Viença, Marot, trouves tu en rime art
Qui serve aux gens, toy qui as rimassé?
Ouy vrayement (respondz je) Henri Macé.
Car voys tu bien, la personne rimante,
Qui au jardin de son sens la rime ente,

---

[28] Clément Marot, *Oeuvres complètes, vol. 1, Les épîtres*, ed. C. A. Mayer (Paris: Nizet, 1977), p. 97, 1–8.

Si elle n'a des biens en rimoyant,
Elle prendra plaisir en rime oyant;
Et m'est advis que, si je ne rimoys,
Mon pauvre corps ne seroit nourry moys
Ne demy jour. Car la moindre rimette,
C'est le plaisir où fault que mon rys mette.

(9–20)

[Now, one day some rhymester asked me the following: "Come here, Marot, do you find in rhyme an art that is useful to people, you who have rhymed?" "Yes, truly," I responded, "Henri Macé. For as you see well, the rhyming person who in the garden of his mind grafts the rhyme—even if this person has no goods from rhyming—will take pleasure in hearing rhyme; and it is evident that, if I didn't rhyme, my poor body would be nourished neither for a month nor half a day. For with the smallest rhyme, it's the pleasure where I must put my laughter (or rice)."]

The uselessness of Marot's poetry vis-à-vis the king reasserts itself in the form of a question by a fellow rhymester: "Trouves tu en rime art / Qui serve aux gens?" However, the different communicative situation allows Marot to answer in the affirmative; he then elaborates a little allegory of the creative process. The affirmative answer is thus staged *for* the king but is not a direct response *to* the king, preserving the latter's independence, and yet showing the useful exchange that poetry can effect between proportionate partners. Marot is offering to the king a poetic version of the *facere quod in se est*, but is formulating it in such a way that it in no way *obliges* the king.

The representation of poetic creation and its merit is a conjoining of *biens* and *plaisir*. Even if the poet has no goods in exchange for his poetry, he will feel pleasure in hearing rhymes. If he did not rhyme, his poor body would not be nourished. So he must "put his laughter in his pleasure," or concentrate on the production of pleasure. Of course the *king's* pleasure was prior to any reward, and prior to this justification, so that the poet hopes for an equivalence between his own pleasure and the king's pleasure. He can thus be sure of the patron's favor and reward. This conjuring of royal pleasure is an attempt to render the sovereign once again commensurable with his subject. Condignity thus emerges as the poet's implicit wish.

A hypothetical contractual relationship with the king is envisaged in the final lines of the passage. If the poet did not produce rhymes, his body would not be nourished, or, implicitly, if he does produce rhymes, he *expects* to be rewarded and nourished: "Si je ne rimoys, / Mon pauvre corps ne seroit nourry moys/ Ne demy jour." Of course the partner in this contract is not stated; Marot is once again unwilling to directly oblige the king. At the same time, by his initial evocation of the king's transcendence he has excluded precisely the obligation he wishes for.

The last line of this section seems to confirm the role of *plaisir* as that which connects the poet and his royal contractual partner: "C'est le plaisir où fault que mon rys mette." Given the preceding allusions to the body and its nourishment, the *rys* can be understood as both laughter and food (rice). Thus material reward and esthetic pleasure are indistinguishable from each other.[29]

The absolute priority of the sovereign's generous decision is reasserted in the conclusion of the poem:

> Si vous supply qu'à ce jeune Rimeur
> Faciez avoir ung jour par sa rime heur,
> Affin qu'on die, en prose ou en rimant:
> Ce Rimailleur, qui s'alloit enrimant,
> Tant rimassa, rima et rimonna,
> Qu'il a congneu quel bien par rime on a.
>
> (20–25)

[So I beg of you that one day you give this young rhymer a reward for his rhyme, so that one may say, in prose or in rhyme: "This rhymester, who was catching a cold, rhymed so much that he got to know which reward one has for rhyme."]

The poet returns to the position of the supplicant, and he begs the king to institute, at some point, a contractual situation: "Qu'à ce jeune Rimeur / Faciez avoir ung jour *par sa rime heur* [italics mine]." The contract is dependent, however, on the free and more or less unforeseeable decision of the sovereign ("ung jour"). So the little vision of reciprocal benefit has been supplanted by the congruity of the poet's and the creature's merit.

The uncertainty endemic to this congruity manifests itself, finally, in the imaginary recording of the reward: one will be able to write an epitaph for the poet, in prose (!) or in rhyme, to remind posterity "quel bien par rime on a." The *bien* is, of course, ambiguous, since it may refer either to the poet's material rewards or to *death*, the recompense the (unrewarded) poet receives. Standing over the grave of Marot, the future rhymester cannot fail to see this irony.

Marot's staging of condignity is an attempt to find a common measure between courtier and sovereign, but in the very gesture of its offering the poem excludes the proportionality necessary to its reward. It opens and

---

[29] Marot's punning and reliance on the plasticity of words might justify an analysis of the word *plaisir* as containing within itself the problem described. It is at the same time *plais/sire*, the seigneur's pleasure, and, anagrammatically, *ris/riz* is contained in the last syllable. So the material, the contractual, is a reading *à rebours* of royal pleasure.

closes by conjuring a decision it describes as excessive and therefore arbitrary. The final suggestion of the poet's grave is not separated from the suggestion of his material reward and happiness, and in a sense this *présence sourde* of death in such a funny *epistre* is, as in Castiglione, the very symptom of the courtier's contradictions.

A more extreme version of flattery and admission of the priority of the prince's favor is found in the poetry of Pierre de Ronsard, whose "La promesse" (1564) contains a bitter satire of the court. Ronsard was fed up with the lack of reward for the polemical pieces he wrote in defense of Catherine de Médicis' policy against the Huguenots, and he manages at the same time to complain about her neglect of him and praise her as a prudent sovereign. Ronsard relates an allegorical *songe* he had one morning in which "Promise" in the form of a lady appears to him. She is distributing favors and honors, and has a large group of courtiers at her side. Her method of distributing these favors and keeping her promises is completely arbitrary:

> Aux uns estoit marastre, aux autres estoit mere,
> L'un devenoit content, sans estre tormenté,
> L'autre attendoit vingt ans sans estre contenté,
> L'autre dix, l'autre cinq: puis en lieu d'une abbaye,
> Ou d'une autre faveur luy donnoit une baye,
> Ou bien un Attendez, ou bien Il m'en souvient,
> Mais oncques en effect ce souvenir ne vient.[30]

[To some she was cruel, to others not, one was made happy, without having been anguished, the other waited twenty years without reward, another ten, another five; then instead of an abbey or another favor she gave him a berry, or else a "Wait!" or "I remember," but never in effect does this memory come.]

In her small *trionfo* she is accompanied by "Dame Fortune," who incarnates the absolutely random success or failure of a courtier's life:

> En pompe, devant elle, alloit Dame Fortune,
> Qui sourde, aveugle estoit, & sans raison aucune:
> Par le milieu du peuple à l'adventure alloit
> Abbaissant & haulsant tous ceulx qu'elle voulloit,
> Et folle, & variable, & pleine de malice,
> Mesprisoit la vertu & cherissoit le vice.

(p. 7, 87–92)

[All trussed up Lady Fortune preceded her; she was deaf and blind, and without any sense: through the middle of the courtiers she went, randomly, lowering and raising all those she wanted, and mad, fickle, full of malice, she despised virtue and loved vice.]

[30] In *Oeuvres complètes* 13:6–7, 76–82.

In spite of these dire circumstances at the royal court, the courtier Ronsard does not give up. "Promesse" tells him that since the arrival of Catherine de Médicis she has changed her ways, as the queen prudently wishes to "choisir / Les hommes vertueux, & en credit les mettre / Les faisant bien heureux [choose virtuous men and give them importance, making them happy]" (p. 14, 270–72), without promises she will have trouble keeping. An equal exchange of virtue, service, and reward is thus projected that enables the queen to respond favorably to Ronsard's supplication without feeling that her "pleasure" was forced ("Ceste Royne . . . ne veult . . . que par la priere on force son plaisir [This queen does not want to have her pleasure forced by supplication]" [pp. 13–14, 267–69]). Again, the projection of an equal exchange includes a reference to the essential priority of the sovereign's pleasure. Again, congruity of merit is the undeniable fact of the courtier's situation.

Merit and Fictional Courts: Rabelais and Marguerite de Navarre

The problems endemic to man's merit in the early Renaissance condition the construction of fictional worlds, especially worlds contained within a larger fictional framework. The texts I am analyzing, Rabelais's *Gargantua* and Marguerite de Navarre's *Heptaméron*, can be understood as miniature courtly utopias, although they certainly differ in other respects. Although an exhaustive study of the literary implications of these questions is beyond the scope of the present chapter, I do hope to show their productiveness.

In Rabelais's famous vision of a courtly society, at the conclusion of *Gargantua* (1534?), one finds a similar interference between condignity and congruity. The building of the abbey of Thélème is the last of a series of fabulously generous rewards offered by Gargantua to the participants in the war against Picrochole and his anarchic army. This war occupies the final half of the novel, and is an illustration of both Grandgousier's and Gargantua's humanist principles regarding the justification and exercise of military force, although the didacticism of these chapters is only intermittent. The war begins with a dispute regarding an exchange of goods: the peaceful shepherds of Grandgousier politely offer to buy some bread (*fouaces*) from the bakers of Lerné who are on their way to the market: "Lesdictz bergiers les requirent courtoisement leurs en bailler pour leur argent, au pris du marché" (23, p. 160).[31] They offer to pay for them with the grapes they are harvesting, based on the current market price. The situation is perfectly banal and telling: equivalent partners exchange goods

[31] Chapter and page numbers in parentheses refer to François Rabelais, *Gargantua*, ed. Ruth Calder and M. A. Screech (Geneva: Droz, 1970). All translations are my own.

based on their inherent value, which is defined by an external measure, the actual market price. This is, of course, a precise reflection of the condignity of merit and its implications.

The *fouaciers*, however, refuse to sell their goods to the shepherds, for no apparent reason whatsoever. They simply insult the shepherds, adding that the latter do not deserve to eat such good bread: "Adjoustans que poinct à eulx n'apartenoit manger de ces belles fouaces, mais qu'ilz se debvoient contenter de gros pain ballé et de tourte" (23, p. 161). The exchange is refused, then, because one side has determined that the bread is of disproportionate value, and that the shepherds do not constitute equal partners in the exchange. As the surprised shepherds point out, this behavior is completely unprecedented and unmotivated. The implication is double: the exchange is now unjustly dependent on an arbitrary decision of the bakers, who, in addition, if they decided to offer the shepherds any *fouaces*, would be acting out of the pure generosity of a superior toward an inferior. For this reason also the *fouaciers* are called "glorieux" by the laughing peasants at the conclusion of the episode.

The silly cause of the Picrocholine War is the abrupt substitution of a congruous exchange for what had been a condign exchange. The bakers decide arbitrarily to estimate the value of their goods as much higher, and thus refuse the external measure of a market price. The exchange can only originate with the willful bakers, and they decide not to be generous. The subsequent war is not, however, the attempt to retrieve a condign exchange, but is instead the continuation of a congruous exchange, in the sense that Grandgousier and Gargantua fight arbitrary miserliness with arbitrary generosity. This choice is important, for it foreshadows the paradoxes of the utopian abbey.

After the failed peace mission of Ulrich Gallet, Grandgousier still hesitates to begin a war, so he attempts to buy peace by delivering to the enemy five cartloads of *fouaces*, 700,003 gold coins, and, *d'abondant*, property rights to the farm of La Pomardière. The cost of the originally lost bread and of the medical services required to treat the injured baker Marquet is of course far less than that of this disproportionately enormous gift. Grandgousier's generosity is simply incommensurable with the original injury. This offer is, however, rejected by Picrochole and his advisors, making war necessary; punishment is predicated upon the absurd refusal of the free gift of grace. Grandgousier is similarly generous with the captain Toucquedillon: after being taken prisoner by Frère Jean, he is allowed to return to Picrochole not only with his life and safe conduct, but with a sword made of gold and precious stones valued at 160,000 ducats and 10,000 *écus*. Once again, the gratuitous generosity of the sovereign nullifies any stable relationship between actions and their reward or punishment.

Gargantua does attempt to justify the sovereign's *liberalitas* in economic terms when he addresses the vanquished remains of Picrochole's army. His reasoning closely follows the pattern of congruous merit: the victor's initial free gift of grace enables the vanquished to merit salvation. The ancestors of Gargantua have always "plus voulentiers erigé trophées et monumens es cueurs des vaincuz par grace que, es terres par eulx conquestées, par architecture [more willingly erected trophies and monuments in the hearts of the vanquished by mercy than in the conquered lands by architecture]" (48, p. 272). The most obvious example of the advantages of generosity is to be found in the war between Grandgousier and the inhabitants of the Canary Islands, during which their king, Alpharbal, was also taken prisoner. Like Toucquedillon in the Picrocholine War, Alpharbal was allowed to return home, by Grandgousier's *incroyable debonnaireté*, "chargé de dons, chargé de grâces, chargé de toutes offices d'amytié [loaded with gifts, loaded with graces, loaded with all the services of friendship]" (48, p. 273). The initial grace infused into Alpharbal made him, in turn, capable of works of incredible charity, as he returned later to Grandgousier offering his country, enormous riches, and himself as slave. The return on Grandgousier's investment was so great that it had to be refused; instead, the islanders were asked to give an annual tribute of two million pieces of gold. They gave two million the first year, 2,300,000 the second, 2,600,000 the third, and so forth. Thus "un bon tour liberalement faict à homme de raison croist continuement par noble pensée et remembrance [a good deed done freely to a man of reason accrues continuously by noble thought and memory]" (48, p. 275). We are no longer in the economy of reward and punishment and exchange of equivalent goods; rather, Grandgousier's and Alpharbal's rival lavishness is a stupendously exaggerated spending gesture that nullifies any inherent value of the things exchanged, emphasizing only its own *gratuité*, in all senses of the word. The islanders will continue to increase the amount of the tribute, says Gargantua, and only the refusal of Grandgousier can stop them. All relations to external values are lost, and the gifts become mere ciphers for the willful pleasure of the sovereign. The inherent value of the gifts themselves is so large that it becomes zero, and the various gifts become *free*—freely given and without a price, or worthless in and of themselves. This generosity has its origin in the free gesture of Grandgousier, whose grace enables his enemy to accomplish charitable deeds and thus become a friend of God. Thus the Rabelaisian giants are benign versions of a free God, infinitely generous but also essentially unconstrained.

The abbey of Thélème is constructed as a reward for the service of Frère Jean, who refuses already extant abbeys: "Si vous semble que je vous aye faict et que puisse à l'advenir faire service agreable, oultroyez moy de faire une abbaye à mon devys [If it seems to you that I have performed for you and can perform in the future pleasing service, permit me to found an abbey according to my own plans]" (50, p. 280).[32] The building of the abbey is to the courtier's service what faith and grace are to charitable works. The inscription on the main portal of the abbey concludes with the following lines:

> Or donné par don
> Ordonne pardon
> A cil qui le donne,
> Et tresbien guerdonne
> Tout mortel preud'hom
> Or donné par don.
>
> (52, p. 293)

[Gold given as a gift demands pardon for him who gives it and gold given as a gift rewards very well all mortal gentlemen.]

Gold given through "don," or charity, implies pardon and thus reward for he who gives. Works of charity are a necessary precondition of faith, and faith is their necessary recompense. Depending on how one interprets the Erasmian (and early scholastic) resonances of these lines, Rabelais more or less presents a version of condign merit: certain actions entail certain compensations in a proportionate exchange. The utopian fiction of the abbey of Thélème is predicated upon the vision of proportionality between service and recompense, and inevitably recalls the company of illustrious and worthy gentlemen and gentlewomen at Urbino.

The following chapters seem to confirm the condign merit of the assembly; the men and women allowed to live in the abbey are "gents liberes, bien nez et bien instruictz, conversans en compaignies honestes, [qui] ont par nature un instinct et aguillon, qui tousjours les pousse à faictz vertueux et retire de vice, lequel ilz nommoient honneur [free persons, well born, well instructed, conversing in honest company, who by nature have an instinct and a spur that always pushes them to virtuous acts and keeps them away from vice; this spur they call honor]" (55, pp. 302–3).[33] The activi-

---

[32] Already this reward is in no direct way linked to Frère Jean's merit: Gargantua's reward depends totally on his own generosity ("si bon vous semble"). Similarly, in chap. 43, when Grandgousier wants to reward the monk for having captured the enemy captain Touquedillon, Frère Jean refuses any money, saying, "Cela ne me mène pas." His nonmonetary motivation underlines the disproportion between his service and his reward, for Grandgousier goes on to give him the fabulous sum of 62,000 *saluz* (an English gold coin from the fifteenth century). Frère Jean refuses, preferring to wait until the war is over. The courtier's modesty is of course here the basic strategy, but modesty or understatement only underlines the fact that a certain power relationship necessitates that modesty, that the gesture of reward originates entirely in the prince and is not already contained within the work of service.

[33] This "aguillon" recalls the "stimulo" in the *Cortegiano* (1.14), which, through fear of

ties at the abbey show them to be singularly cultivated and valorous, as far as both their intellectual and their physical lives are concerned. Rabelais reacts against the traditional order of monasteries and convents by refusing to allow any external rule or obligation; instead, they should do what they like: "Faictz ce que vouldras." Yet this rejection of external obligation entails a social obligation that seems curiously arbitrary: "Par ceste liberté entrerent en louable emulation de faire tous ce que à un seul voyoient plaire. Si quelqu'un ou quelcune disoyt: 'Beuvons,' tous beuvoient; si disoit: 'Jouons,' tous jouoient; si disoit: 'Allons à l'esbat es champs,' tous y alloient [By this freedom all began to emulate each other in doing what they saw pleased a single member. If one of them said: "Let's drink," all drank; if he or she said: "Let's play," all played; if he or she said: "Let's go have fun in the fields," they all went there]" (55, p. 303).[34] The apparently haphazard selection of what pleases one member, for whatever reason, becomes totally determining for everyone else. There is no sense in which something may be more or less pleasing, more or less worthy of attention. This lack of gradation corresponds inversely to the power that the selection of a pleasing thing entails. The refusal of any external rule leads to the absoluteness of individual whim. In his eagerness to reject ecclesiastical orders and their "servitude," Rabelais has built a contradiction into his fiction, for it is precisely the acceptance of an external obligation or rule that assures the proportion between merit and recompense. So Frère Jean's meritorious service is contradicted by the structure of the society he founds. The little courtly society of Thélème is in fact a benign version of

---

infamia and hope of praise, spurs nobility on to virtuous acts. For an interpretation that equates the "aguillon" with *synderesis*, or the incitement to do good that is within fallen man (a counterpart to the "fomes peccati"), see H. D. Saffrey, " 'Cy n'entrez pas, hypocrites . . .': Thélème, une nouvelle académie? [Rabelais, *Gargantua*, chap. LII (LIV)]," *Revue des sciences philosophiques et théologiques* 55 (1971): 593–614. However, the incitement of *well-born* persons to virtue is a commonplace humanist justification of nobility; see, for example, Josse Clichtove, *Le traicte de la vraye noblesse translate nouvellement de latin en francoys* (Paris: Jean Longis, 1529), chap. 6: Children from noble families can profit so well from their heritage "que par la contemplation de la vertu & gloire paternelle ilz soient stimulez et incitez à lensuyvre" (f. 5ᵛ). The stimulation to do good that is within natural man is a Stoic tradition; in Philibert de Vienne's satire of court life, he describes the "first nature" of man, before his transformation by the court: "Nature ha semé dedens noz espritz quelques petites estincelles de bons vouloirs . . . Ces petites estincelles sont petits esguillons, qui nous induisent & incitent à faire les choses qui sont bonnes de soy" (*Le philosophe de court* [Lyons: Jean de Tournes, 1547], p. 18). In Guillaume Du Vair's *La philosophie morale des stoïques* (ed. Guy Michaut [Paris: Vrin, 1946]), we find a similar language: "Le bien, en vérité, n'est pas exposé ici en vue à tout le monde; la nature n'en a semé ça-bas que de faibles étincelles" (p. 64). See also Maxwell Gauna, "Fruitful Fields and Blessed Spirits, or Why the Thelemites Were Well Born," *Etudes rabelaisiennes* 15 (1980): 117–28.

[34] Similarly, all men dress like the women, and all women dress the same, by their "franc vouloir" (54, p. 297, var. l. 6).

Ottaviano's arbitrary despot free from constraint. Rabelais has represented *en petit* a substitutable God's *potentia absoluta*. The introduction of "freedom" into the court of Thélème undermines the premise on which the abbey was built, that is, the proportion between Frère Jean's agreeable service and his just reward by Gargantua.

The Picrocholine War and the abbey of Thélème are not the only illustrations of generosity and congruous merit in the works of Rabelais; one may argue that the relationship between Pantagruel and Panurge in the other novels hinges on a free and seemingly unmotivated decision by Pantagruel to endow Panurge with the capacity to please him. It is not in the least obvious why Pantagruel chooses Panurge as a lifelong companion, but that is of course precisely the point.[35]

The relationship between Panurge and his giant patron is characterized not only by literal, physical incommensurability, but also by an apparently essential irrelevance of Panurge's actions to Pantagruel's attitude towards his friend. Whatever tricks Panurge has up his sleeve, however cowardly he may behave, Pantagruel steadfastly maintains his affection for him. The beginning of the *Tiers livre* is a case in point. Panurge has squandered the immense revenue of the domain of Salmigondin and has plunged himself into debt. Pantagruel strongly disapproves of his friend's conduct, but Panurge mounts a mock (?) defense of debtorship that fails to persuade his patron but that is effective, since Pantagruel agrees to pay his creditors. During his encomium of debts, Panurge compares the borrowing of money to the creation of the world: "Dea en ceste seule qualité [i.e., being in debt] je me reputois auguste, reverend, et redoubtable, que, sus l'opinion de tous Philosophes (qui disent rien de rien n'estre faict), rien ne tenent ne matière première, estoys facteur et createur [By God, in this quality alone I thought myself august, respectable, and to be feared: that in spite of the opinion of all philosophers (who say that nothing can come from nothing), having nothing, nor any first matter, I was maker and creator]" (3, p. 39). The connection between credit and the production of something from nothing is made in Plutarch, but the use of the word *createur* points to an additional source.[36] As opposed to pagan philosophers who posited an eternal universe shaped by God, medieval Christian theo-

---

[35] See my discussion of choice in Rabelais, below, Chapter Four.

[36] In Plutarch's brief essay *De vitando aere alieno* (from the *Moralia*), usurers are described as making fun of the scholars of nature, who say that nothing is born from what is not. For in the case of usurers, τόκος (either an offspring, a child, or interest) is born out of nothing (ἐκ τοῦ μηκέτ' ὄντος) and out of what lacks substance or support (μηδ' ὑφεστῶτος). Plutarch uses the verb γίγνεσθαι (to become, to be born out of); the active sense of "create" is less evident here, and specific to Rabelais's formulation, which is informed by theological argumentation.

logians insisted precisely on God's creation of the world from nothing.[37]
Panurge's quip is perhaps primarily an imitation of Plutarch, but the structure of his argument is such that it ties in precisely with the problem of
arbitrary generosity: as Panurge's money comes from nothing and is not
the result of an exchange of commensurable goods, Pantagruel's generosity
similarly is never merited by Panurge. When Pantagruel decides to "de-
liver" Panurge from his past by paying his debts, Panurge emphasizes the
incommensurable reward this gesture represents:

> Le moins de mon plus (dist Panurge) en cestuy article sera vous remercier; et,
> si les remercimens doibvent estre mesurez par l'affection des biensfaicteurs, ce
> sera infiniment, sempiternellement: car l'amour que de vostre grace me portez
> est hors le dez d'estimation, il transcende tout poix, tout nombre, toute me-
> sure, il est infiny, sempiternel. Mais le mesurant au qualibre des biensfaictz et
> contentement des recepvans, ce sera assez laschement. Vous me faictez des
> biens beaucoup, et trop plus que ne m'appartient, plus que n'ay envers vous
> deservy, plus que ne requeroient mes merites, force est que le confesse; mais
> non mie tant que pensez en cestuy article. (5, p. 56)

> [The least I can do (Panurge said) is to thank you; and, if thanks must be
> measured by the affection of the benefactors, thanks will be infinite and eter-
> nal: for the love that your grace has for me is outside of all estimates, it tran-
> scends all weight, number, measure, it is infinite and eternal. But if you mea-
> sure thanks according to the good deeds and the contentment of the
> recipients, that will be doing it loosely. You are doing much good for me, and
> more than belongs to me, more than I have deserved from you, more than my
> merits required, I must confess; but not at all as much as you think in this
> case.]

Just as Frère Jean did not feel he deserved to be rewarded so generously by
Gargantua, during the war against Picrochole, so Panurge feels he does
not deserve his patron's generosity. The latter is literally unmeasurable: it
is infinite and eternal, that is, divine. What is more, the recipients of Pantagruel's generous gesture have in no way performed a service that would
merit such a reward. In a way, Panurge's little rejoinder at the end of the
passage underlines his undeserving nature; his acknowledgment that Pantagruel's affection is infinite is confirmed by his reluctance, for Panurge is
only reluctantly grateful for something he does not deserve in the first
place. It is therefore all the more astounding that Pantagruel would choose
him as a recipient of his *biensfaictz*. That is, of course, the point: it is only
Pantagruel's decision to find Panurge agreeable that actually makes him

---

[37] See my brief discussion of this distinction, and the attendant *artifex/creator* distinction,
below, Chapter Three.

agreeable. Panurge's merit, then, is congruous, dependent on his patron's generosity.

The movement from condign to congruous merit in the representation of social relations at the court is symptomatic of an increasing insistence in Renaissance literature on a principle of the arbitrary governing esthetic authority. The subversion of proportionate reward is accompanied by the emphasis on *decorum*, on relational esthetic qualities, which are, paradoxically, all the more determining and absolute for having been produced by the assumption of an initial arbitrariness or lack of external obligation. It is clear that the late scholastics would never speak of God's *arbitrariness* as such (his *liberalitas*, his *contingent relationship to creation*, are contextually more apt terms); it is similarly clear that Castiglione would not speak in a systematic way about the prince's arbitrariness, although the principle of *Fortuna* comes close to it, and he would certainly not admit to the necessary arbitrariness of absolute power. The concept of imitation and the social homogeneity of the Italian elite guarantee at least a practical means of avoiding the ultimate consequences of a relational esthetics. In other words, inherently valuable and pleasing behavior always *seems* possible to attain, since one feels one can imitate, and since the behavior in question is empirically not so diverse as to exclude an appearance of order and rules, although in fact there can be none.

The structural arbitrariness latent in courtier esthetics can be related fruitfully to a sense of unmotivatedness in literature in the early modern period. In spite of gestures pointing to a prior tradition and authority determining literary creation, the literary text often whimsically excludes just such authority, or invests *itself* with the authority to create a fictional world, as if nothing had preceded it. We have seen this autonomy in the working of Rabelais's courtly utopia, and another brief analysis of a French rewriting of Boccaccio's *Decameron* will suggest some of its other manifestations.[38]

In the prologue to Marguerite de Navarre's *Heptaméron* (published in successive versions from 1558 on) we find a miniature court stranded in the Pyrenees, intent upon entertaining itself during the construction of a bridge over a flooded river. The prologue to the tales is essentially a conflation of Boccaccio's introduction to the *Decameron* and the first chapters of the *Cortegiano*, especially in regard to the choice of *divertissement*. Two things have to be determined: who shall lead and which game shall be played. In the *Decameron* the first choice is described in somewhat greater detail; Pampinea decides that there should be a leader for each day, for she

[38] For an ahistorical discussion of this literary autonomy, see Eugenio Donato, " 'Per selve e boscherecci labirinti': Desire and Narrative Structure in Ariosto's *Orlando furioso*," in *Literary Theory/Renaissance Texts*, ed. Patricia Parker and David Quint (Baltimore: Johns Hopkins Univ. Press, 1986), pp. 33–62, and below, Chapter Three.

has thought about these things since she first suggested the retreat from plague-ridden Florence.[39] Since it is so hot in the afternoon, she suggests that the company retreat to a cool, shady place and tell stories. Everyone agrees.

In the *Heptaméron* everyone is essentially united by chance, or "miraculeusement" (although the possibility of miracles is doubted by the most devout member, Oisille), during several days of floods and attacks by men and animals in the Pyrenees. Contrary to the *Decameron*, there is no prior organization or selection in the courtly society, although, obviously, the group assembled is highly homogeneous. The selection of a leader seems less important than the choice of a game, and Marguerite de Navarre devotes several pages of the prologue to the latter. The noble company turns first to Oisille, the oldest and most experienced member of the group. Her proposal is to read the Scriptures, but another member of the group would prefer corporeal exercise or pleasure. Oisille then refuses to choose an activity and leaves the selection to "la pluralité des opinions" (p. 8).[40] This should be taken to mean "multiplicity" rather than "plurality," from the Latin *plures* (several, plural, multiple). So the decision is once again deferred, as no external condition seems to dictate who should choose which activity, once age and experience have been excluded as criteria. Hircan is the first "opinant"—he proposes an activity that he hopes would be as agreeable to another person in the company as to himself. His wife, Parlamente, correctly interprets this as sex and rejects it as not being an activity in which all can participate. She is then chosen to select a game:

Hircan dist à toutes les dames: "Puisque ma femme a si bien entendu la glose de mon propos et que ung passetemps particulier ne luy plaist pas, je croy qu'elle sçaura mieulx que nul autre dire celluy où chascun prendra plaisir; et de ceste heure je m'en tiens à son oppinion comme celluy qui n'en a nule autre que la sienne." A quoy toute la compaignie s'accorda. Parlamente, voiant que le sort du jeu estoit tombé sur elle, leur dist ainsy. (p. 9)

[Hircan told all the women: "Since my wife has so well understood the meaning of my statement and since a private pastime does not please her, I believe that she will know better than anyone how to determine the pastime that will be pleasing to all, and from now on I will conform to her opinion as someone

---

[39] "Ma per ciò che le cose che sono senza modo non possono lungamente durare, io che cominciatrice fui de' ragionamenti da' quali questa cosí bella compagnia è stata fatta, pensando al continuar della nostra letizia, estimo che di necessitá sia, convenire esser tra noi alcun principale, il quale noi ed onoriamo ed ubidiamo" (Giovanni Boccaccio, *Il Decameron*, ed. Charles Singleton [(Bari): Laterza, 1966], 1:24).

[40] All quotations are from Marguerite de Navarre, *L'Heptaméron*, ed. Michel François (Paris: Garnier, 1967).

who has no other opinion than hers." The entire group agreed to this. Seeing that she had drawn the lot, Parlamente spoke in this way.]

The choice of Parlamente is more or less haphazard ("le sort du jeu"), although it seems to be motivated by her display of interpretive skills. She is able to interpret Hircan's allusion, and it *displeases* her: therefore she will be able to choose what is pleasing to *all*. This is a version of Rabelais's *faire tous ce que à un seul voyoient plaire*. The choice of Parlamente, then, wavers between pure chance and internal motivation (her interpretive skills), and this choice is accepted by all. The hesitant choice of a game highlights the arbitrary yet absolute reward for multiple "opinions," although in the *Heptaméron*, as opposed to the *Cortegiano*, perhaps a more decisive role is played by interpretation. Once again, though, prior or external conditions setting up proportionate reward are rejected.

As in Rabelais's antimonastic utopia, we find in the prologue to the *Heptaméron* a hypothetical reconstitution of an ideal court society. Although individual differences between the members of this society are stressed by Marguerite de Navarre, as they are in the *Cortegiano*, in the structure of choices made by the members one finds at the same time an arbitrariness and a conformity that recall the prince's court. At the end of the prologue it remains to be decided who will begin the storytelling: "Simontault commença à dire: 'Qui sera celluy de nous qui aura commencement sur les autres?' Hircan lui respondit: 'Puisque vous avez commencé la parolle, c'est raison que nous commandez; car au jeu nous sommes tous esgaulx' [Simontault began to say: 'Who will be the one to begin before the others?' Hircan responded: 'Since you have begun talking, you will take precedence; for in the game we are all equal']" (p. 10). The very equality of the participants in the game, or rather, the lack of inherent distinctions of merit, makes the choice of precedence a haphazard matter: the only legitimation of precedence is the circumstance of having begun to talk about it. Authority, then, is not invested from the outside, but derives from the act of its assumption; it is completely internal to its exercise. The lack of accessible external legitimation is a sign of the sovereign's power, even in the *Heptaméron*, which at first reading seems not to be connected with the king. However, in Parlamente's description of her "game," she refers to the success of Boccaccio's novellas with the king François Ier and the royal court (p. 9).[41] A French version of the *Decameron* was conceived by the dauphin and some ladies of the court; they intended to "assembler jusques à dix personnes qu'ilz pensoient plus dignes de racompter quelque chose

---

[41] For a suggestive discussion of the expression of royal power in the *Heptaméron*, see Peter Brockmeier, *Lust und Herrschaft: Studien über gesellschaftliche Aspekte der Novellistik: Boccaccio, Sacchetti, Margarete von Navarra, Cervantes* (Stuttgart: J. B. Metzler, 1972), pp. 54–82; he insists on the preabsolutist tendencies of the collection.

[assemble up to ten persons whom they thought worthier of recounting something]" (p. 9) but never got around to it. The haphazardous meeting of the ten *devisants* at Notre Dame de Serrance is, then, an indirect representation of the dauphin's choice and, finally, caused by the king's *pleasure*. The king's reward of merit, or "dignity," is coextensive with the risky and unmotivated coming-together of the noble company.

The replacement of condign merit by congruous merit organizes some of the basic issues of courtly literature, and the nostalgia produced by courtly civilization is principally a desire for the now past ideal of condignity. Courtly civilization is, on the other hand, *based* on the contradiction between the imitation of illustrious examples and the nature of the power that structures this civilization. This contradiction is brought to the fore in a work that takes up some of the ethical problems addressed in the fourth book of the *Cortegiano*, and that may serve as both a summary of and a conclusion to the questions raised here.

Louis Le Caron's *Dialogues* (1556) is a collection of Platonic musings about the nature of sovereignty, justice, and poetry, and contains two pieces in which the philosopher "Le Caron" explains the responsibilities of the prince to "Philarete."[42] The first chapter, "Le Courtisan, que le Prince doit philosopher, Ou de la vraic sagesse & Roiale philosophie," is essentially a monologue by Le Caron, who first of all proclaims the affinity of kings and God. The king "represente entre les hommes la semblance de Dieu [represents among men the semblance of God]" (p. 71); the king's authority "n'est une election ou sort des hommes, ains un don de Dieu [is not elected or chosen by men, but is a gift of God]" (p. 70). The king should, however, rule by justice and truth, and should compel his people to live by justice (pp. 88–89). The force of laws is based on two things:

Toute la force des lois est appuiée sus deux choses, desquelles est entretenuë la chose publique, à sçavoir le loier ou guerdon, et la peine. Car le vertueux labeur merite d'estre orné et enrichi d'honneur, de digne recompense & illustre gloire. . . . Rien n'est mieux-seant et convenable à la dignité du Roi, que la juste liberalité, laquelle decore et recompense châcun de telz loiers qu'il merite: et ainsi excite le peuple à l'amour et bienveullance de son seigneur. (pp. 92–93)

[The whole force of laws is based on two things through which public life is maintained: reward, and punishment. For virtuous labor deserves to be decorated and enriched with honor, worthy reward, and illustrious glory. . . . Nothing is more fitting to the dignity of the king than just liberality, which

[42] Louis Le Caron, *Les dialogues* (Paris: Jean Longis, 1556). Page numbers refer to the edition by Joan A. Buhlmann and Donald Gilman (Geneva: Droz, 1986).

decorates and compensates each one with those rewards that he merits, and thus incites the people to love and good will toward their sovereign.]

In the ideal state virtuous labor is rewarded proportionately to its merit: this is guaranteed by the fact that it is fitting to royal dignity to be "justly" generous. The proportionality of service and reward is based on the king's knowledge of philosophy, which teaches him "la prudence, le bien, le mal, le vrai, le faux, la justice, l'injure, la liberalité, la force et noblesse de coeur, la temperance, brief en quoi gist la science roiale [prudence, good, evil, truth, falsehood, justice, injustice, liberality, force and nobility of the heart, temperance, in sum, that which royal science consists of]" (p. 115). This is an optimistic version of merit, where in spite of relational language ("mieux seant & convenable"), philosophy is an external constraint to the king, whose inherent value depends on the knowledge of certain ethical values or concepts. Arbitrariness is seemingly excluded: "Quel desordre seroit au ciel si le Soleil empruntoit sa lumiere de la Lune, inconstante et volage? Aussi quelle police au roiaume, si le Prince ne dependoit, que de la fortune? [What disorder would be in the heavens if the sun took its light from the changing and fickle moon? So, what order would be in a kingdom, if the prince depended on chance only?]" (pp. 102–3). The prince is not merely generous, his is a *juste liberalité*.

This Platonic vision of monarchy comes close to condign merit, although Le Caron does not delineate his position until the logical consequences of royal power are pointed out to him by another character, a gentleman in the service of the duke of Vendôme, in the following dialogue. He is aptly called the "Courtisan," and he denies any external restraint on the power of the prince:

J'ai accordé le prince se devoir proposer l'utilité publique. Mais [ce] seroit rendre le Roi le plus serf de touts ses sujets, s'il n'estoit maistre de sa volunté, constituant ce qu'il estime meilleur: car parlant de l'utilité publique j'enten celle du prince, laquelle châcun doit reputer commune: par ce qu'en tout il [chacun] se doit accommoder et flechir au Roi, duquel est la souveraine puissance. (p. 130)

[I have agreed that the prince should hold before his eyes the public good. But if the king were not master over his own will, choosing what he deems best, he would be the most enslaved of all his subjects. For in speaking of the public good I understand the prince's, which everyone must hold to be the common good, because in all things the subject must accommodate himself to the king, who has sovereign power.]

The courtier summarizes this position by identifying justice and the pleasure of the prince: "J'ai tousjours dit rien ne devoir estre appellé juste, que ce qui plaist au prince [I have always said that nothing should be called just except that which pleases the prince]" (p. 130).[43] The courtier has forced the issue by pointing out the prince's *potentia absoluta*, and the ensuing disproportion between subjects' service and the generous reward by the sovereign. Any other conception of their relationship would lead to the constraining of the prince.

So wisdom is not something prior to or outside of a set of social relationships; instead, it is the constant observation and following of the opinions of the multitude: "La plus grande sagesse a tousjours esté estimée de servir au tems: et n'est moins excellent, que difficile de flechir et façonner sa maniere de vivre aux muables raisons de la multitude: et promptement s'accommoder à touts les evenements des choses et diversitez des tems [The greatest wisdom has always been held to be service to one's own time. It is no less excellent than difficult to adapt one's manner of living to the changing reasons of the multitude, and to accommodate oneself to all events and diversity of one's time]" (p. 141).[44] This *reductio ad absurdum* of relational thinking is already structurally contained in the congruity of merit Castiglione is obliged to admit; it is no less present in the bizarre freedom of Rabelais's abbey of Thélème, nor is it foreign to the "equality" of the storytellers of the *Heptaméron*. The nominalist impulse of courtier esthetics is implied by the definition of absolute power of the despot-prince, which in turn is modeled on a certain relationship between God and his creatures. God is the paradigm for the all-powerful in Christian culture, and the paradoxes of power and its relationship to the less powerful are conceptually mediated through theological distinctions. Congruity of merit is precisely such a distinctive concept, for it appears to reconcile the natural efforts of man with an absolute priority of God's grace. In the Renaissance courtly society is an esthetic, secular version of that relationship, and the insistence on the relational qualities of the courtier is implied by the increasing distance between the sovereign and what are no longer his vassals, but his subjects.

[43] For a more extensive discussion of the connection between sovereignty and "pleasure," see below, Chapter Five.

[44] A very similar development can be found in Philibert de Vienne's *Le philosophe de court*; whereas our former nature made us seek those things that are good in themselves, the court makes us seek those things that please: "Nous trouvons bon & reputons estre le seul bien, ce qu'il [sic] plait & est trouvé bon au monde: & en ce plaisir des hommes nous constituons nostre vertu. La vertu donc des hommes ne gist pas en cela qui est bon de soy, suyvant l'ancienne Philosophie: mais en ce qui leur semble bon, qui n'est autre chose, sinon une mode de vivre" (pp. 26–27). The protean nature of the courtier is of course another commonplace of the anticourt tradition. See Eneo Silvio Piccolomini, *De curialium miseriis* (composed 1444), ed. Wilfred P. Mustard (Baltimore: Johns Hopkins Univ. Press, 1928), p. 52; see again Philibert de Vienne, *Le philosophe de court*: "Il ne fault point donques blasmer ceste facilité d'esprit, qui fait que l'homme selon le plaisir des autres, se change & transforme" (p. 99).

THREE

THE FREE CREATOR: CAUSALITY AND
BEGINNINGS

Omne ergo, quod movetur, oportet ab alio moveri.
(Aquinas, *Summa theologiae*, following Aristotle)

La gloria di colui che tutto move,
per l'universo penetra.
(Dante, *Paradiso*)

Ce voyant quelqu'un de ses amis, luy demanda quelle cause le
mouvoit à son corps, son esprit, son tonneau ainsi tormenter.
(Rabelais, *Tiers livre*)[1]

T HE FORM of a book's beginning is the form of a writer's authority.[2] This beginning may be either the literal beginning, the exordium to the actual work, or a reflection in any part of the book on
the conditions preceding it and to which it displays its connections. What
the book says or implies about its provenance, its dependence, about whatever has preceded it and without which it would not have come into existence: that is the form of its connection to the surrounding culture and
world. It is also the form of the power that writing intends; this is especially the case in a culture that conceives of previous events or writing as
more meaningful than itself owing to their temporal priority. *Form* in an
Aristotelian sense is emphasized here, for authority, power, and begin-

---

[1] Aquinas: "Therefore it is necessary that everything that is moved is moved by something
else"; Dante: "The glory of God who moves everything, penetrates throughout the universe";
Rabelais: "Seeing this, one of his friends asked what cause moved him to torment in such a
way his body, his mind, and his barrel." Unless indicated otherwise, translations are my own.

[2] "Every sort of writing establishes explicit and implicit rules of pertinence for itself: certain
things are admissible, certain others not. I call these rules of pertinence *authority*—both in the
sense of explicit law and guiding force (what we usually mean by the term) and in the sense
of that implicit power to generate another word that will *belong to* the writing as a whole"
(Edward Said, *Beginnings: Intention and Method* [New York: Basic Books, 1975], p. 16). On
literary problems of authorship and authority, see also the suggestive general discussion by
Jacqueline T. Miller, *Poetic License: Authority and Authorship in Medieval and Renaissance Contexts* (New York: Oxford Univ. Press, 1986), pp. 3–33.

nings of writing are not invariable elements of all literature, but are essentially different in different kinds of books, in different cultural contexts.

An example of the diversity of forms of authority is the difference between a "modern" and a "premodern," or medieval, sense of beginning. The medieval writer, and in many ways the ancient poet, write as continuers of writing; they seem caused to write by someone or something external to themselves. Whether as a translator of culture and empire, or as a poet inspired by the Muses, an *afflamen*, a *spiritus* (or by a generous patron), the writer's creation is generated from a principle outside of himself. The writer is in some ways a mediation between the work and an anterior power.[3] Although obviously there are differences between these anterior powers, as a patron is not in every way comparable to a Muse, they are all outside of the writer and prior to him.

In a "modern" view, the writer is seen as the absolute origin of the work. He denies filiation with anterior writing or conditions of writing; he is implicitly free of prior determination and is free to choose. The writer is *alone* before the blank page, is not a conduit of culture and experience but their creator.[4] These are fairly commonplace descriptions of the creative process that in their vagueness do not really convey the intricate set of cultural conditions determining a writer's authority. In a primarily oppositional definition the *emergence* of a modern sense of beginning may be difficult to discern or even talk about, since *emergence* seems to be excluded by the structure of the definition itself. The purpose of this study is to provide an analogical model that will contain the possibility of that emergence, and it is to theology that it will have recourse, as it is within theology that the pertinent issues are endlessly debated and refined.

[3] On the *spiritus* see D. P. Walker, *Spiritual and Demonic Magic from Ficino to Campanella* (Leiden: Warburg Institute, 1958); on the poet's inspiration see the introduction in Durling, *Figure of the Poet*, and a typical Renaissance example in Marco Girolamo Vida, *De arte poetica* (1517), 2.432–33. (ed. and trans. Ralph G. Williams [New York: Columbia Univ. Press], 1976). For the notion of medieval authorship in this light, see Roger Dragonetti, *La vie de la lettre au moyen âge (Le conte du Graal)* (Paris: Seuil, 1980), pp. 41–61, and, for a study of the inspirational importance of the patron, Douglas Kelly, "The Genius of the Patron: The Prince, the Poet, and Fourteenth-Century Invention," *Studies in the Literary Imagination* 20 (1987): 77–97, and "Le patron et l'auteur dans l'invention romanesque," in *Théories et pratiques de l'écriture au moyen âge*, ed. Emmanuèle Baumgartner and Christiane Marchello-Nizia (Paris: Centre de recherches du Département de Français, Fontenay/Saint-Cloud, 1988), pp. 25–39. For an interesting discussion of the "efflorescent death of inspiration" and the emergence of "imagination," especially in English medieval and Renaissance literature, see John Guillory, *Poetic Authority: Spenser, Milton, and Literary History* (New York: Columbia Univ. Press, 1983).

[4] See Said, *Beginnings*, pp. 66–67, on the distinction between dynastic and intentional beginning, and, for the modern writer's essential solitude in writing and alienation from the written word, Maurice Blanchot, *L'espace littéraire* (Paris: Gallimard, 1955), pp. 9–28.

Causation as a Theological Problem

The cultural paradigm for individual "creation" in medieval and Renaissance society is, as has been pointed out with great frequency, God's creation and conservation of the world.[5] The divine analogy both defines the act of human creation and relegates it to a certain status within Creation, emphasizing that, whereas God could create something out of nothing, man, in the medieval view, could only fashion preexistent material.[6] The link between Creation and Creator allows the consideration of the creative act through consideration of its effects in the created world. This link was a constant presupposition of medieval theology. One of the more important conditions of God's connection to the created world is the notion of causality and all of its ramifications in scholastic philosophy. One can hardly find a more complex and far-reaching question; its very pervasiveness and the interest devoted to it in medieval and early modern theology and philosophy suggest its fruitfulness in intellectual culture in general. Hence the vicissitudes of causality should provide a perspective through which the created *fictional* world is related to its author, *artifex* or *creator*, in literature. It is this relationship, set in the context of causality, that will be examined here.[7]

[5] For a survey of the history of the divine analogy for human creation, see Vinzenz Rüfner, "*Homo secundus Deus*: Eine geistesgeschichtliche Studie zum menschlichen Schöpfertum," *Philosophisches Jahrbuch* 63 (1954): 248–91; see also Hans Robert Jauss, "Poiesis," trans. Michael Shaw, *Critical Inquiry* 8 (1982): 591–608, esp. pp. 593–99. In both cases the theological side of the analogy is not very extensively worked out.

[6] According to the scholastics, man cannot create *de nihilo*, but can only form an already existent material. This is the distinction between *creator* and *artifex* that Peter Lombard makes in his *Sentences*: "Ex qua ratione proprie dicitur creator, et quid sit creare, quid facere. Creator enim est, qui de nihilo aliqua facit, et creare proprie est de nihilo aliquid facere; facere vero, non modo de nihilo aliquid operari, sed etiam de materia. Unde et homo vel angelus dicitur aliqua facere, sed non creare; vocaturque factor sive artifex, sed non creator. Hoc enim nomen soli Deo proprie congruit, qui et de nihilo quaedam, et de aliquo aliqua facit. Ipse est ergo creator et opifex et factor" (*Sententiae in IV libris distinctae*, 3d ed. [Grottoferrata: Collegium S. Bonaventura, 1971], vol. 1, pt. 2, p. 330 [II d 1 c 2]). This essential distinction between human creation and divine creation is never really in question, of course, among scholastic theologians. See Ockham, *Quodlibet* II q 9: "Utrum creatura possit creare." The answer is no, if "to create" is taken in the sense of "producere aliquid sine passo praesupposito tempore vel natura" (*Opera theologica* 9:150). I will be arguing, however, that nominalist undermining of causality, and argumentation *de potentia Dei absoluta*, provide paradigms for the radicalization of human creation in literature of the Renaissance.

[7] On the explicit relationship between Aristotelian causality and authorship in scholastic prologues and Bible exegesis, see Minnis, *Medieval Theory of Authorship*, esp. pp. 75–94, and Concetta Carestia Greenfield, *Humanist and Scholastic Poetics, 1250–1500* (Lewisburg, Pa.: Bucknell Univ. Press, 1981) (on the relationship between scholasticism and art). I am not interested in what the scholastics themselves may have said about human writing or literary activity, except in a general way. Rather, literary practice seems determined in a more funda-

The symptom of causation is movement, in a general sense—that is, all qualititative and quantitative change observable in created beings. Things move in the world, and this movement implies a cause or mover which is different from the thing moved.[8] That cause or mover is also caused or moved in some way, although specific cause-effect relationships can sometimes begin and end completely.[9] According to the scholastics, when the causal chain is followed back, one must come to a first cause, a *prima causa efficiens*, or *primum mobile*, which sets everything in motion.[10] This *primum mobile* can be identified with God[11] and, more importantly, with the act of

mental way by paradigmatic distinctions governing the relationship between God and his creatures that are elucidated in scholasticism and often have no explicit connection to literary activity.

[8] See Saint Thomas Aquinas, *Summa theologiae* Ia q 2 a 3; q 25 a 1; *Contra gentiles* 1.2 c 65. See also A. Chollet's article "Cause" in the *Dictionnaire de théologie catholique*, vol. 2, pt. 2, 2014 sq.; on movement and its causation, see Aristotle, *Physics*, 200b 12–202b 29, and especially *Metaphysics*, 1012b 22–32, 1071b 2ff. Movement and causation are not always explicitly connected by all scholastics, although overall their connection is evident: see, for example, Roy R. Effler, O.F.M., *John Duns Scotus and the Principle 'Omne quod movetur ab alio movetur'* (St. Bonaventure, N.Y.: Franciscan Institute, 1962); Effler shows that Scotus disconnected the two issues (pp. 43–45). See also his historical overview, pp. 1–31.

[9] Aristotle excludes an infinite regression of causes, in *Metaphysics*, 994a 1–994b 5, and posits an eternal unmoveable substance causing actual movement.

[10] That is, infinite regression in essentially ordered causes is impossible. See Duns Scotus, *Ordinatio* I d 2 p 1 q 1–2 n 53: "Essentialiter ordinatorum infinitas est impossibilis" (in *Opera omnia*, ed. P. Carolus Balić et al. [Vatican: Typis Polyglottis Vaticanis, 1950–1966], 2:157). One of the reasons for this is the hierarchical organization of the causal chain (the prior cause is more perfect than the effect, or the later cause): "Quia superior causa est perfectior in causando, ex secunda differentia [see below, note 14]; ergo in infinitum superior est in infinitum perfectior, et ita infinitae perfectionis in causando, et per consequens non causans in virtute alterius, quia quaelibet talis est imperfecte causans, qui est dependens in causando ab alia" (*Opera omnia*, ed. Balić, 2:158; ed. Lucas Wadding [Paris: L. Vivès, 1891–1895], 8:418). A regression to the most perfect would mean that the latter is uncaused, since independence from a cause is more perfect than dependence on a cause.

[11] See Aquinas's famous argument conflating the uncaused first cause and the being/essence identification in God, in *De ente et essentia* (1256): "But all that belongs to anything is either caused from principles of its nature, as for instance risibility in man, or accrues to it through some extrinsic principle, as for instance light in air from the influence of the sun. But it cannot be that existence itself should be caused by the form of quiddity of the thing, caused, I say, as by means of an efficient cause, because thus something would be the cause of itself and would bring its very self into existence, which is impossible. Therefore it follows that everything such that its existence is other than its nature has existence from another (*ab alio*). And because everything which exists by virtue of another is reduced to that which exists in virtue of itself (*per se*), as to its first cause, it follows that there must be something which is the cause of the existence (*causa essendi*) of all things, because it is very existence alone; otherwise the causes would proceed to infinity, since everything which is not existence alone would have a cause of its existence, as has been said. It is clear, therefore, that an intelligence is form and existence, and that it has its existence from the first being which is existence alone, and this the first cause which is God" (*Concerning Being and Essence*, trans. George G. Leckie [New

Creation, so that not only does God first move the universe, but he creates what he moves. This creationist modification of the causal chain is an important correction brought by Aquinas and Christian medieval theologians in general to the eternal universe implied by Aristotelian-Averroist metaphysics.[12] The image of the causal chain is sometimes confusing, as it obscures another concept of God as cause, namely, his function as sustaining or conserving cause of the present universe. So any present event is dependent on God both as the temporally first cause and the basic sustaining cause. Emphasized, then, is the fact that God does not *necessarily* create the universe and conserve it; the latter's existence is contingent, in the sense that it is God's decision to create the universe that enables it to exist, not an ineluctable necessity outside of God, or something inherent in the universe's essence.[13] The existence of God does not absolutely imply the existence of the universe, although the converse is true.

The relationship between the existence of God and the existence of the universe is essential to various aspects of the problem of causality and its interpretation in the Middle Ages. Seen from the perspective, this time, of the cause, a relationship of causation means that when one thing exists, another also exists. When fire exists, so does heat, smoke, and so on. In scholastic thought, however, the relationship between cause and effect is not one of mere succession, for, since the effect is dependent on the cause for its existence, the cause is thought to be ontologically more perfect than the effect.[14] The causal chain is, then, at the same time a hierarchy of beings, which leads to the most perfect being and cause, God. The causal

---

York: Appleton-Century-Crofts, 1937], pp. 24–25). See also Scotus, *De primo principio*, esp. c 3, in *Opera omnia*, ed. Wadding, 4:750–62.

[12] See Etienne Gilson, *L'être et l'essence* (Paris: Vrin, 1948), pp. 46–77.

[13] See the decree of March 7, 1277, by the Sorbonne (and the bishop Etienne Tempier) declaring the following statements (among many others) to be errors: "21. Quod nichil fit a casu, sed omnia de necessitate eveniunt, et, quod omnia futura, que erunt, de necessitate erunt, et que non erunt, impossibile est esse, et quod nichil fit contingenter, considerando omnes causas"; and especially "53. Quod Deum necesse est facere, quicquid inmediate ab ipso.—Error, sive intelligatur de necessitate coactionis, quia tollit libertatem, sive de necessitate inmutabilitatis, quia ponit impotentiam aliter faciendi" (in H. Denifle and E. Chatelain, eds., *Chartularium universitatis parisiensis* [Paris: Delalain, 1889], 1:545–46). See also Aquinas, *Summa theologiae* I q 19 a 4, "Utrum voluntas Dei sit causa rerum?"

[14] Scotus, for example, distinguishes between essentially ordered causes ("causae per se sive essentialiter ordinatae") and accidentally ordered causes ("causae per accidens sive accidentaliter ordinatae"). In essentially ordered causes the second depends on the first, whereas in accidentally ordered causes this is not the case; the first essential cause must necessarily be present for the second to be produced; essentially ordered causes have a completely first cause, whereas in accidentally ordered causes infinite regression is possible, and so on. An important difference concerns the ontological hierarchy of causes: "Differentia secunda est quod in per se ordinatis est causalitas alterius rationis et alterius ordinis, quia superior est perfectior, in accidentaliter autem ordinatis non. . . ." (*Ordinatio* I d 2 p 1 q 1–2 n 50 [ed. Balić, 2:154; ed. Wadding, 8:417]).

relationship is conceived as a transmission of Being, where the source of Being is naturally more perfect than the receiver. The universe is not immediately caused in all of its present effects by God, although he is the first efficient cause; rather, there are secondary causes that explain the relative imperfection of the created world in time. If, *a contrario*, God were the only immediate cause of all events, then presumably the universe would be timeless, infinite, and perfect, since all events would receive their being immediately from the divine nature.

This hierarchical, mediated view of causality is attacked by nominalist theologians of the fourteenth century.[15] In William of Ockham's writings the relationship between cause and effect is not seen as the relationship of the more perfect to the less perfect, for a necessary ontological hierarchy among causes is untenable.[16] Moreover, God's will and his essence are identical, and he immediately causes *all* events, although secondary causes are not superfluous. Thus there is no difference in degree of perfection between causes, and causality is conceived of merely as necessary succession or sequence, not as a transmission of Being.[17] Ockham generally attacks Scotus's distinction between essential and accidental causal orders (which had allowed the definition of a perfect first cause as God), an attack which makes the provableness of God as *prima causa efficiens* extremely difficult,[18] although God as immediate sustaining cause of events is not

[15] For a general discussion, definitions, and a *mise-en-garde* concerning nominalist critiques of causality, see William J. Courtenay, "The Critique on Natural Causality in the Mutakallimun and Nominalism," *Harvard Theological Review* 66 (1973): 77–94.

[16] See Ockham, *Sent.* I d 2 q 10: "Contra secundam differentiam [between essential and accidental causes; see note 14], quando accipit quod causae essentialiter ordinatae sunt alterius rationis et alterius ordinis, quia causa superior est perfectior, aut accipitur superioritas pro prioritate secundum perfectionem, aut pro prioritate secundum illimitationem. Si primo modo, hoc esset petere quod causae sunt alterius ordinis, quia perfectior est perfectior; igitur oportet quod accipiat secundo modo et dicat quod omnis causa illimitatior est perfectior causa magis limitata. Sed hoc est simpliciter falsum, quia aliquando causa illimitatior est simpliciter imperfectior et aliquando perfectior" (*Opera theologica* 2:349). On Ockham's critique of Scotus, see Marilyn McCord Adams, *William Ockham* (Notre Dame, Ind.: Univ. of Notre Dame Press, 1987), 2:772–84; she claims that Scotus is more equivocal about priority and perfection than Ockham allows.

[17] See Ockham, *Sent.* I d 45 q unica, "Utrum voluntas Dei sit causa immediata et prima omnium eorum quae fiunt" (*Opera theologica* 4:661–69), and the analysis by Klaus Bannach, in *Die Lehre von der doppelten Macht Gottes bei Wilhelm von Ockham: Problemgeschichtliche Voraussetzungen und Bedeutung* (Wiesbaden: Franz Steiner, 1975), pp. 295–97. See also Aristotle, *Metaphysics* 1013a 24–35. McCord Adams, *William Ockham*, pp. 784–95, discusses the degree of Ockham's skepticism concerning causality.

[18] Ockham, *Sent.* I d 2 q 10: "Utrum sit tantum unus Deus." One of the models for causation is the generation of men; now it is difficult to disprove the possibility of an infinite regression of generations, and it is difficult to disprove the claim that one man can be a total cause for another man (i.e., one does not need a divine uncaused cause in generation). Given these two difficulties, "difficile esset probare quod iste processus in infinitum [of causes] non

doubted. Moreover, the evidence of movement does not imply the existence of a mover, since it is not impossible for a thing to move itself (as in the case of angels, the soul, and gravity).[19] However, both a first mover and a causal chain begun by God are the preferable or more probable explanations, although they are not certain. God could have created a different world, or several worlds.[20] In the case of Ockham we have a transferral of God's contingent work *ad extra* (to anything outside of himself) to the created world, in the sense that the unnecessary creation of the world corresponds to the (logically) unnecessary connection between the world and God.

The most radical critique of causation, and thus the most extreme infusion of contingency into the logical structure of experience, is found in what we know of the work of Nicolas d'Autrecourt. He argues in the following way: Causality means that when one affirms one thing, one can also affirm another. If the second thing is the same as the first, all one is doing is affirming the identity of a thing with itself. If the second thing is not the same, nothing permits one to affirm or deny the thing, for the only principle of absolute certainty, the principle of noncontradiction, does not guarantee it. Logically the relationship between cause and effect is neither necessary nor evident, although in the realm of experience it is evident.[21] A similar critique of causality is found in the work of Pierre d'Ailly, who emphasizes that the principle of causality is not a metaphysical law but is essentially dependent on the will of God.[22] Thus the contingency of God's

---

esset possibilis nisi esset unum semper manens a quo tota ista infinitas dependeret" (*Opera theologica* 2:355). See on this question Gilson, *La philosophie au moyen âge*, p. 649, and Bannach, *Die Lehre von der doppelten Macht Gottes*, pp. 278–97.

[19] "[P]ossum rationabiliter dicere aliquid seipsum movere sicut anima et angelus, qui producunt varios suos actus et gravitas ipsa quae movendo seipsam descendit" (Ockham, *Centiloquium*, quoted in Bannach, *Die Lehre von der doppelten Macht Gottes*, p. 279 n. 17). Bannach comments: "Immerhin weist diese spätere Kritik Ockhams auf den Kern des thomasischen Arguments hin: nämlich daß die stete Veränderung des Geschaffenen (also nicht nur Orts—sondern auch Quantitäts—und Qualitätsveränderungen, jede Art von Seinsveränderung) die Annahme der Existenz Gottes als desjenigen, der diese ständige Veränderung des Geschaffenen verursacht, erzwingt" (p. 279). On self-movement see also Aristotle, *Physics* 254b 7. See also McCord Adams, *William Ockham*, pp. 827–28.

[20] Gilson, *La philosophie au moyen âge*, p. 650.

[21] Ibid., pp. 666–67; Paul Vignaux quotes d'Autrecourt: "Ex eo quod aliqua res est cognita esse, non potest evidenter, evidentia reducta in primum principium vel in certitudinem primi principii, inferri quod alia res sit" (in *Dictionnaire de théologie catholique* 10:566). On d'Autrecourt's critique of causality, see also Julius Rudolph Weinberg, *Nicolaus of Autrecourt: A Study in 14th-Century Thought* (Princeton: Princeton Univ. Press, 1948), pp. 31–37, 47–50; Mario Dal Pra, *Nicola di Autrecourt* (Milan: Bocca, 1951), pp. 116–23.

[22] See *Sent.* IV q 1a: "Licet ad praesentiam causae secundae proprie dictae sequatur effectus non solum ex voluntate Dei, sed ex virtute ipsius causae et ex natura rei: tamen quod ad praesentiam alicuius causae sequatur aliquis effectus virtute ipsius causae seu ex natura rei, solum est ex voluntate Dei," quoted by Bernhard Meller, *Studien zur Erkenntnislehre des Peter*

creation has been transferred, in a way, to the logical connection of causes and effects in the created world. The unnecessary creation of the world corresponds to the unnecessary relationship between causes and effects within the created world.

To summarize the shifts in notions of causality relevant to the issues that will be discussed: First, the Thomist-Scotist view of a mediating, hierarchical causal chain leading from Creation to Creator is criticized by nominalist theologians, who insist on God's immediate causation of effects and on the lack of any immanent hierarchy in created phenomena. Thus, from the point of view of the creature, there is no reasonable and certain way of ordering phenomena according to differences in degree of Being. Second, although the link between God and Creation is immediate, it is also, paradoxically, more obscure, as effects are equally caused by him, but not ordered to each other in a way that leads inherently to a divine first cause. God causes everything, but one may also say that he causes nothing, from the point of view of the reasoning creature. Third, priority in causation is not necessarily felt to be more valuable than posteriority—the cause is not necessarily more perfect than the effect. In the created order, origin does not enjoy the ontological prestige of divine origin, partly because the latter is absolutely effective, without eliminating secondary causes.

The corrosiveness of nominalist argumentation is often attributed to the redefinition of God's faculties or powers. Whereas in the Thomist tradition reason, understanding, or knowledge (*intellectus*) is conceptually (as opposed to temporally) prior to will in God, thereby guaranteeing an order fundamental to God's actions, or to which his actions are bound, in the nominalist critiques of the fourteenth and fifteenth centuries God is viewed as not subject to any anterior necessity. Thus his will is thought of as conceptually prior to his actions.[23] This does not lead to disorder, for God has decided to enter into a pact with man and his creation, to which he binds himself (exercising his *potentia ordinata*). However, his absolutely prior, unbound, unnecessary power is the constant possibility of hypothetical (and, according to some, in the case of miracles, real) transgression, or rather, suspension, of creation's laws. This is his *potentia absoluta*,[24] which

---

von Ailly (Freiburg: Verlag Herder, 1954), p. 115 n. 130. Meller further characterizes d'Ailly's views of causality: "Diese Ausführungen zeigen klar, daß das Kausalgesetz nach Ailly kein metaphysisches Grundprinzip ist, das allgemeine and unumstößliche Geltung hat. In der kontingenten, geschaffenen Welt besteht zwischen Ursache und Wirkung kein notwendiges, inneres Abhängigkeitsverhältnis, sondern nur eine äußere, zufällige Aufeinanderfolge" (p. 115).

[23] On this question see Oakley, *Omnipotence*, pp. 41–65. In humanist-Augustinian thought of the fourteen and fifteenth centuries, the will is valorized above reason or understanding; see Trinkaus, *In Our Image and Likeness*, esp. 1:51–102, on Coluccio Salutati. See also below, Chapter Four, on the will in Rabelais.

[24] See Bannach, *Die Lehre von der doppelten Macht Gottes*, pp. 13–17, for this concept in

allows for the projection of radical contingency into the logical structure of the creation.[25] Everything could have been different, even if we are sure that things will not be different. There were other possibilities open to God when he decided to create, and there was nothing outside of God forcing him to choose this order of creation. The adoption of God's point of view, then, permits the nominalist critique of causality and movement, and yet does not, in undermining Creation's rational connections to the Creator, deny God himself, for it is on the principle of God's contingent creative act that the critique is based. Paul Vignaux has characterized in this way Ockham's use of the concept of God's power:

> L'univers de ce nominalisme est l'univers d'un théologien que la Révélation a introduit au point de vue divin: il n'a pas du réel une autre appréhension que l'incroyant, mais, croyant, il en affirme des prédicats spécifiquement théologiques; en les pensant soumises à une *potentia absoluta*, il juge des choses comme Dieu les voit.[26]

> [The universe of this nominalism is the universe of a theologian whom Revelation has introduced to the divine point of view: he does not have a different apprehension of what is real than the nonbeliever, but, as he does believe, he attributes specifically theological attributes to the real; in thinking them to be submitted to God's *potentia absoluta*, he judges things as God sees them.]

An example of Ockham's reasoning will illustrate the way in which the philosopher-theologian-logician places himself implicitly in the position of God. In the *Quodlibeta* VI q 1, Ockham poses the question whether man can be saved without possessing the habit of grace, that is, the habit of charitable and meritorious works in the eyes of God ("utrum homo possit salvari sine caritate creata"). In the scholastic manner, arguments for and against are rehearsed. The more obvious answer to the question is no, "quia quicumque salvatur est carus Dei; sed nullus potest esse carus Deo sine caritate, igitur nullus potest salvari sine caritate [for whoever is saved is a friend to God; but no one can be a friend of God without grace, therefore no one can be saved without (infused) grace]." However, the argument for salvation without the habit of grace (as opposed to *caritas in-*

Duns Scotus, and pp. 17–25, for Ockham's definition of the distinction, and McCord Adams, *William Ockham*, pp. 1186–1207. See also Oakley, *Omnipotence*; Oberman, *Harvest of Medieval Theology*, pp. 30–38; Courtenay, "Nominalism and Late Medieval Religion," esp. pp. 37–43; Vignaux, *Le nominalisme au XIVe siècle*.

[25] It must always be emphasized that the strong empirical bent, that is, the reliance on the evidence of experience, of nominalists such as Ockham, d'Autrecourt, and Jean de Mirecourt, distinguishes them essentially from skeptics, and that their critique *de potentia Dei absoluta* is not conceived of, at least by them, as an undermining of religion itself, but rather as a use of theological precepts in the domain of philosophy that in many ways strengthens the otherness of faith and does not lead to a deist or atheist rationalism. Renaissance fideism can fruitfully be seen in this light.

[26] Vignaux, *Le nominalisme au XIVe siècle*, p. 96.

creata) is based on what is in an absolute sense possible for God to do: "Deus potest omne absolutum distinctum ab alio separare et in esse sine eo conservare; sed gratia et gloria sunt duo absoluta realiter distincta; igitur potest gloriam in anima conservare et gratiam adnihilare [God can separate everything absolutely distinct from anything else and conserve its being without the other; grace and glory are two really absolutely distinct things; therefore he can conserve glory in the soul and eliminate grace]."[27] This reasoning is based on the distinction between God's ordained and absolute powers, which Ockham goes on to define. He emphasizes that it is not a matter of two really different powers in God, but instead two ways of understanding the words *posse aliquid* as applied to God. Ordained power is defined as God's power to act according to laws instituted by himself; absolute power is the power to do anything that does not involve a contradiction:

> Sed est sic intelligenda quod 'posse aliquid' quandoque accipitur secundum leges ordinatas et institutas a Deo, et illa dicitur Deus posse facere de potentia ordinata. Aliter accipitur 'posse' pro posse facere omne illud non includit contradictionem fieri . . . et illa dicitur Deus posse de potentia absoluta. (VI q 1 a 1)[28]

> [But the expression "to be able to do something" is to be understood in this way when it means according to the laws ordained and instituted by God: so it is said that God is able to do something through his ordained power. Otherwise "to be able" means to be able to do anything that does not entail a contradiction . . . so it is said that God is able to do something through his absolute power.]

So God can, absolutely speaking, reward a particular man with salvation in spite of the fact that this man does not, through a habit of grace, merit God's saving grace. A biblical example is the rapture of Paul (2 Cor. 12:1–4), who was not, up until that point, a friend of God.

The only limitation to God's power is the principle of noncontradiction, which is thus the only substantial definition of God's *potentia absoluta*.[29] Now Ockham depends on the principle of noncontradiction in his own reasoning, and in a decisive way, for logical contradiction is taken as the only *certain* means of excluding a proposition, or, conversely, logical noncontradiction of any proposition means that one cannot deny its possibility. An example is given in *Quodlibeta* II q 5, "utrum Deus potuit fecisse mundum ab aeterno [whether God could have made the world in eter-

---

[27] Ockham, *Opera theologica* 9:585.

[28] Ibid., p. 586. See, for a detailed discussion of this passage, Bannach, *Die Lehre von der doppelten Macht Gottes*, pp. 17–19.

[29] On the importance of this principle in Ockham, which is not really a limitation of God's power but which enables it in the first place, see Miethke, *Ockhams Weg zur Sozialphilosophie*, pp. 137–56, esp. pp. 139–41.

nity]." The affirmative argument is: "Quia non includit contradictionem; igitur potuit fieri a Deo" [It does not entail a contradiction; therefore it could have been made by God]." The negative is: "Tunc infinita essent pertransita [In that case infinite things would be transitory]." Ockham does not actually endorse one or the other, but declares that the question cannot be answered positively: "Ad istam quaestionem dico primo quod neutra pars quaestionis potest sufficienter probari: pars negativa non, quia nulla apparet contradictio manifesta; nec affirmativa, quia rationes non sufficienter concludunt quin possint solvi [To this question I say first of all that neither side of the question can be sufficiently proven: not the negative side, since there appears no obvious contradiction; neither the positive, since the arguments do not sufficiently conclude, such that they cannot be solved]."[30] The proposition, as contrary as it may be to the anti-Averroist theological tradition, cannot be excluded because it does not lead to or contain a manifest contradiction. Ockham's use of this principle is frequent and decisive.[31] Noncontradiction becomes, then, both the criterion of God's absolute power and the epistemological measure of things for the human philosopher. The latter places himself into a *hypothetical* situation that is similar to the *actual* situation of God. Ockham can entertain all propositions about the world that do not contain a contradiction, as God can *do* anything that does not lead to a contradiction. Human epistemological judgment mimics God's *potentia absoluta*.

To put it in simpler terms, one can say that in fourteenth-century nominalist theology the following two issues are relevant to literary authority: the undermining of Thomist causality, and argumentation *de potentia Dei absoluta*, which tends to place the human interpreter in the perspective of God. The nominalist scholastic tradition, through the reading of the works of Scotus and Ockham and their successors in the *via moderna*, preserves and augments these problems and arguments in the following two centuries. It is this shifting view of causality that can be related to the way in which literary authority and beginning operate in the Renaissance, and that will form the ground of the analyses to come.

Authority as Prior Cause

Before turning to Rabelais and Montaigne, it seems appropriate to describe briefly the sort of literary authority consonant with the creature's

---

[30] Ockham, *Opera theologica* 9:128. See also his *Quaestiones variae* 3, which takes up the same issue (8:59–97).

[31] See the other instances of its use in the *Quodlibeta* (e.g., III q 10; IV qq 4, 8, 10, 22; V q 18; VI qq 4, 6, 13). Ockham is of course more famous for his "razor," *pluralitas non est ponenda sine necessitate* (*Quodlibeta* II q 15; III q 6; IV qq 26, 27, 30, etc.).

status as moved by an agent external to itself. The most obvious example of a work in which this problem is overtly addressed, and which is an endless source of edifying paradoxes, is Saint Augustine's *Confessions*. His autobiographical writing is grounded in prior constraint and causation. The first book begins with an invocation of God's greatness, power, and wisdom, in an almost exact quotation of Ps. 146:5–6, and goes on to describe the relationship to God that allows man to praise him:

> Magnus es, domine, et laudabilis valde: magna virtus tua, et sapientiae tuae non est numerus. et laudare te vult homo, aliqua portio creaturae tuae, et homo circumferens mortalitatem suam, circumferens testimonium peccati sui et testimonium, quia superbis resistis: et tamen laudare te vult homo, aliqua portio creaturae tuae. tu excitas, ut laudare te delectet.

> [Great art thou, O Lord, and greatly to be praised: great is thy power, and thy wisdom is infinite. And man, who being a part of what thou hast created, is desirous to praise thee; this man, bearing about his own mortality with him, carrying about him a testimony of his own sin, (even this testimony, that God resisteth the proud;) yet this man, this part of what thou hast created, is desirous to praise thee; thou so provokest him, that he even delighteth to praise thee.][32]

Human creation is praise of God; this praise is caused by God himself, who provokes man ("excitas"). Thus God causes the writer to write, strictly speaking. Not only is God the first mover, but that with which the writer Augustine begins is God's word, that is, a quotation from the Bible. God determines the act of writing and its product, and the writer is conceived essentially as a mediation between God and the book. The authoritative voice, then, is not the "narrator" or even the *sujet de l'énonciation*, but rather the prior, external Word. This is perhaps the most extreme example of the individual writer's absorption into prior theological authority and causation.

In the Renaissance, hexameral epic also carefully links its own discourse to the Bible and identifies its own cause as God, that is, as a source much greater than the individual writing. The literary material consists of the creation of the world by God, and human description of Creation is both praise of God's work and already encompassed in that work. In this sense the hexameral poet's authority is similar to Augustine's status as a creature whose praise of the Creator is already caused or at least provoked by the latter. Man's praise of God will not add anything to God, since man's work is the effect of a superior cause.

Guillaume Salluste Du Bartas's *La sepmaine* (1578), a poem describing

---

[32] Saint Augustine, *Confessions*, ed. W.H.D. Rouse, trans. William Watts (Cambridge, Mass.: Harvard University Press, 1912), pp. 2–3.

the first seven days of the created world, invokes God in its exordium; God's inspiration of the poet is simultaneously, on the intradiegetic level, the beginning of Creation:

> Toy qui guides le cours du ciel porte-flambeaux,
> Qui, vray Neptune, tiens le moite frein des eaux,
> Qui fais trembler la terre, et de qui la parole
> Serre et lasche la bride aux postillons d'Aeole,
> Esleve à toy mon ame, espure mes esprits,
> Et d'un docte artifice enrichi mes escrits.
> O Pere, donne moy que d'une voix faconde
> Je chante à nos neveux la naissance du monde.
> O grand Dieu, donne moy que j'estale en mes vers
> Les plus rares beautez de ce grand univers.
> Donne moy qu'en son front ta puissance je lise:
> Et qu'enseignant autruy moy-mesme je m'instruise.
>
> . . . .
>
> L'immuable decret de la bouche divine,
> Qui causera sa fin, causa son origine:
> Non en temps, avant temps, ains mesme avec le temps.
>
> (1.1–12, 19–21)[33]

[You who guide the course of the torch-carrying sky, who, true Neptune, hold the wet bridle of the waters, who make the earth tremble, and whose word tightens and relaxes the bridle of the postilions of Aeolus, raise my soul to you, purify my spirits, and enrich my writings with learned artwork. Oh Father, grant me that I may sing to our grandsons the birth of the world with a fluent voice. Oh great God, grant me that I may display in my verses the rarest beauties of this great universe. Grant me that I be able to read your power in its face, and that by instructing others I may instruct myself. . . . The immutable decree of the divine mouth that will cause its end, caused its beginning: not in time, before time, but with time itself.]

The poet creates nothing, strictly speaking, for he is nothing but a conduit of "instruction." He reads about God's power in the universe, and in instructing himself he teaches others. The universe, caused by God, causes the poem, formally. Inversely, the poet reads the book of the world in order to write his own book.[34] The poet is then imitating God, whose spirit is described as writing the book of the universe:

[33] Guillaume Salluste Du Bartas, *La sepmaine* (text of 1581), ed. Yvonne Bellenger, 2 vols. (Paris: Nizet, 1981).

[34] "Le monde est un grand livre, où du souverain maistre / L'admirable artifice on lit en grosse lettre. / Chasque oeuvre est une page, et chaque sien effect / Est un beau charactere en tous ses traits parfaict. . . . Ainsi donc, esclairé par la foy, je desire / Les textes plus sacrez de

Ainsi qu'un bon esprit, qui grave sur l'autel
De la docte memoire un ouvrage immortel,
En troupe, en table, au lict, tout jour, pour tout-jour vivre,
Discourt sur son discours, et nage sur son livre:
Ainsi l'Esprit de Dieu sembloit, en s'esbatant,
Nager par le dessus de cest amas flottant.

(1.289–294)

[Just as a good spirit, which engraves on the altar of learned memory an immortal work, in a group, at table, in bed, every day, in order to live always, talks about its work (or reasons about its reasoning), and swims above its book, so the Spirit of God seemed, frolicking, to swim above this floating mass.]

So the individual poet at least affirms that he does not constitute anything distinct from God and his creation, and his activity, the writing of his book, is already prefigured in God's writing of the world.[35] Authority is completely derivative, an effect of prior formal and efficient causes.

As a work of allegorical imagination, and thus somewhat less determined by the need to transcribe preexistent material than hexameral epic, Dante's *Divina commedia* (composed ca. 1307–1321) begins by projecting a prior, external constraint within which there is individual variation: "Nel mezzo del cammin di nostra vita / Mi ritrovai per una selva oscura. [Midway through our life I found myself in a dark forest]." Although the poem comes into being essentially through an act of individual recognition ("mi ritrovai"), the individual is on a path that is prescribed, that belongs to "us." "Nostra vita" also projects, in an uncanny way, a transcendent observer who observes us on our path (as opposed to, say, "life in general," or "my life"). In spite of individual choices, then, the path of the poet is essentially determined and enabled by an order transcending the individual. In addition, Dante's exemplary voyage, by the very fact of its exemplariness, is derived from an authority that grounds and surpasses the individual poet and "us."[36]

---

ces Pancartes lire: / Et depuis son enfance, en ses ages divers, / Pour mieux contempler Dieu, contempler l'univers" (Du Bartas, *La sepmaine* 1.151–54, 175–78). See, on this topos, Curtius, *European Literature and the Latin Middle Ages*, pp. 321–26.

[35] See, on the cosmic status of poetry, Robert Griffin, "Cosmic Metaphor in *La concorde des deux langages*," in *Pre-Pléiade Poetry*, ed. Jerry C. Nash (Lexington, Ky.: French Forum, 1985), pp. 15–30, and Luzius Keller, *Palingène, Ronsard, Du Bartas: Trois études sur la poésie cosmologique de la Renaissance* (Bern: Francke, 1974). Du Bartas, however, does affirm his poetic autonomy more strongly in the last book of his epic. See Jan Miernowski, "L'accès aux vérités spirituelles: Continuités et ruptures des codes intertextuels dans *La sepmaine* de Du Bartas," in *Continuités et ruptures dans l'histoire de la littérature*, ed. Michèle Weil, Halina Suwala, and Dominique Triaire (Geneva: Champion-Slatkine, 1988), pp. 33–45.

[36] The extent of theological grounding of the *Commedia* is a matter of critical debate. See

Secular versions of external authority are numerous, ranging from inspiring patrons to more or less fictitious prior manuscript or oral traditions. In Chrétien de Troyes's *Li contes del Graal* (before 1184), the author prefaces the romance with an encomium of Philip of Flandres, his patron. The dominant metaphor describing the poet's relationship to his patron is agricultural and economic; Chrétien is also recalling the biblical parable of the sower (Matt. 13:4–23):

> Qui petit seme petit quialt
> Et qui auques recoillir vialt,
> an tel leu sa semance espande
> que fruit a cent dobles li rande;
> car an terre qui rien ne vaut
> bone semance i seche et faut.
> Crestïens seme et fet semance
> d'un romans que il ancomance,
> et si le seme an si bon leu
> qu'il ne peut estre sanz grant preu,
> qu'il le fet por le plus prodome
> qui soit an l'empire de Rome:
> c'est li cuens Phelipes de Flandres.
>
> (1–13)[37]

[Whoever sows little reaps little, and who wants to harvest should spread his seed in a place that will give him hundredfold returns, for in land that is worth nothing, good seed drys up and dies. Chrétien sows a novel that he begins, and sows it in such a good place that it cannot be without great profit, as he does it for the most valorous man of the Roman empire: the count Philip of Flandres.]

Robert Hollander, "Dante *Theologus-Poeta*," in *Studies in Dante* (Ravenna: Longo, 1980), pp. 39–89, he bases his interpretation on the work of Charles Singleton. See especially his conclusion: "Dante creates a fiction which he pretends to consider not to be literally fictitious, while at the same time contriving to share the knowledge with us that it is precisely fictional" (p. 86). In any event the *Commedia* flows out of something prior, namely, Christian inspiration, but in Dante's doubleness he does announce the autonomy and imperialism of fiction we observe in many Renaissance texts. See, however, Dante's (?) letter to Can Grande della Scala, in which he rehearses the argument for the existence of a first mover, and the perfection of a first cause, commenting specifically on the opening of the *Paradiso*, cited as an epigraph to this chapter (in *Dantis Alagherii epistolae: The Letters of Dante*, rev. ed., ed. C. G. Hardie, trans. Paget Toynbee (Oxford: Clarendon, 1966), 10.20–27 [pp. 182–89]).

[37] Chrétien de Troyes, *Le conte du Graal (Perceval)*, in *Les romans de Chrétien de Troyes*, vol. 5, ed. Félix Lecoy (Paris: Champion, 1973). For other examples of explicit prologues to medieval romances, see Ulrich Mölk, *Literarästhetik des 12. und 13. Jahrhunderts: Prologe, Exkurse, Epiloge* (Tübingen: M. Niemeyer, 1969).

Chrétien sows and reaps his *romans* in a good field—a field that more or less *is* his patron Philip of Flandres. The poet explains later on that by virtue of his patron's love of justice and the church, and his exercise of charity, he is better than even Alexander. The agricultural metaphor is puzzling to modern readers: What, precisely, does Chrétien sow? In what sense can he be said to reap a harvest? Is the harvest the romance itself, the approbation of the patron, or the poet's monetary reward? Chrétien's language is quite explicit: he sows the romance ("fet semance d'un romans"), which flourishes in the field of the patron. The little allegory resists an easy decoding, as it mixes the literal with the figurative. What is important here is the *dependence* of the writer-farmer, whose writing of the *Contes del Graal* somehow is literally connected to and produced by the favor and charity of his patron-soil. There is no question of an autonomous creation on the part of the poet, whose work is inserted into a seasonal agricultural cycle, and who is only one of the elements necessary to the final product.

The end of Chrétien's prologue underlines the poet's dependence on a prior cause, as he fulfills the command of the patron and is given the "book" of his novel:

> Donc avra bien sauve sa peinne
> Crestïens, qui antant et peinne
> a rimoier le meillor conte,
> par le comandement le conte,
> qui soit contez au cort real:
> ce est li contes del graal,
> don li cuens li baille le livre,
> s'orroiz comant il s'an delivre.
>
> (61–68)

[Therefore Chrétien will have his work safe, Chrétien, who is attentive and labors to rhyme the best story, by the order of the count, that is recounted at the royal court: this is the story of the Grail, of which the count gave him the book, so hear how he manages.]

Chrétien depends on the count's charity and other qualities in order to have some reward for his "peinne," or for his labors to bring fruit ("avra bien sauve sa peinne"); in some sense his patron's qualities are a guarantee of the work's qualities, as if they had been transferred there. The poet's work is, of course, produced on command, and the count explicitly gives him the "book." Does this mean the material object on which the poet may write his *romans*? Or does it refer to the subject matter? In any case the patron again determines what is written and how it is written, and it is through this prior authority that the poet is able to write "le meillor conte . . . qui soit contez an cort real."

A similar interference, or rather collaboration, between material production, the patron's command, and writing is found in Antoine de la Sale's *Jehan de Saintré* (composed ca. 1456), one of the first "modern" novels in other respects.[38] The writer explains his decision to write the story of the sire of Saintré and the lady of the "Belles Cousines." He addresses his patron, Jean d'Anjou:

> Aprés mes treshumbles et tresobeissans recommandacions, pour obeir a voz prieres qui me sont entiers commandemens, me suis delicté a vous faire quatre beaus traictiez, en deux livres pour les porter plus aisiement, dont ce premier parlera de une dame des Belles Cousines de France, sans autre nom ne surnom nommer, et du tres vaillant chevalier le sire de Saintré.[39]

> [After my very humble and very obedient recommendations, in order to obey your requests (or invitations), which are for me truly commandments, I took pleasure in making for you four beautiful treatises, in two books so that I could carry them more easily, of which the first will speak of a lady of the Belles Cousines de France, without naming any other name or surname, and of the very valiant knight, lord of Saintré.]

The patron invites, prays the writer ("voz prieres") to write a certain book; these "prayers" become commandments ("entiers commandemens"), and the writer finds joy in executing the commandments ("me suis delicté"). The theological language reinforces the patron's authority, without which the production of *Jehan de Saintré* would have been impossible. The writer has introduced, of course, a slight doubt about the ultimate origin of this chain of authorizing gestures, as he begins his sentence with "Aprés mes treshumbles et tresobeissans recommandacions." It is unclear if Antoine de la Sale is referring to recommendations concerning the present work, or general recommendations concerning his own qualities and willingness to execute the patron's projects (which the adjective "tresobeissans" seems to indicate). In any case the work is an effect of the authorizing wish of the patron and, interestingly, of material restrictions governing writing, as the writer put his texts into two books, which are more easily carried than four separate treatises. The writer is, then, much more *scripteur* than *écrivain*; writing is primarily material production.

Another example of external secular authorization occurs at the beginning of the immensely popular *roman-fleuve* of chivalry, the *Amadis de Gaule*, whose French and Spanish translator-editor-writers continue and augment a (probably fictitious) account of the anonymous, obscure origin

---

[38] For example, as analyzed by Julia Kristeva, in "Narration et transformation," *Semiotica* 1 (1969): 422–48.

[39] Antoine de la Sale, *Jehan de Saintré*, ed. Jean Misrahi and Charles A. Knudson (Geneva: Droz, 1967), p. 1, 1–11.

of the manuscripts recounting the story of Amadis and his descendants. As the account goes, the first three books of the *Amadis*, through the negligence of bad writers or translators, had to be extensively corrected and improved; the fourth book (on Esplandian, son of Amadis) was found in the form of an old parchment under a tombstone in a hermitage close to Constantinople and brought to Spain by a Hungarian merchant, and so on and so forth.[40] The novel begins by implicitly connecting its characters to the Bible. According to the French translation of 1540, "Peu de temps apres la passion de nostre Saulveur Jesuchrist, il fut ung Roy de la petite Bretaigne nommé Garinter, instruict en la loy de verité, et grandement decoré de bonnes et louables vertuz, qui eut d'une noble dame son espouse, deux filles [Shortly after the Passion of our Saviour Jesus Christ, there was a king of Brittany named Garinter, instructed in the law of truth, and much decorated with good and praiseworthy virtues, who had two daughters of a noble lady, his wife]" (p. 1). The temporal proximity to Christ's death, and the indication that Garinter was Christian, constitute an authoritative guarantee of the novel's truth content, and present its adventures as somehow closely linked to biblical narrative.[41] The fabulous origin of the book, with its resonances of archeological mystery and precarious transmission (a commonplace which Ariosto and Rabelais do not tire of mocking while using it), is linked, then, to the book's content, equally distant in time and thus close to the Word. The disinterment of the parchment under a *tumba di piedra* relates, implicitly, to the disinterment of Christ and the spread of his gospel, through the myth of Joseph of Arimathea, who figures prominently in the authorizing of medieval romance (such as the *Queste del Saint Graal*). So secular authority of manuscript transmission is fused with theological authority; the individual writer is presented more or less as a conduit for the truth or for an ancient history that, although in need of a scribe, is always far greater than the individual recording it.[42]

[40] Nicolas de Herberay des Essarts, trans., *Amadis de Gaule*, bk. 1, ed. Hugues Vaganay and Yves Giraud (Paris: Nizet, 1986), 1:xvii, and, for Montalvo's original version, 2:493.

[41] Compare another more obvious example of theological authorization of romance, Pulci's exordium to the *Morgante*: "In principio era il Verbo appresso a Dio, / ed era Iddio il Verbo e il Verbo Lui; / questo era nel principio, al parer mio, / e nulla si può far sanza Costui" (1.1.1–4). The degree to which irony undermines this beginning is of course difficult to gauge. For a fine discussion of medieval invocations of the Creator in the prologues of medieval fiction, see C. Stephen Jaeger, "Der Schöpfer der Welt und das Schöpfungswerk als Prologmotiv in der mittelhochdeutschen Dichtung," *Zeitschrift für deutsches Altertum und deutsche Literatur* 171 (1978): 1–18.

[42] Montalvo's prologue to the *Amadis de Gaula* is in fact more complex than that, for he questions the exactness of many historians, and laments the absence of worthy poet-historians to commemorate (and amplify) the deeds of King Ferdinand in his conquest of Grenada (see *Amadis* 2:491). Ariosto, of course, suggests that in the end poets are more important than the heroes they describe, for the latter would soon be forgotten without epics (see *Orlando*

I am taking the preceding examples of authority and external causation as a simplified background against which the emergence of radical beginnings in Rabelais and especially Montaigne can be measured. I will suggest, although this point is often obscured by the literary argument, that theological reinterpretations of the relationship between Creator and Creation are at least a conceptual model for the positing of radical self-authorization. The habit of reasoning from God's perspective in nominalist theology is conceptually analogous to the emergence of a more "modern" view of literary creation and authority, for the assumption of God's point of view brings with it an altered perception of the human creator's relationship to his creation. I am tempted to say furthermore that the theological analogy is a strong one, as it is both commonplace in Christian culture and exceptionally refined. Renaissance self-authorization does not come from the outside, so to speak, but is at least structurally contained in conceptual developments within late scholasticism.

Source and Movement: From *Pantagruel* to the *Tiers livre*

When Rabelais published his first novel, *Pantagruel*, in 1532, he took some of his material from popular literature concerning the giant Gargantua, and he was careful to insert his own contribution into a category of well-selling books relating to characters from the legend of Merlin and King Arthur. The prologue to *Pantagruel* begins in a way reminiscent of the book he refers to immediately, the *Grandes et inestimables Cronicques du grant et enorme geant Gargantua*:

> Trèsillustres et trèschevaleureux champions, gentilz hommes et aultres, qui voluntiers vous adonnez à toutes gentilesses et honnestetez, vous avez n'a guères veu, leu et sçeu les *Grandes et inestimables Chronicques de l'énorme géant Gargantua*, et, comme vrays fidèles, les avez creues tout ainsi que texte de Bible ou du sainct Evangile, et y avez maintesfois passé vostre temps avecques les honnorables dames et damoiselles, leur en faisant beaux et longs narrez, alors que estiez hors de propos: dont estes bien dignes de grand louenge. (pp. 3–4)[43]

> [Very illustrious and chivalrous men of battle, noblemen and others, who like to occupy yourselves with noble and honest things, you have recently seen, read, and learned the *Great and Immeasurable Chronicles of the Enormous Giant Gargantua*, and, as true faithful ones, have believed them just as the text of the

---

furioso 35.22–30). I am emphasizing the aspects of the *Amadis* that repeat medieval authorization of romance.

[43] Quotations are from Verdun-L. Saulnier's edition of the 1532 text (Geneva: Droz, 1965). Translations of Rabelais's texts are my own.

Bible or the holy gospel, and have often passed the time with honorable ladies, recounting long and beautiful stories from those chronicles, when you had nothing left to say; for this you are quite worthy of great praise.]

The opening of Rabelais's novel not only contains an explicit reference to the source of the book, but also parodies the opening of his intertext. The latter is a somewhat slight booklet, published anonymously the same year as *Pantagruel*, that locates its own authority in the tales surrounding Arthur and Merlin, similarly to the Breton material authorizing the *Amadis de Gaule*: "Tous bons chevalliers et gentilz hommes vous debvez sçavoir que au temps du bon roy Artus il estoit ung grant philosophe nommé Merlin, Lequel estoit expert en l'art de nigromance plus que nul homme du monde. Lequel jamais ne cessa de secourir l'estat de noblesse, dont il merita par ces faictz estre appellé prince des nigromanciens. [All good knights and noblemen, you must know that in the time of the good king Arthur there was a great philosopher named Merlin, who was expert in the art of necromancy more than anyone in the world. He never ceased helping the nobility; by these deeds he deserved to be called prince of the necromancers]."[44] Rabelais parodies the opening address to the noblemen, as well as the usefulness to nobility of Merlin, who by his marvelous deeds helped Arthur get out of tight spots. Rabelais's beginning does not insert his own text into a tradition flowing out of the deeds of Merlin, but rather refers simply to another book that itself claims to flow out of that tradition. His ironic mention of the Bible makes fun precisely of the traditional claim of authority of medieval romance, although certainly in the various *Chroniques gargantuines* themselves such playfulness is not uncommon.[45] His

[44] *Les Grandes et inestimables Cronicques: du grant et enorme geant Gargantua: Contenant sa geneallogie, La grandeur et force de son corps. Aussi les merveilleux faictz d'armes qu'il fist pour le Roy Artus, comme verrez cy après* (1532), in *Les chroniques gargantuines*, ed. Christiane Lauvergnat-Gagnière and Guy Demerson (Paris: Nizet, 1988), pp. 115–16. See François Cornilliat, "L'autre géant. Les *Chroniques gargantuines* et leur intertexte," *Littérature* 55 (1984): 85–97.

[45] The narrator of the *Grandes et inestimables Cronicques* ironically disputes information about the nourishment of the child Gargantua with other transmitters of the chronicles ("acteurs"), citing in his support "Morgain" (King Arthur's sister?) (in *Les chroniques gargantuines*, p. 120). Various versions, such as the undated *Grande et merveilleuse vie du trespuissant et redoubté roy de Gargantua* and the *Croniques admirables du puissant Roy Gargantua*, specify that they are a translation from the Latin, which itself was a translation from the Greek (in *Les chroniques gargantuines*, pp. 153, 165). The narrator-translator of the latter insists on the truthfulness of his account, citing in his support both recent historiographers and characters in medieval romance (pp. 165–67). This playful insistence on truthfulness is taken to the extreme by the narrator of the *Voyage & navigation que fist Panurge, disciple de Pantagruel aux isles incongneues & estranges, et de plusieurs choses merveilleuses difficiles à croyre qu'il dict avoir veues . . .* (1538) (ed. Christiane Lauvergnat-Gagnière and Guy Demerson [Paris: Nizet, 1982]) in his prologue (pp. 1–2) and throughout the text. See also the editors' introduction, pp. xxxvi–xli. Mocking the tradition is not, however, the same thing as leaving it behind.

reference to the "beaux et longs narrez" contained in the *Chroniques* is also ironic, as his "source" is all of sixteen octavo sheets long. Rabelais devotes most of the prologue to a highly ambiguous praise of his immediate predecessor, as he recounts various uses of the *Chroniques*, such as a makeshift conversation piece, a way of avoiding boredom during the hunt, a remedy for toothaches, and a consolation for syphilitics. He ends by praising its commercial success, as in two months its printers sold more copies of it than they sold copies of the Bible in nine years (p. 6). The "source" Rabelais is reaching back to is not really a prior *auctor* in whose reserve of material Rabelais will find the inspiration for a continuation, although formally that seems to be what the prologue is defining. Rather, by describing the *present* "usefulness" and commercial success of this little book, Rabelais establishes himself not as a continuer of tradition, but as someone wishing to share the success of a contemporary. Rabelais is not inspired by the *Chroniques*' material, but by its saleability. The material itself is treated sardonically. In a sense, he is reflecting a secularization of the book that the invention of printing has allowed.[46] Rabelais is not augmenting a tradition, but is using his "source" as way of increasing the rate of reproduction by printing of his own text. The source is an advertising instrument. He then offers to his reader another book of the same nature ("de mesmes billon"), his *Pantagruel*, which will be more worthy of trust than its predecessor.

Rabelais's beginning does imitate the pointing to a prior cause that we have seen in the medieval literary tradition, but this gesture is virtually emptied of any real significance. Rabelais tends to preserve the formal structure of authority, in that he displays his models, but in fact these models do not constitute a prior, greater cause in a chain of determination. Rather, Rabelais *chooses* to write books that for all their reminiscence of prior material are willful (but neither arbitrary nor useless) productions of the creator Rabelais. In the prologue to *Pantagruel* this actual independence of the writer is implicit in the motivation of his writing through concerns of saleability, but Rabelais's autonomy becomes more manifest in the succeeding books, especially in the elaborate prologue to the *Tiers livre*.

---

[46] Printing is a theme of the prologue, as Rabelais recommends learning by heart the *Chroniques*, in case the art of printing should cease and all books perish (p. 4). I am not sure that the sense of printing's precariousness expressed by that comment is completely ironic, as François Ier did attempt, however briefly and unsuccessfully, to suppress printing altogether in early 1535, in the aftermath of the affair of the Placards. For a differing interpretation of those lines, see Michael B. Kline, *Rabelais and the Age of Printing* (Geneva: Droz, 1963), pp. 11–13 on *Pantagruel*. See Lucien Febvre and Henri-Jean Martin, *L'apparition du livre* (Paris: Albin Michel, 1958), p. 428. Elizabeth L. Eisenstein, in *The Printing Press as an Agent of Change* 1:400–1, discusses literary careers and printing, with reference to Rabelais (interpreting inaccurately the prologue's ironic allusion to the *Chroniques*' success); see, nevertheless, her suggestive chapter on "self-consciousness" and printing, pp. 225–72.

Already in the prologue to his *Gargantua* (1534?), in which literal and figurative interpretation play a preponderant role,[47] Rabelais discusses the composition of his book in terms that underline his choice, in spite of references to ancient authors. He asks his reader why he would not look for a deeper meaning in Rabelais's text, although while composing it he himself did not think of such meaning more than the reader himself. Instead, Rabelais composed while eating and drinking—activities that are not, however, incompatible with the presence of deeper significance in his book:

> Car, à la composition de ce livre seigneurial, je ne perdiz ny emploiay oncques plus, ny aultre temps que celluy qui estoit estably à prendre ma refection corporelle, sçavoir est, beuvant et mangeant. Aussi est ce la juste heure d'escrire ces haultes matieres et sciences profundes, comme bien faire sçavoit Homere, paragon de tous philologes, et Ennie, pere des poëtes latins, ainsi que tesmoigne Horate, quoy q'un malautru ait dict que ses carmes sentoyent plus le vin que l'huile. (p. 17)

> [For, composing this seignorial book, I never lost nor used more time or other time than the time that was allotted to my physical replenishment, that is, drinking and eating. Also that is the right time to write about these high subjects and deep knowledge, as Homer, model of all lovers of knowledge, and Ennius, father of Latin poets, knew so well, according to Horace, although a miserable fellow said that his songs smelled more of wine than of oil.]

The deeper meaning in Rabelais's text is not derived from Homer and Ennius, although in a superficial way the author is imitating them by composing while eating and drinking. The "haultes matieres et sciences profundes" are not located necessarily in a filiation of wisdom stretching back to a first cause (Homer); rather, Rabelais makes them up as he eats and drinks. This does not mean that they are not there before him, although that too could be the case. We do not know, and we cannot determine these

---

[47] See the enduring debate on the interpretation of interpretation in the prologue to the *Gargantua*; especially the fine study by Edwin M. Duval, "Interpretation and the 'Doctrine absconce' of Rabelais's Prologue to *Gargantua*," *Etudes rabelaisiennes* 18 (1985): 1–17 (arguing against a conception of the prologue in terms of allegorical vs. literal reading, and for a reading in terms of *moral* interpretation). See also Terence Cave, Michel Jeanneret, and François Rigolot, "Sur la prétendue transparence de Rabelais," *Revue d'histoire littéraire de la France* 86 (1986): 709–16, and the response by Gérard Defaux, "Sur la prétendue pluralité du prologue de 'Gargantua': Réponse d'un positiviste naïf à trois 'illustres et treschevaleureux champions,' " *Revue d'histoire littéraire de la France* 86 (1986): 716–22. The very concern with interpretation of his books that characterizes Rabelais's prologues is a sign of the fact that it is not a matter of Rabelais interpreting a previous *auctor*, and thus continuing a tradition, but of Rabelais placing himself at the starting point, as a first text to be read correctly. On Rabelais's text as creating an interpretative community, see Quint, *Origin and Originality*, pp. 176–88.

things by recourse to a prior tradition, for Rabelais's locating himself in tradition is essentially a formal exercise.

It is only with the third book that these hints at authorial autonomy are developed in an explicit way. In the prologue to the *Tiers livre* (1546) Rabelais offers the reader an extensive parable of the creative process in terms of movement. He recounts an anecdote concerning Diogenes, first related by Lucian in *How to Write History*, which figures as well in Guillaume Budé's *Annotationes in Pandectas* (1535).[48] Diogenes is praised by Rabelais at the outset as being nearly perfect (only God *is* perfect, of course), and presumably the anecdote from Lucian will justify Rabelais's and Alexander's high opinion of the Cynic. Philip, king of Macedonia, is about to lay siege to the city of Corinth, and through spies its inhabitants have learned of his intentions. They begin frantic preparations to defend their city, and Rabelais describes in quite appropriate detail their frenetic activity. Diogenes observes the ceaseless movement about him and, after several days of silent contemplation, starts his own imitative version of siege preparations by doing all and sundry things to his barrel. Again there follows a copious enumeration of movements. Rabelais is extensively amplifying both Lucian and Budé:[49]

> [Il] y roulla le tonneau fictil qui pour maison lui estoit contre les injures du ciel, et, en grande vehemence d'esprit desployant ses braz, le tournoit, viroit, brouilloit, [barbouiloit,] hersoit, versoit, renversoit, [nattoit, grattoit, flattoit, barattoit,] bastoit, boutoit, butoit, tabustoit, cullebutoit, trepoit, trempoit, tapoit, timpoit, estouppoit, destouppoit, detraquoit, triquotoit. . . . (p. 11)

> [There he rolled the barrel of clay which served as a house against the weather, and, with a great vehemence of spirit, unfolding his arms, turned, twisted, mixed, soiled, thrashed, poured, overturned, stroked, scratched, caressed, churned, packed, kicked, struck, pummeled, knocked over, trampled, drenched, clanged, stopped up, unstopped, changed direction, stopped it. . . .]

---

[48] See, following Jean Plattard, Michael Andrew Screech, *Rabelais* (Ithaca: Cornell Univ. Press, 1979), pp. 217–18, and his edition of the *Tiers livre* (Geneva: Droz, 1964), p. 9 n. 46. For a good discussion of the literary consequences of the allusion to Diogenes' barrel, see Floyd Gray, "Structure and Meaning in the Prologue to the *Tiers livre*," *L'esprit créateur* 3 (1963): 57–62. The Diogenes allusion is discussed by many critics as an emblem of Rabelaisian writing: see in particular Alfred Glauser, *Rabelais créateur* (Paris: Nizet, 1964), pp. 22–25.

[49] Lucian: "He belted up his philosopher's cloak and very busily by himself rolled the crock in which, as it happens, he was living up and down Cornel Hill" (*How to Write History* 3, ed. and trans. K. Kilburn, in *Lucian* [Cambridge, Mass.: Harvard Univ. Press, 1959]), 6:5. Budé is also relatively laconic: "Dolium illud suum . . . subvolvere, devolvere, ultro citròque versare per vicinum urbi collem coepit" (*Annotationes . . . in quatuor & viginti Pandectarum libros* [Paris: R. Estienne, 1535], [p. ii]).

Whereas the siege preparations of the Corinthians all made sense, that is, each activity corresponded to a (military or sexual) function in defense of the city, Diogenes' activity is not functional or teleological, as the eventual comparison with Sisyphus seems to illustrate.[50] Not only do the activities described not integrate themselves into a purposeful contextual whole, but they seem to be determined by poetic concerns rather than by real actions.[51] The series of predicates is ordered by rhyme, paronomasia, alliteration, assonance, parechesis, and tautology.[52] In response to the goings-on about him in the "real world," Diogenes has produced a referentially senseless yet poetically intricate web of activities. Of course, it is Rabelais who has produced the amplification of Lucian, and it is unlikely that a real Diogenes should have performed all of these movements so that their descriptions in French could be so poetically interconnected. Diogenes' activity is a formal parody of the Corinthians; Rabelais's writing is a textual remotivation of what is deprived of referential teleology, Diogenes rolling a barrel up and down a hill.

Rabelais then states that he is imitating Diogenes' imitation of the Corinthians. He is similarly "moved" by the activity around him in France: "Je pareillement, quoy que soys hors d'effroy, *ne suis toutefoys hors d'esmoy*, de moy voyant n'estre faict aulcun pris digne d'oeuvre, et consyderant par tout ce tresnoble royaulme [de France,] deça, dela les mons, un chascun aujourd'huy soy instantement exercer et travailler. . . . [Similarly I myself, even though I am not in trouble, am still moved, and seeing that no one considers me worthy of any work, and seeing that everywhere in this noble kingdom of France on this and that side of the mountains everyone is exercising himself and working . . .]" (p. 12; italics mine). The Diogenes-Rabelais analogy is evident: neither is considered worthy of the military activity that occupies everyone else around him. However, whereas Diogenes parodies the Corinthians' beelike industriousness, we learn that Rabelais's activity is not taken directly from his context. There is no direct

[50] In Budé's preface, Sisyphus is elsewhere an example of futile activity: "Satius siquidem esse dictabat Attilius ociosum esse quàm nihil agere, id est quàm inaniter vexari, ut Sisyphus ille in fabulis, voluens & ipse saxum, sudans nitendo nec proficiens hilum" (*Annotationes*, [p. iii]). I cannot agree with critics who see a didactic intent in Diogenes' movements, for, although the Cynic may have often been used to point out the folly of man's endeavors, this is certainly not the case in any explicit way in Rabelais's prologue, and would furthermore imply that Rabelais was making fun of patriotic activities about him in France. See Kennedy, *Rhetorical Norms in Renaissance Literature*, pp. 116–17; Kennedy follows Walter Kaiser and Alice Berry in this interpretation.

[51] In the sense of Roman Jakobson's "poetic function," in *Essais de linguistique générale*, trans. Nicolas Ruwet (Paris: Minuit, 1963), pp. 218–19.

[52] For a more detailed study of Rabelais's devices here, see Marcel Tetel, *Etude sur le comique de Rabelais* (Florence: L. S. Olschki, 1964), p. 103.

cause moving him after all; rather, he decides freely not to hide his gift of writing, but to do what he does best:

> *Prins ce choys et election*, ay pensé ne faire exercice inutile et importun si je re-muois mon tonneau Diogenic, qui seul m'est resté du naufrage faict par le passé on far de Mal'encontre. A ce triballement de tonneau que feray je en vostre advis? Par la vierge qui se rebrasse je ne scay encores. Attendez un peu que je hume quelque traict de ceste bouteille: c'est mon vray et seul Helicon, c'est ma fontaine Caballine, c'est mon unicque Enthusiasme. Icy beuvant je delibere, je discours, je resoulz et concluds. Après l'epilogue je riz, j'escripz, je compose, je boy. (p. 14; italics mine)

> [Having made this choice, I thought that I would not be doing a useless and importune thing if I moved about my Diogenic barrel, which alone survives after the shipwreck at the light of the Misfortune (?). With this moving about of my barrel what will I end up doing? By the virgin who takes up her clothes I do not know yet. Wait a bit for me to drink from this bottle: it is my true and only Helicon, my fountain of inspiration, my only enthusiasm. Drinking here I deliberate, I reason, I resolve and conclude. After the epilogue I laugh, I write, I compose, I drink.]

Rabelais underlines the fact that there is no necessary subject prior to his choice of writing as an activity ("que feray je?"). The inspiration will come as he drinks, laughs, and writes. Whereas Diogenes had imitated real, useful activity around him, Rabelais creates from within himself, separated from his context.[53] His creation will derive its meaning and content from the act of writing itself, not as an imitation of Diogenes' futile torments of his barrel. Rabelais himself, then, will be the first cause, the unmoved mover of his creation, even though the analogy between Diogenes and Rabelais is, on the surface, undeniable.

A close analysis of this anecdote reveals, then, two conflicting views of the creative process, one clearly mimetic, the other nonmimetic. Diogenes' parody of real circumstances is very different from Rabelais's creation of his novelistic universe. The author of the *Tiers livre* has precisely *not* been content to amass futile activities in parody of useful ones: "Tant s'en fault que je reste cessateur et *inutile* [I will surely not remain a do-nothing and useless]" (p. 15; italics mine).[54] The wine of his writing will entertain and

---

[53] I am not excluding eucharistic associations of the wine here; I am emphasizing the narrator's independence from Diogenes. See, for the Christian connotations of the wine, Florence M. Weinberg, *The Wine and the Will: Rabelais' Bacchic Christianity* (Detroit: Wayne State Univ. Press, 1972), and more recently, Quint, *Origin and Originality*, pp. 183ff.

[54] The *usefulness* of Rabelais's text is an addition or distinction vis-à-vis Diogenes: in Lucian, Diogenes only wants "not to be thought the one idle man in the midst of all these workers"—ὡς μὴ μόνος ἀργεῖν δοκοίην ἐν τοσούτοις ἐργαζομένοις (*How to Write History* 3)— the contrast is simply between working (ἐργάζεσθαι) and not working (ἀργεῖν). Rabelais's

encourage (pp. 15–16), and will not be merely an image of what everyone around him is doing. The mimetic creative process is caused by the Corinthians' movements; the nonmimetic resembles the mimetic but in fact depends on a choice to create, and an independence of the material created.

The conflicting modes of creation are parallel to a twofold relationship to Lucian, who, according to Michael Andrew Screech, is here "being paraded as source and model."[55] Certainly the explicit example of Diogenes followed by Rabelais suggests the implicit acceptance of Lucian by the writer Rabelais as authority and model to be imitated. Rabelais is ostentatiously conforming to a humanist-Platonic convention of inspiration. He is looking backward in time for authorization of his literary creation, to a more perfect source. Rabelais seems to be setting up a chain of inspiration or causation: the impending siege by Philip of Macedonia inspires the Corinthians to fortify their city, which inspires Diogenes to roll his barrel (which inspires Lucian to write about historiography), which inspires Rabelais to drink from *his* barrel. Through Lucian, the Renaissance writer is able to attach himself to this causal and inspirational chain. The return to Diogenes through Lucian is also a retrieval of a model more perfect than the epigone. The Diogenes anecdote is an attempt to retrieve a more perfect, past state of affairs.

As I have pointed out, however, there are essential differences between Diogenes' activity and Rabelais's creation: the content of the former is irrelevant to any purpose and irrelevant as well to the content of writing. The form of Diogenes' activity is mimetic, as opposed to Rabelais's self-authorized and self-inspired, nonmimetic creation. Rabelais's simultaneous and mutually implicating drinking, laughing, and composing contrast with Diogenes' frenetic movements imitating the Corinthians' frenetic activity. So there is no *substantial* link between Diogenes and Rabelais, or rather, the Cynic is a *pretext*; his example is an example only because Rabelais chooses to write and whimsically sets up Diogenes (whom he may admire on other counts) as a source. Rabelais is thus making the exemplary cause (Diogenes) an *effect* of his own efficient cause of writing, thus suggesting that a mimetic model of literary creation is a result of choice, and is not predetermined by a condition outside of the writer.

Diogenes does not want to be seen as the "seul cessateur et ocieux" (*Tiers livre*, p. 12); Budé's Diogenes has similar concerns: "Voluo (inquit ille) ego quoque dolium, ne unus inter tot operi intentissimos cessator esse videar" (*Annotationes*, [p. ii]). The difference between not being idle and being useful should be maintained, given the lack of usefulness of Diogenes' Sisyphean efforts. Not being "lazy" is, by the way, a commonplace justification for writing romances or novels; see the prologue to the *Amadis de Gaule* (p. xvii). Also, the readers of novels are called "oisifz cessartz" in one of the dedicatory poems to the *Amadis*, by Antoine Macault.

[55] Screech, *Rabelais*, p. 220.

Rabelais begins, then, in a profoundly ambivalent way, as he both "parades" a mimetic creative process, the structure of which demonstrates imitation of real, antecedent conditions by an *auctor* (Diogenes), and shows the latter's imitation by the epigone Rabelais. Writing is "dynastic" and introduces a chain of causation that, perhaps inevitably, involves a movement from the more perfect to the less perfect. Beginning is viewed from the epigone-creature's point of view, in which "a priori" constraints are acknowledged. Yet, as we have seen, Rabelais then emphasizes the writer's choice, his uncertainty regarding his material, and seems to establish the parameters of the process of creation *as* he is composing ("Icy beuvant je delibere, je discours, je resoulz et concluds. Après l'epilogue je riz, j'escripz, je compose, je boy"). He ends up denying a predisposition of his material, the content of which is made up as he goes along. Thus the writer's *will*, rather than a prior plan, is the most important element of creation. Rabelais is proposing a pact with the reader in his fictional universe, a pact which depends on himself, absolutely, for the first impetus. The writer is not looking at himself as creature and epigone, but instead is taking the position of God, who is exercising his absolute power through his willful beginning. Rabelais's flippant references elsewhere to the reader and to his material confirm this lack of prior constraints and conventions in his creation.[56]

Rabelais's variations on models of authority and beginning are essentially playful, although evangelical themes traverse the prologues and the novels themselves and are an important feature of his "message." The theological provides a set of structures within which literary experimentation is not felt to be foreign. An evangelical message is not incompatible with a certain levity. Rabelais comments on his creation and causality playfully, but he is nonetheless guided by certain conceptual principles. In fact, as we have seen, divine creation constitutes an intellectual and logical substratum through which literary creation can be understood as an arrogation of the powers of a *prima causa efficiens* to reenact creation of a contingent universe.

Montaigne's Beginning, or, Authorizing the Subject

In March of 1580, just before the publication of what turned out to be the first two books of the *Essais*, Montaigne wrote a brief prologue, "Au lecteur," the first lines of which set up a version of authority reminiscent of

---

[56] See the prologue to the *Pantagruel*, which maintains, in parody, a dynastic view of beginning, by inscribing itself into a tradition of filiation with the *Grandes et inestimables Chroniques*. The addresses to the reader, however, range from praise to imprecation, thus emphasizing the willfulness of the author, on whom everything depends.

the Word and yet finally different from Augustine's projection of external, prior causation: "C'est icy un livre de bonne foy, lecteur. Il t'advertit dès l'entrée, que je ne m'y suis proposé aucune fin, que domestique et privée [This here is a book of good faith, reader. It lets you know from the very beginning that I had no goal in mind except a domestic and private one]" (p. 3; my translation).[57] The deictic beginning ("This here is . . .") apparently establishes a distinction between a *sujet de l'énonciation*, the subject telling the reader about the book, and the *sujet de l'énoncé*, the subject represented in the book. The former *points* to the latter. At the beginning of the book an exteriority (and, in terms of the reader, a priority or anteriority) is projected outside of the book.[58] The function of this exteriority is to guarantee the "good faith" of the book. The deictic beginning, in its act of separation between exterior subject and book, establishes the authority of the voice pronouncing the words, "C'est icy. . . ." The pointing is, as it were, outside of truth or falsity. It leads the reader away from the status of the subject pointing and to the object pointed to, thereby *assuming* the legitimacy and authority of the subject pointing. This assumption means that the use of the deictic at the absolute beginning of the text precludes any cause or condition prior to the subject that is pointing to the book. The subject pronouncing "C'est icy un livre" is not somehow caused by some other condition that allows it to point to the book of good faith. The deictic functions precisely as a pure beginning, as the projection of authoritative transcendence. In this sense, also, the subject of the enunciation is a first cause, a *primum mobile*. In clear distinction to Augustine's perspective, Montaigne begins as God would begin, in a gesture of pointing that projects the act of creation, judges it, and grounds its creature, the book, in a discursive instance of Being prior to any beings, an *esse* grounding the *ens*.

The subject enunciating the deictic performs in this sentence an act not of identification but of predication: "C'est icy un livre *de bonne foy*, lecteur." The sequence deictic-copula-[deictic]-noun-predicate (unconsciously, I think) imitates the eucharistic *Hoc est [enim] corpus meum*.[59] In fact, Mon-

---

[57] All references are to the edition by Pierre Villey, 2 vols. (Paris: Presses univ. de France, 1924, 1965). Unless noted otherwise, all translations are from *The Complete Essays of Montaigne*, trans. Donald M. Frame (Stanford: Stanford Univ. Press, 1957).

[58] This prologue was most likely written after the main section of the book had been composed, and so it does not represent the historic beginning of the *Essais*, but a conceptual beginning (in the sense of inserting the book into a schema of authorization or justification, locating its origins and spiritual provenance, etc.) for the author, and a temporal beginning for the reader, for the prologue is what the reader begins with. It is, as Montaigne himself says, the "entrée" to the book.

[59] Montaigne elsewhere is aware of theological disputes centering on the deictic *Hoc*. See the discussion by Antoine Compagnon in *Nous, Michel de Montaigne*, pp. 32–44. For a brilliant analysis of the eucharistic phrase as a fulcrum of theories of reference and signification, see Louis Marin, *La critique du discours: Sur la "Logique de Port-Royal" et les "Pensées" de Pascal*

taigne's sentence in more than one way recalls the eucharistic phrase. The paradox of Christ's multiplication and identity in the consecrated bread parallels the paradox of the book, that is, of Montaigne's multiplication of himself in pages of printed words, and of printing as repetition of the unique. Similarly, Christ's affirmation of real presence—*corpus meum*—constitutes a model of (once again paradoxical) self-sameness and self-transparency. The transubstantiated bread is Christ, in spite of its appearance as bread. Montaigne's book is "de bonne foy," that is, without ulterior motives, disguises, or stratagems. The subject represented in the book is immediately apprehended in its entirety, in spite of the mediation of writing, printing, and reading.

The first sentence of the *Essais* projects a pure first cause and establishes the "rules of pertinence" by imitating the transubstantiating force of a sacramental formula. The book offers itself and authorizes itself in a simultaneous movement. The final element of the sentence addresses the reader, who is invited to consume the book and thereby gain knowledge of its author, who is implied but not stated. The reader is thus placed in the position of the creature who moves through the created world to its Creator—*fides quaerens intellectum*. The Creator/author may reveal himself in the book, although the authorizing instance of the deictic maintains a distinction between the author pointing and the pointed-to, represented author in the book of good faith.

I have been suggesting all along a close analogy between the beginning of the *Essais* and theological notions of causality and authority. In sharp contrast to Augustine, as I have pointed out, Montaigne puts himself in the place of God. This profound transformation, not of functions or structures of authority but of the content and the agents of authority, is prefigured in the nominalist argumentation *de potentia Dei absoluta*. As such, Montaigne's modern self-authorization is an unwitting version of what is already contained in the logical developments of late scholasticism.

The second sentence of the prologue introduces a twist into what seems like a smooth secular version of theological authority: "Il t'advertit dès l'entrée, que je ne m'y suis proposé aucune fin, que domestique et privée." The first sentence is now reformulated, and by this seeming redundancy the distinction between the authorizing subject of the deictic and the book pointed to is lost, for it is the *book* that proclaims its good faith, not a voice external to it. And the book does so by pronouncing its own beginning, "C'est icy. . . ." What was external, prior, becomes part of the book itself. The book moves itself, authorizes itself, simply by beginning arbitrarily. The model of external causation is undermined, and the text consumed is no longer a conduit to the transcendent subject, who is now encompassed

(Paris: Minuit, 1975), and, underlying the representation of royal power, Louis Marin, *Le portrait du roi* (Paris: Minuit, 1981), pp. 147–68.

by his creation, instead of being outside of it. The ground of the book becomes the book itself; Being is no longer distinct from beings.

The conflation of deictic voice and the text it points to precludes, then, any recourse to an authority other than the text itself. Either of two conclusions can be drawn from this conflation: either there is *no* authority to the text—that is, it is paradoxically uncaused—or the authority or cause is utterly distinct from what it causes. Either no one caused the book or the book is entirely independent of its author. There is no reason to associate the "good faith" of the book with an unquestioned external authority; the book is all there is. Perhaps there is an author, but no necessary connection exists between creator and creation. I would maintain that the two conclusions are equivalent, and that they are the symptom of an insistent critique of causality in Montaigne.[60]

The exclusion of an *auctor* as first cause in Montaigne's *Essais* should strike the reader as absurd, as contrary to the autobiographical project Montaigne had espoused and consistently defended by the time he wrote the prologue to the *Essais*. In fact, the second sentence of the prologue uses the first person: "Je ne m'y suis proposé aucune fin, que domestique et privée." What is the status of the *je* here? Since the *book* ("*Il* t'advertit") tells the reader that "I had no other goal in mind," the *je* seems to be a creation of the book, not vice versa. Thus the first person is a *persona* conceptually posterior to the text that contains it. The symbiotic relationship between Montaigne and his book, which he describes elsewhere, is a thematic instance of this curious discursive feature of the prologue.[61]

Montaigne's *Essais* begin in a way that disconnects authorship and authority from causality, and thus makes it difficult to consider the text as an effect of a beginning impetus, as linked to the will of a unique creator. Yet the *contingent* relationship between creator and creation was already implied, by the emphasis on the priority of God's will (as opposed to his

[60] See Montaigne, *Essais* II, 12, p. 601: "Aucune raison ne s'establira sans une autre raison: nous voylà à reculons jusques à l'infiny." The subject of the first essay of the first book ("Par divers moyens on arrive à pareille fin") is of course an indication of what will follow.

[61] The famous formula "Je suis moy-mesme la matiere de mon livre" is only one instance of the book's active, and Montaigne's passive, role in this paradoxical relationship. Although the paths to the conclusion are different, I would agree with Claude Blum, in "Les *Essais* de Montaigne: Les signes, la politique, la religion," in *Columbia Montaigne Conference Papers*, ed. Donald M. Frame and Mary B. McKinley (Lexington, Ky.: French Forum, 1981), p. 27: "Le 'je' ne se définit plus par son action sur le monde, sur l'Histoire; nouveauté inouïe dans l'art de l'autoportrait littéraire: le portrait et le peintre ne pensent plus le monde sur lequel ils n'ont plus de prise; ils sont pensés, compris par lui. La fameuse passivité montaignienne a sa source dans cette révolution où émerge surtout ce qu'on peut appeler la conscience du 'sujet'—conscience étrange qu'aura bientôt l'Homme de ne plus penser ce qui l'entoure mais d'être pensé par lui. Il n'est plus à découvrir, ce 'moi' profond qui fondait l'être entier, ce moi qui ressemblerait, tout au bout, tout au fond de lui-même, à tous les autres puisqu'il est devenu inaccessible." As I will suggest, especially in the next chapter, the paradoxes of God's absolute freedom are the conceptual substratum of the inaccessible modern subject.

intellect, wisdom, etc.). Rabelais freely chooses to create, independently of external conditions. The radical critique of causality leads, however, to an even deeper break between creation and creator, to an expulsion of the notion of a foreseeable, knowable God acting in some understandable way in his universe. In the autobiography of Montaigne this expulsion is adumbrated by a narrative voice that generalizes its *potentia absoluta* in the sense that it cannot be assigned a stable existence outside of the text, but is produced by the vicissitudes of the text. This means that it is completely disjoined from the text, and is essentially irrecoverable since indistinguishable.

Problems of authority in Montaigne lead naturally to problems of the self, since the self is often taken to be a grounding of the book, a stable refuge.[62] At least logically (though not, perhaps, historically or socially), the definition of the self encounters the same problems as the definition of an essentially free creator. Montaigne sketches out the forms of this definition in the following way: "Et puis, me trovant entierement despourvu et vuide de toute autre matiere, je me suis presenté moy-mesmes à moy, pour argument et pour subject" (II, 8, p. 385) [And then, finding myself entirely destitute and void of any other matter, I presented myself to myself for argument and subject (p. 278)]. The self as theme is *emptied out* of all "other material"; in order that the self be perfectly self-conscious, mediation of any alien matter has been eliminated. Self-sameness is, then, based on the exclusion of obstructions and constraints. It is the relationship of *moy* to *moy-mesmes*; there is nothing one can say about it. It is anterior to any thematic material, for it is based on exclusion, or emptying out. God's *potentia absoluta* works similarly, in that any order or disposition posited prior to God's will is felt to be a constraint, a submission of God to something outside of himself. The essentially contingent relationship of God to Creation implies an essentially empty God; he is free of ordering principles to which his actions are bound (unless he himself freely enters into a promise to be bound). Thus Montaigne's discursive undermining of authorial causation is related to the transparent self-possession constituting the beginning of the autobiographical project.

The First Cause of Custom: *Essais* I, 23

If the deictic "C'est icy" initiates a vertiginous questioning of literary authority in the little preface to the reader, it remains to be seen how Montaigne follows through in the body of the essays. In fact, he seems both not

---

[62] See, for example, Hugo Friedrich, *Montaigne* (Bern: Francke, 1949); Richard L. Regosin, *The Matter of My Book: Montaigne's 'Essais' as the Book of the Self* (Berkeley: Univ. of California Press, 1977); and Glyn P. Norton, *Montaigne and the Introspective Mind* (The Hague: Mouton, 1975).

to want to begin and not to want to end, in an increasingly conversational flow that is in itself the writer's way of prolonging life.[63] The constant revising and adding (of which especially modern readers are aware) make for an essentially nonchronological text, an antihierarchical succession of reflections and examples. When something comes *after* something else in Montaigne's essays, this does not mean that it is either more or less important; being *first* is often equally unimportant.[64] Clearly the ancients' "firstness" confers no particular privilege on them if the Renaissance can discover American Indians who are greater than the Ancients in courage and social organization although temporally and geographically far removed.[65] What prevents us from discovering other worlds, given that no one could foresee or even imagine the discovery of America?[66] The search for a first cause seems, on the whole, irrelevant, as experience is resistant to hierarchical ordering. Discovery of a first cause is more a satisfaction of curiosity than the retrieval of a more perfect state of being.

Among the apparently "Pyrrhonist," skeptical essays we find a piece on the ambiguous value of custom, "De la coustume et de ne changer aisément une loy receüe [Of Custom and Not Easily Changing an Accepted Law]" (I, 23), that begins in a typically inconspicuous way. Montaigne recounts an anecdote he may have found in Erasmus or various ancient sources:

> Celuy me semble avoir tres-bien conceu la force de la coustume, qui premier forgea ce conte, qu'une femme de village, ayant apris de caresser et porter entre ses bras un veau des l'heure de sa naissance, et continuant tousjours à ce faire, gaigna cela par accoustumance, que tout grand beuf qu'il estoit, elle le portoit encore. Car c'est à la verité une violente et traistresse maistresse d'escole, que la coustume. Elle establit en nous, peu à peu, à la desrobée, le pied de son authorité: mais par ce doux et humble commencement, l'ayant rassis et planté avec l'ayde du temps, elle nous descouvre tantost un furieux et tyrannique visage, contre lequel nous n'avons plus la liberté de hausser seulement les yeux. (pp. 108–9)

[63] On the analogy between fictive closure and death, see above, Chapter One, on hypothetical necessity in Pulci's *Morgante*.

[64] This does not mean that the *Essais* are not meticulously *composed*. See Edwin M. Duval, "Montaigne's Conversions: Compositional Strategies in the *Essais*," *French Forum* 7 (1982): 5–22, and, regarding their detailed legal argumentative structure, André Tournon, *Montaigne: La glose et l'essai* (Lyons: Presses univ. de Lyon, 1983).

[65] See *Essais* I, 31 ("Des cannibales"), pp. 203–4, and in particular: "Il me semble que ce que nous voyons par experience en ces nations-là, surpasse, non seulement toutes les peintures dequoy la poësie a embelly l'age doré, et toutes ses inventions à feindre une heureuse condition des hommes, mais encore la conception et le desir mesme de la philosophie" (p. 206). These are strong words.

[66] See *Essais* III, 6 ("Des coches"): "Nostre monde vient d'en trouver un autre (et qui nous respond si c'est le dernier de ses freres, puis que les Daemons, les sybilles et nous, avons ignoré cettuy-ci jusqu'asture?)" (p. 908).

[That man seems to me to have very well understood the power of habit who first invented this story: that a village woman, having learned to pet and carry in her arms a calf from the hour of its birth, and continuing always to do so, gained this by habit, that even when he was a great ox she still could carry him. For in truth habit is a violent and treacherous schoolmistress. She establishes in us, little by little, stealthily, the foothold of her authority; but having by this mild and humble beginning settled and planted it with the help of time, she soon uncovers to us a furious and tyrannical face against which we no longer have the liberty of even raising our eyes.] (p. 77)

Montaigne's beginning is weak. Rather than anchoring his discussion in a *sententia*, or better, in an ancient authority, he designates someone ("Celuy") whose only distinguishing feature is that he or she "conceived" well the force of custom in "forging," that is, assembling, inventing, or fashioning, an anecdote that he proceeds to retell. The first one to tell the well-conceived story is anonymous. Montaigne's beginning is, then, just as "doux et humble" as the beginning of custom, and just as innocuous as the little calf that becomes a bull. Similarly, the initial episode is disappointing in retrospect, for the commentary Montaigne adds does not really correspond to the story's import. There is no hint, either in Montaigne's own recounting of the story or in his possible sources, of the *tyrannical* or *violent* nature of custom.[67] There is no suggestion that somehow the woman was *forced* to continue to carry the ever heavier animal, just that the habit of doing so *enabled* her to continue. We discover, then, in a comparatively innocent (if bizarre) tale a "tyrannical" and "violent" meaning revealed by Montaigne's commentary. Or, the meaning Montaigne "reveals" is in fact not contained in the original story, but arises because Montaigne says it is there.

The beginning of "De la coustume" is weak, in that it is a pointing to an anonymous source and is no real beginning: it is not a kernel of truth out of which the essay will flow. It does, however, mimic *custom*, for an inauspicious beginning leads to a formidably resistant habit, or, in this case, to

---

[67] In Quintilian (*Institutio oratoria* 1.9.5) the story's protagonist is Milo, who carried a calf every day until it became a bull, at which time he was strong enough to continue to carry it. This is also the version in Erasmus's adage "Taurum tollet, qui vitulum sustulerit" (Chil. I, Cent. II, Ad. 51), although Erasmus mentions an obscene meaning given to the saying by Petronius (*Satyricon* 25.6, in *Opera omnia* [Loudun: P. Vander Aa, 1703], 2:90e). Another possible source is Stefano Guazzo's *La civil conversatione* (1574), bk. 3: "Milo was able to carry a bull, bicause he used to carry hym a calfe" (trans. George Pettie [1581] [repr. London: Constable, 1925], 2:70). The fear-inspiring nature of the full-grown bull is contained in Ovid, *Ars amatoria* 2.341: "Quem taurum metuis, vitulum mulcere solebas [The bull you fear, you were wont to stroke as a calf]" (2d ed., ed. G. P. Goold, trans. J. H. Mozley [Cambridge, Mass.: Harvard Univ. Press, 1979]). However, *carrying* the calf is always thought of as making one *able* to carry the bull.

strong pronouncements on the violent nature of custom. This mimicry is evident in the metaphorical language of the beginning. The initial anecdote uses the figure of birth ("l'heure de sa naissance") explicitly, and implicitly, in the figure of pregnancy ("porter"). The introduction to the anecdote had already announced this language, as the anonymous inventor of the tale "conceives" the force of custom. The furtive or hidden process by which custom establishes itself ("peu à peu, à la desrobée") and the seed imagery ("rassis et planté") confirm the sexual-biological metaphors Montaigne uses in the tale itself. One conceives, is pregnant, and gives birth to a child, just as one begins an essay, and just as custom is born.[68] This mimicry is nevertheless purely *formal*, in the sense that the initial anecdote does not contain within itself the authority and the meanings that become ascribed to it in the context of Montaigne's commentary. This is a situation similar to Rabelais's parody of Diogenes' parody: the typical gesture that points to a previous, more perfect source is here essentially poetic or formal. It is not a conferral of substance, and the gesture of beginning, if anything, points to the factitious and weak nature of the first instance.

If the beginning of "De la coustume" is a nonbeginning, so is custom itself. Custom is, in fact, just *there*. One should treat custom as if it were detached from any etiological chain, for if one searches for the first cause, disappointment and "disgust" will result:

> Autrefois, ayant à faire valoir quelqu'une de nos observations, et receüe avec resolue authorité bien loing autour de nous, et ne voulant point, comme il se faict, l'establir seulement par la force des loix et des exemples, mais questant tousjours jusques à son origine, j'y trouvai le fondement si foible, qu'à peine que je ne m'en dégoutasse, moy qui avois à la confirmer en autruy. (pp. 116–17)

> [Once, having to justify one of our observances, which was received with steadfast authority far and wide around us, and preferring to establish it, not as is usually done, merely by force of laws and examples, but by tracking it to its origin, I there found its foundation so weak that I nearly became disgusted with it, I who was supposed to confirm it in others.] (p. 84)

Following a causal chain back to the first cause does not mean retrieving a more perfect state, but rather its contrary. The fact, however, that a law or custom[69] has a "weak" beginning does not entail a reduction in its force. A

---

[68] This seed imagery is taken up farther along; speaking of the early signs of cruelty in children, Montaigne comments: "Ce sont pourtant les vrayes semences et racines de la cruauté, de la tyrannie, de la trahyson: elles se germent là, et s'eslevent apres gaillardement" (*Essais* I, 23, p. 110). We "drink" the orders of custom "avec le lait de nostre naissance" (p. 115); custom's laws are "infuses en nostre ame par la semence de nos peres" (p. 116).

[69] This essay arguably concerns the distinction between customary and civil law; however, it seems that Montaigne conflates the two, in order to simply pose the question of changing

custom's foundation may be insignificant (like the calf, or the one who thought of the calf story), but it may still be "well-conceived" and should not be changed. The implication of the "disgusting" origin is that one should treat custom as uncaused, or as having caused itself. Otherwise we fall into untenable and savage opinions:

> Les premieres et universelles raisons sont de difficile perscrutation. Et les passent noz maistres en escumant, ou, ne les osant pas seulement taster, se jettent d'abordée dans la franchise de la coustume, où ils s'enflent et triomphent à bon compte. Ceux qui ne se veulent laisser tirer hors de cette originelle source faillent encore plus et s'obligent à des opinions sauvages, comme Chrysippus qui sema en tant de lieux de ses escrits le peu de compte en quoy il tenoit les conjonctions incestueuses, quelles qu'elles fussent. (p. 117)

> [The first and universal reasons are hard to scrutinize, and our masters either skim over them lightly or, not even daring to touch them at all, cast themselves immediately into the protection of custom, where they puff themselves up and enjoy a cheap triumph. Those who will not let themselves be dragged out of this original source err even more and bind themselves to barbarous opinions, like Chrysippus, who in so many places strewed his writings with remarks displaying the little account he took of incestuous unions, of whatever kind they might be.] (p. 84)

Not accepting the fait accompli of custom means risking "savage" opinions, such as the condoning of incest. Custom is motivated in the sense that it can protect from unnatural opinions, but it is not motivated by its origin, or by a first principle. It is, in a strange way, self-motivated, not attached to a causal chain, but nevertheless legitimate.

Montaigne reverses, however, his argumentation when he goes on to say that those who wish to free themselves from the violent prejudice of custom will find their judgment shaken, but in a more certain state.[70] This, however, does not authorize any modification of existing custom, for the

---

any "loy receüe," that is, any law in force. Determining the origin of a custom and the origin of, say, a fragment in the *Digests* involves a difference of degree rather than nature. The question is more one of the distinction between a decree without precedent and the application of precedent, or in a more general sense any introduction of new laws supplanting old ones. For an excellent discussion of the role of legal commentary in the *Essais*, see Tournon, *Montaigne*.

[70] "Qui voudra se desfaire de ce violent prejudice de la coustume, il trouvera plusieurs choses receues d'une resolution indubitable, qui n'ont appuy qu'en la barbe chenue et rides de l'usage qui les accompaigne; mais, ce masque arraché, rapportant les choses à la verité et à la raison, il sentira son jugement comme tout bouleversé, et remis pourtant en bien plus seur estat" (*Essais* I, 23, p. 117). This reversal may find one explanation in the fact that the prior passage is a late addition, whereas the following one continues the text of the 1580 edition. However, on paradoxical argument *in utramque partem* in this essay, see Tournon, *Montaigne*, pp. 81–84.

same "disgust" that accompanied the discovery of the "weak" first cause characterizes the introduction of any new state of affairs. Montaigne refers here to the religious wars and the Reformation:

> Je suis desgousté de la nouvelleté, quelque visage qu'elle porte, et ay raison, car j'en ay veu des effets tres-dommageables. Celle qui nous presse depuis tant d'ans, elle n'a pas tout exploicté, mais on peut dire avec apparence, que par accident elle a tout produict et engendré: voire et les maux et ruines, qui se font depuis sans elle, et contre elle. (p. 119)

> [I am disgusted with innovation, in whatever guise, and with reason, for I have seen very harmful effects of it. The one that has been oppressing us for so many years is not the sole author of our troubles, but one may say with good reason that it has accidentally produced and engendered everything, even the troubles and ruins that have been happening since without it, and against it.] (p. 86)

The instituting of a new first cause is "disgusting," in whatever form this cause may present itself, although, in keeping with his skeptical view of causation, Montaigne mitigates the efficaciousness of the changes envisaged by the Reformers. First, it is only by accident that the Reformation engendered the religious wars; second, the causal chain is unforeseeable in all of its effects, which sometimes even go "against" the first cause. In other words, when we change the inertia of custom, things happen that in no way have to do with the original intent or nature of the cause. A good and reasonably motivated first cause does not confer onto its effects its own goodness and reasonableness. Catastrophic unpredictability is the alternative to the albeit arbitrary precedent of custom.

So what does it mean to free oneself from the violent tyranny of custom? Given that both custom and its alternative, chaotic reform, are less than desirable, the first being unmotivated and the second unpredictable, how is the observer to react? The solution, I am suggesting, is structurally similar to the argumentation *de potentia Dei absoluta* that we have observed in the late scholastic corrosion of causality. When the skeptical observer frees himself from the arbitrary bonds of custom, and envisages a reasonably motivated alternative, it is precisely only a *hypothetical* move, not an *actual* change of the order of things. The Montaignian reader is one who can entertain propositions that, when put into practice, radically alter the face of the current order. We can entertain, in other words, the vision of a different world or order, or envisage the intervention of a new cause. The point is, however, that these propositions are only hypothetical; it is highly undesirable that the current order actually be modified as a result; and it is highly improbable that it will be. Montaigne's skepticism is in at least this respect analogous to the nominalist view of a contingent universe. This contingency is the result of a conceptual stance taken by the human observer, who places himself or herself, hypothetically, in the position of a God who, *de potentia absoluta*, can institute himself as primary cause at any moment, can separate apparent cause from effect, and so forth. It is nevertheless highly unlikely that he should in fact change the actual order he has committed himself to.

This detached reasoning *de potentia absoluta* takes on literary forms in Montaigne's *Essais* in two ways, although both end up producing the same effect. The first is the peculiar practice of addition and correction, from the 1580 to the 1588 editions, and the handwritten corrections after the 1588 edition. Modern editions distinguish the different chronological levels of the text, although the contemporary reader would not, presumably, have been aware of them. Montaigne's interminable adding and intermittent correcting give the impression of the simultaneous presence of all chronological events determining the text's composition. The author intervenes, as it were, at any and all points. I do not think that this confusion of chronological levels is meant to show the gradual unfolding and development of a thought, to introduce time into the portrait of the man Montaigne. It is, rather, the opposite: The author does not just intervene in the final stages of the textual development of an argument, to give the "ripest" and most mature judgment. Rather, *any* stage or moment in the argument could have been inserted at any point. In other words, any moment of the text could be directly caused by the author, rather than the consequence of an earlier event or point on the same chronological plane. This immediacy subverts the notion of a linear unfolding over time of the text, impelled by a beginning (in 1580), and ending with a mature conclusion.

Illustrations of the textual contingency of the *Essais* can be found everywhere; a particularly telling example in "De la coustume" concerns the habit of blowing one's nose in public. The context of the anecdote is as follows: Montaigne wants to show that anything can become a custom, and that human imagination can produce any sort of usage, which then establishes itself as a "reasonable" law. He begins his enumeration of bizarre customs, in the 1588 edition, with "Il est des peuples où . . ." [There are countries where . . .]" and gives three examples. The first two involve modes of greeting and the custom of spitting, whereas the third concerns a nation in which the most esteemed friends of the king collect his excrement in linen. At this point Montaigne ostentatiously interrupts his enumeration with "Desrobons icy, la place d'un compte" (p. 111) [Let us here steal room for a story (p. 80)]. He goes on to relate the habit of an acquaintance who refused to use a handkerchief to blow his nose, saying that linen was too delicate to receive such a dirty bodily excretion. The example undoubtedly is meant to show that our own customs are not *so* different from a custom that requires a king's excrement to be gathered by his favorites.

The French example is a later insertion, and the way in which Montaigne introduces it seems to emphasize the fact that it is an insertion into a prior text. Stealing space for a tale, "desrober la place d'un compte," supposes a preestablished order into which the author furtively inserts room for another example, as if the space belonged to an anterior body of text, and this text had priority over the insertions that followed. Montaigne seems here to be overtly demonstrating the chronological difference between the French anecdote and its context. However, the effect is not one of evolution or development, but instead one of complete contingency. The French anecdote is not, say, the conclusion of the argument, but instead one of many similar examples, and it does not introduce any truly different material into the argument.[71] If we interpret "Desrobons icy, la place d'un compte" as a gesture of an author who is indicating a later insertion, we will have the impression that the author is constantly rereading his own text and is willing to jump in and intervene, changing the order of his fictional world. What is prior is strangely not prior, for it is under constant supervision and reapproval by the author, who can change it at will. The pointing out of chronological difference has led to the abolishing of chronology, under the power of an ever present and immediate author. This is another way of saying that, in Montaigne's *Essais*, the diegetic universe in which one represented event entails another represented event is replaced by a universe in which everything *could* be caused directly by an intervening author-God. It is a universe ruled not by custom but by decree. This is precisely the point: reading the *Essais*, we are in the realm of the hypothetical, the trying-out of other worlds.

The "stolen" tale of blowing one's nose is placed toward the beginning of a long series of examples of strange customs. Montaigne's use of lists of examples is the second way in which *de potentia absoluta* reasoning takes a literary form. The most effective use of such lists is to be found in his skeptical *summa*, the "Apologie de Raimond Sebond" (II, 12), which is less a concise argument than an immense collection of examples tending to show how little privilege man can claim in the general order of things. In the early part of the essay, Montaigne considers various capabilities that are claimed to be uniquely human, and shows by examples how in each case one can find corresponding abilities among animals. Thus speech is not a purely human function, for communication is not limited to vocal articulation: gestures and expressions form just as complicated a "language," and animals are capable of using such sign systems. Montaigne demonstrates

---

[71] A few lines earlier Montaigne had given a similarly curious contemporary example, of a crippled man from Nantes who, having been born without arms, learned to shoot a pistol, write, play cards, and so on with his feet.

the importance of gestures by providing a list of things we humans do with our hands and our head:

> Quoy des mains? nous requerons, nous promettons, appellons, congedions, menaçons, prions, supplions, nions, refusons, interrogeons, admirons, nombrons, confessons, repentons, craignons, vergoignons, doubtons, instruisons, commandons, incitons, encourageons, jurons, tesmoignons, accusons, condamnons, absolvons, injurions, mesprisons, deffions, despitons, flattons, applaudissons, benissons, humilions, moquons, reconcilions, recommandons, exaltons, festoyons, resjouissons, complaignons, attristons, desconfortons, desesperons, estonnons, escrions, taisons; et quoy non? d'une variation et multiplication à l'envy de la langue. (p. 454)

> [What of the hands? We beg, we promise, call, dismiss, threaten, pray, entreat, deny, refuse, question, admire, count, confess, repent, fear, blush, doubt, instruct, command, incite, encourage, swear, testify, accuse, condemn, absolve, insult, despise, defy, vex, flatter, applaud, bless, humiliate, mock, reconcile, command, exalt, entertain, rejoice, complain, grieve, mope, despair, wonder, exclaim, are silent, and what not, with a variation and multiplication that vie with the tongue.] (p. 332)

One common element in this vertiginous list is that we do these things with our hands, but another common element is the grammatical form of the list's elements, which begin to function poetically the further we proceed, lulled by the assonance of *-ons*. Montaigne is implying both that this could go on forever and that *anything* is possible: "et quoy non"?[72] This vertiginous listing of examples has the paradoxical effect of reducing each example's force as a particular illustration of what reality is like. The poetic self-generation of verbs corresponds to a sense of detachment in Montaigne's hypothetical argumentation.

On a more general level of the rhetorical disposition of his argument, Montaigne proceeds similarly. Moving from language to other qualities of human society, he shows how in every case there are numerous examples of animals or insects possessing a similar quality. These demonstrations are

---

[72] The Villey edition indicates that Montaigne has imitated here Quintilian, who in the *Institutio oratoria* shows how gestures should accompany the voice in a speech. Hands almost speak for themselves, for "Annon his poscimus, pollicemur, vocamus, dimittimus, minamur, supplicamus, abominamur, timemus, interrogamus, negamus; gaudium, tristitiam, dubitationem, confessionem, paenitentiam, modum, copiam, numerum, tempus ostendimus?" (11.3.86; ed. and trans. H. E. Butler [Cambridge, Mass.; Harvard Univ. Press, 1922]). Quintilian's list is "balanced," in the sense that he divides the sentence equally between verbs in the first person plural (mixing active and passive endings) in the first half, and nouns constituting the direct objects of "ostendimus" in the second. Montaigne's amplification of the verb forms deprives the sentence of its measure; the sentence seems to engender itself similarly to Rabelais's amplification of Lucian.

punctuated by "Quant à . . . [As for . . .]," such as "Quant à la mesnagerie," "Quant à la guerre," "Quant à la fidelité," "Quant à la gratitude" [As for domestic management; As for war; As for fidelity; As for gratitude], and so forth (pp. 473–83). Each time an aspect of human society is pointed to, counterexamples surge forward, discouraging any imprudent confidence on the part of the reader.[73] Again, anything is possible. So why begin here and not there, why choose this and not that?

This returns us to the problem of custom. Montaigne proceeds, after the nose-blowing intercalation, to a list of startling and often disgusting practices that contains some of the formal elements we will see used later in the "Apologie de Raimond Sebond." This particular list is introduced by "Il est des peuples où . . . ," which is reduced later to "Il en est où . . ." and even further to "Où . . . ," the author having been driven to stylistic impatience by the wealth of examples:

> Il en est où il se void des bordeaux publicz de masles, voire et des mariages; où les femmes vont à la guerre quand et leurs maris, et ont rang, non au combat seulement, mais aussi au commandement. Où non seulement les bagues se portent au nez, aux levres, aux joues, et aux orteils des pieds, mais des verges d'or bien poisantes, au travers des tetins et des fesses. Où en mangeant on s'essuye les doigts aux cuisses et à la bourse des genitoires et à la plante des pieds. (p. 112)

> [There are places where there are public brothels of males, and even marriages between them; where the women go to war alongside their husbands, and take their place not only in the combat but also in command. Where they not only wear rings on the nose, lips, cheeks, and toes, but also have very heavy gold rods thrust through their breasts and buttocks. Where in eating they wipe their fingers on their thighs, on the pouch of their genitals, and on the soles of their feet.] (p. 80)

The list goes on, for another two pages. The only thing connecting all these strange, anonymous examples is the *où*, "where." The only common element is the author's gesture of designation, which is a gesture without commentary. These examples are at the same time completely diverse and completely similar in the sense that they are repetitively strange. Anything is possible, and it is sufficient for the author to summon up another place for another bizarre custom to appear. The examples are also entirely simultaneous and without any apparent hierarchy or order. This is the most obvious demonstration of textual contingency; the text's only connecting tissue is the author's willful designation of places, unreal not only because of their strange customs but also in that the author refuses to give names to

---

[73] Another such list contains, ironically, different definitions of God, from Thales to Epicurus, engendering similar confusion (see *Essais* II, 12, pp. 514–16).

any of them. Rather than referring us back to reality in all of its bewildering diversity, Montaigne's designation of bizarre customs constructs a hypothetical world essentially dependent on the author's whim.

The essay on custom concludes with a paragraph defending those leaders who take the law into their own hands when extreme circumstances dictate extreme actions. It is not clear how, after destroying all conceptual bases for such "nouvelleté," Montaigne can justify this recourse, given that extreme circumstances were certainly a justification for the parties in the religious wars. Yet bending the laws, when the defense of the social order requires it, is the privilege of the one who leads. This privilege was put to good use by Philopoimen, according to Plutarch: "C'est ce dequoy Plutarque loüe Philopaemen, qu'estant né pour commander, il sçavoit non seulement commander selon les loix, mais aux loix mesme, quand la necessité publique le requeroit" (p. 123) [This is what Plutarch praises Philopoimen for: that, being born to command, he knew not only how to command according to the laws, but how to command the laws themselves, when the public necessity required it (p. 90)]. Montaigne's text is very close to the Greek version, a copy of which he owned. Where Montaigne and Jacques Amyot, the best-known French translator of Plutarch in the sixteenth century, use "commander . . . aux loix," the Greek original is τῶν νόμων ἄρχειν. In an uncanny way, the Greek verb ἄρχειν (archein) incarnates important aspects of the question that Montaigne addresses in this essay, and that I have raised throughout the chapter. For archein means both "to command" or "to lead" and "to begin," such that τῶν νόμων ἄρχειν can mean both "to command the laws" and "to begin the laws."[74] Montaigne has shown that there is no hierarchically ordered chain of causation in the diversity of human conduct, and he has similarly shown the weakness of a (temporal) first cause. Yet that very absence of a priori order is a mark of his authority, in that all elements of the textual order are contingent upon his will. So Montaigne's arche is a perpetual beginning, or an omnipresent beginning; it is thus also a sovereignty absolved of the order it sustains.

Radical beginning and the debunking of authority are most explicit, finally, in *Don Quixote* (1604, 1614). The prologue to the first part is no longer a source of authority: the topics normally required for its establishment are furnished by a "friend" who gives advice on how to write authoritative prologues to the writer, who is completely devoid of inspiration.

[74] In Henri Estienne's *Thesaurus graecae linguae* (ed. Carolus Benedictus, 8 vols. [Paris: Firmin Didot, 1831–1865]) we find for ἄρχω both "incipio, initium facio" and "principatum obtineo, impero, imperium teneo." Similarly, the noun ἀρχή (*arche*) (used in the opening of Saint John, ἐν ἀρχῇ ἦν ὁ λόγος, "In the beginning was the Word") means both "beginning" and "power" or "sovereignty."

The narrator presents, through conversation with this friend, a list of possibilities (*sententiae*, biblical quotations, *auctores*, and so on), from which the writer refuses to choose. The implication is that any recourse to authority has nothing to do with the book itself, which in essence remains "a child of [the narrator's] brain." Even the parent-child topos is problematic, though, for the narrator emphasizes that he is not all that attached to his book-child after all: "But I, though in appearance Don Quixote's father, *am really his step-father*, and so will not drift with the current of custom, nor implore you, almost with tears in my eyes, as others do, dearest reader, to pardon or ignore the faults you see in this child of mine [italics mine]."[75] The text is, then, without external grounding, and a product of a slightly unreliable narrator whose whim decides its fate; the text is not a continuous *effect* of a causal order. *Don Quixote* is the terminus ad quem of the emergence of radical beginning, and the inauguration of a long period of ostentatious narrative experimentation, from *Jacques le fataliste* to the *nouveau roman*.

[75] Miguel de Cervantes Saavedra, *The Adventures of Don Quixote*, trans. J. M. Cohen (Harmondsworth: Penguin, 1950), p. 25.

FOUR

FREE CHOICE IN FICTION: WILL AND ITS OBJECTS

IN RABELAIS

THE FINAL CHAPTERS of Rabelais's *Gargantua* (1534?) are devoted to the utopian antimonastery, the abbey of Thélème, whose device "Faictz ce que vouldras" apparently summarizes the freewheeling spirit of at least the first two Rabelaisian novels. Indeed the inhabitants of Thélème tend to do what they will, in a somewhat uniform way, as they are all well-born, educated, and naturally inclined to do good. Much ink concerning this episode has been spilled, and some attention has focused on the connection between the device and the name of the abbey. *Thélème* undoubtedly stands for the Greek θέλημα, "will"; this noun is particularly frequent in the New Testament (although θέλειν occurs quite often in classical sources) and usually refers to the divine will.[1]

The connection between the abbey's device and its name is obvious; furthermore, Rabelais seems to connect divine and human will, although exactly how they are connected is not clear. If Rabelais's utopian vision is a product of will, θέλημα or *voluntas*, rather than, say, wisdom or knowledge, and if the utopian vision governed by will informs the writer's literary production as a whole, then the conceptual complexities of will in the early modern period are most relevant to an interpretation of Rabelais's oeuvre.[2]

---

[1] See, on the etymology of *Thélème*, Michael Andrew Screech, "Some Stoic Elements in Rabelais's Religious Thought (The Will-Destiny-Active Virtue)," *Etudes rabelaisiennes* 1 (1956): 73–97, esp. pp. 84–86; Per Nykrog, "Thélème, Panurge et la Dive Bouteille," *Revue d'histoire littéraire de la France* 65 (1965): 385–97; and Weinberg, *The Wine and the Will*, pp. 127–28. See also Quint, *Origin and Originality*, pp. 197–98; he emphasizes the Augustinian source ("Dilige, et quod vis fac"), following Jean Paris. For an interpretation of Thélème as a society of Stoic sages, see Gordon Braden, *Renaissance Tragedy and the Senecan Tradition: Anger's Privilege* (New Haven: Yale Univ. Press, 1985), pp. 80–83. On Stoicism and Rabelais, see also Jerry C. Nash, "Rabelais and Stoic Portrayal," *Studies in the Renaissance* 21 (1974): 63–82. A differing interpretation of Thélème and its structure (linking it exclusively with Francesco Colonna's architectural-allegorical *Songe de Poliphile*) can be found in Gilles Polizzi, "Thélème ou l'éloge du don: Le texte rabelaisien à la lumière de l'*Hypnerotomachia Poliphili*," *Réforme, Humanisme, Renaissance* 25 (1988): 39–59.

[2] An emphasis on the will (as opposed to the intellect, or rather, knowledge and understanding) is often said to characterize humanism, in its preference for the ethical and rhetorical over the metaphysical. See Trinkaus's reading of Petrarch's *Secretum* (*In Our Image and Likeness* 1:3–17) as a good example of this view. As will be obvious from the following pages, my account of the scholastic discussion of divine will is intended to show that this move into

Although the Stoic and humanist-evangelical sources of Thélème have been emphasized repeatedly, relatively little attention has been paid to the theological complex informing the concept of will, and to the ways in which the vicissitudes of this concept may provide a conceptual key to structural features of Rabelais's work.[3] This is what I propose to explore in this chapter, first by laying out some relevant problems related to the definition of the will, and then by demonstrating Rabelais's modulation of those problems.

Antecedent and Consequent Will of God

One of the most interesting problems surrounding God's will and its relationship to man's will is the interpretation in medieval theology of 1 Tim. 2:4: "[Deus] qui vult omnes homines salvos fieri [God who wishes that all men be saved]"[4] in the Saint Jerome translation, or "qui cunctos homines vult salvos fieri" in Erasmus's version. The Greek original is "ὃς πάντας ἀνθρώπους θέλει σωθῆναι," and the major Greek commentator on this verse, Saint John Damascenus, uses θέλημα to designate God's will in this affair in his *De fide orthodoxa* (translated into Latin in 1512). θέλημα is

---

the ethical in fact does not escape metaphysics, or, conversely, late scholastic metaphysics contained within itself developments that either announce or parallel humanist concentration on rhetorical action. In opposition to the pessimistic emphasis on the frailty of human will that we see in Petrarch, the concentration on divine will as prior to his *intellectus* is a reflection of God's power and freedom. The various distinctions governing the absolutely free will provide, as we shall see, a code through which human will can be reimagined in literary representation. The priority of the will over knowledge does not leave man in a quandary, but instead provides him with the freedom to act, because he is free from necessitating conditions. In this I disagree with the view of will in Ascoli, *Ariosto's Bitter Harmony*, p. 77, although the following formulation is very appropriate: "The moment of choice becomes a point of radical suspension of the hierarchy of faculties through which human consciousness is interpreted in the Renaissance" (p. 78), which is, I argue, a structural divinization of the will. Weinberg's discussion of various forms of human will in Rabelais is essential (*The Wine and the Will*, pp. 124–41), although I do not think that the Neoplatonic and scholastic strains are so easily conjoined, precisely because the will's priority over knowledge is not an obvious feature of Neoplatonic thought. I emphasize the divine paradigms of will underlying the human will's literary representation.

[3] Some useful work has been done on the scholastic sources of Rabelais; see, for example, Etienne Gilson, "Notes médiévales au *Tiers livre* de Pantagruel," *Revue d'histoire franciscaine* 2 (1925): 72–88, and the chapter on "Rabelais franciscain" in his *Les idées et les lettres* (Paris: Vrin, 1932), pp. 197–241. Gilson's work is focused on terminological explanations. See also A. J. Krailsheimer, *Rabelais and the Franciscans* (Oxford: Clarendon, 1963), especially on Scotus (pp. 295–99). Krailsheimer, however, relies exclusively on Gilson in his account of Scotist theology, and views the connection between Rabelais and theology in an essentially topical way.

[4] Unless indicated otherwise, all translations are my own.

rendered as *voluntas* by Saint Thomas Aquinas when he refers to this problem in *De veritate* q 23 a 3.[5] The problem is the following: God wishes to save all men, but some men are damned. That means that human will can impede divine will. Therefore, God's will (or God, for that matter) is not all-powerful.[6]

The scholastic solution to this dilemma is the following: One must distinguish between different meanings of *vult*. God's will can be defined by a series of distinctions that represent not different wills (since God's essence and his will are identical) but different names for his will.[7] Two aspects of his will are to be distinguished: his *voluntas signi* and his *voluntas beneplaciti*. The former is his "external" will, that is, the signs of his will to man (*prohibitio, praeceptum, consilium, impletio, permissio* [prohibition, precept, counsel, fulfillment, permission]). The latter is his "good pleasure," that is, his "internal" will, the internal working of his decisions concerning Creation. His *voluntas beneplaciti* can be broken down into two aspects, his *voluntas antecedens* and his *voluntas consequens*. The former is a general will or wish for Creation, such as the general wish that all men be saved. However, this antecedent will can be impeded by man's free actions, which can be sinful and thus entail damnation. It is through God's consequent will that God acts and wills absolutely efficaciously. God wishes all men to be saved, *antecedenter*, but damns some of them, *consequenter*.[8]

---

[5] See Louise-Marie Antoniotti, O.P., "La volonté divine antécédente et conséquente selon Saint Jean Damascène et Saint Thomas d'Aquin," *Revue thomiste* 65 (1965): 52–77. The scholastic theologians glossing this verse always use *voluntas*, of course.

[6] The problem is succinctly put in Lombard's *Sentences* (I d 46 c 1): "Dictum est enim in superioribus, et auctoritatibus communitum, quod voluntas Dei, quae ipse est vocaturque beneplacitum eius, cassari non potest, quia illa voluntate *quaecumque voluit fecit in caelo et in terra*; cui, teste Apostolo, *nihil resistit*. Augustinus in Enchiridion: 'Quaeritur ergo, quomodo accipiendum sit quod Apostolus de Domino ait: *Qui vult omnes homines salvos fieri*. Cum enim non omnes salvi fiant, sed plures damnentur, videtur utique non fieri quod Deus vult fieri, humana scilicet voluntate impediente voluntatem Dei' " (vol. 1, pt. 2, p. 312).

[7] Ockham insists on this point: "Circa primum sciendum quod ista distinctio non est alicuius quod est realiter in Deo et realiter Deus, quia in Deo non est aliquo modo multiplex voluntas, immo etiam divina voluntas nullo modo distinguitur ab essentia. Sed istae distinctiones sunt nominum et dictionum quae significant ipsam voluntatem quae Deus est" (*Ordinatio* I d 46 q 1, in *Opera theologica* 4:671). See Marilyn McCord Adams, *William Ockham* 2:1170–73, for a discussion of Ockham's use of the antecedent/consequent distinction.

[8] These distinctions are a scholastic commonplace and usually arise in commentaries on Lombard's *Sentences* (I d 46 c 1); see, for example, Saint Thomas Aquinas, *Commentum in quatuor libros sententiarum* I d 45 q 1 a 4, d 46 q 1 a 1, *De veritate* q 23 a 2–3; Bonaventure, *Commentarius in I. Librum sententiarum* d 40 a 3 q 1, d 46 a unicus q 1; Alexander of Hales, *Glossa in quatuor libros sententiarum* (Quaracchi: Collegium S. Bonaventura, 1951) I d 40, 21; John Duns Scotus, *Quaestiones in librum primum sententiarum* d 46 q unica (Commentarius 1a); Gregory of Rimini, *Lectura super primum et secundum sententiarum*, ed. A. Damasus Trapp Osa and Venicio Marcolino (Berlin: Walter de Gruyter, 1981), I d 46–47 q 1 a 1; Ockham, *Ordinatio* I d 46 q 1. A good summary is found in Altensteig, *Vocabularius theologie*,

Consequent will, then, is in some ways the crucial aspect of God's will. It is, as it were, the most "internal" and inaccessible feature of God's will, for it is his essential ability to do otherwise. It is his private pleasure. Even if he has announced that he wishes the salvation of all men, he can, by virtue of his consequent will, do anything he pleases. The other use of this special feature of God's will is the preservation of man's free will in scholastic, especially late scholastic, theology. Man's free will comes after God's antecedent will, but before his consequent will, although temporal terms can be misleading here. In that sense God's final decisions can be based on man's merit, or can take his merit into consideration. The preservation of man's free will thus does not seem to exclude the preservation of God's absolutely free and efficacious will.

Given these underlying distinctions concerning divine will, there are two issues that interest me more specifically, as they are relevant to the representation of will in literary texts: the relationship of God's will to his intellect or goodness and the so-called problem of future contingents. God's will is increasingly defined in its independence from his goodness as a final cause, and it is increasingly difficult to reconcile God's foreknowledge and omnipotence with man's free will in relationship to events that are not necessary but contingent. The conflict between man's free will and God's will determining future contingent events is so thorny precisely because of an analogy between human will as an ability to do otherwise and God's *voluntas beneplaciti consequens*. This analogy, I am claiming, is also evident in the "emptying-out" of both God's and man's will: the will is conceived of more and more as not determined by the *intellectus* or by its objects as final cause, but instead as an essentially free power *ad oppositum*.[9]

This shift in views of divine and human will accounts for the representation of individual decision or choice in Rabelais. The will as determined by its object is superseded by the will that derives its power and orientation

---

pp. 974–76. Consequent will is conceived by Scotus as identical to *impletio* (a feature of revealed will): "Quinto, velle fieri, et sic est *impletio*, et coincidit cum voluntate efficaci sive beneplaciti" (in *Opera omnia*, ed. Wadding, 10:769–70). See also Johann Gerhard, *Loci theologie . . .* (Jena: T. Steinmann, 1610), "Locus secundus: De natura Dei," 271; he also discusses Calvinists' arguments against the distinction. Gerhard emphasizes the internal-external distinction: "Voluntas beneplaciti est internus actus divinae voluntatis, quo aliquid vult; voluntas signi non est internus actus, sed externum signum divinae voluntatis, quo significat se aliquid velle" (quoting Suarez, p. 359). For a discussion of the political analogies to the antecedent-consequent distinction, see Patrick Riley, *The General Will before Rousseau: The Transformation of the Divine into the Civic* (Princeton: Princeton Univ. Press, 1986), pp. 3–63.

[9] The "empty" will is described somewhat hyperbolically but suggestively by Jan Miel in *Pascal and Theology* (Baltimore: Johns Hopkins Univ. Press, 1969), pp. 40–42. A more balanced view is put forth by more recent studies of the problem of the will in late scholastic theology. See below, especially the studies by Wolter and Bonansea.

from itself. This latter conception is also highly problematic narratively, as a completely autonomous will is also ipso facto unrepresentable. The reasons for a decision can never be sufficient to explain the decision, and are moreover irrelevant to the decision. I will be arguing that this epistemic shift underlies the thematic conflict between Pantagruel and Panurge which constitutes the dynamic of Rabelais's novels.

Will, Final Cause, and "Voluntarism"

Aquinas does not allow for any principle outside of God's will that could move it, except one: God's knowledge of the Good, which acts as a final cause determining his will (although one can speak only metaphorically about relationships within God):

> Ad tertium dicendum, quod voluntas non movetur nisi a fine: finis autem voluntatis divinae est ipsa sua bonitas quae est idem quod voluntas secundum rem; et ideo non sequitur quod Deus sit movens motum, proprie loquendo, quia omne movens est aliud a moto. Sed forte propter hoc Plato posuit quod primum movens seipsum movet, inquantum cognoscit se et amat se . . . et hoc non nisi metaphorice dicitur, sicut etiam dicitur, quod finis movet.[10]

> [It should be said that the will is not moved except by the end. The end of divine will is his own goodness, which is the same as his will, in reality, and it therefore does not follow that God is a mover moved, properly speaking, because each mover is different from what is moved. But perhaps because of this Plato claimed that the first mover moves himself, inasmuch as he knows himself and loves himself . . . and this is said only metaphorically, so it is still said that the end moves.]

Although God's goodness does not constitute an external constraint, since it is a part of God himself and not essentially "other" to the will, the latter is constrained by the internal necessity of conforming to the end of its actions, God's goodness. Knowledge of the end determines, then, the immediate cause of an action. God's will cannot will something contrary to God's goodness. God wills something external to himself because it is good.

[10] Saint Thomas Aquinas, *Commentum* I d 45 q 1 a 1 (in *Opera omnia* [Parma: P. Fiaccadori, 1856–1873; New York: Musurgia, 1948–1950], vol. 6). See also *De veritate* 23 a 4: "Voluntas igitur divina habet pro principali volito id quod naturaliter vult, et quod est quasi finis voluntatis suae; scilicet ipsa bonitas sua, propter quam vult quidquid aliud a se vult" (in *Opera omnia*, vol. 9). See also Seeberg, *Lehrbuch der Dogmengeschichte*, pp. 398–401, and B. M. Bonansea, O.F.M., *Man and His Approach to God in John Duns Scotus* (Lanham, Md.: Univ. Press of America, 1983), pp. 51–89, who contrasts Aquinas's "intellectualism" with Scotus's "voluntarism," with some qualifications.

The contrary formulation is frequently found in later scholastics. Speaking about meritorious goodness, Scotus states, "Dico quod sicut omne aliud a Deo, ideo est bonum, quia a Deo volitum, et non e converso, sic meritum illud [Christ's] tantum bonum erat, pro quanto acceptabatur, et ideo meritum, quia acceptatum, non autem e converso, quia meritum est, et bonum, ideo acceptatum [I say that just as everything other than God is good because it is willed by God and not vice versa, so this merit [Christ's] was good to the extent that it was accepted. It was not the other way around, namely, because it was merit and good, therefore it was accepted]."[11] In Pierre d'Ailly's commentary on the *Sentences* we find similar statements that seem to concede a general freedom from constraint to God's will, such as "Divina voluntas nullam habet rationem propter quam determinetur ut velit [Divine will has no reason or order according to which it is to be determined how it wills]" and "Hec ideo praecipit bona quia bona sint. Et prohibet mala quia mala sint. Sed sicut declaravi tunc hec ideo bona sunt quia praecipiuntur et mala quia prohibentur [This (will) thus prescribes the good because it is good. And proscribes evil because it is evil. But as I have declared already, these are good because they are prescribed and evil because they are prohibited]."[12] In Altensteig's dictionary of scholastic terms, the discussion of God's antecedent will similarly affirms the independence of his will from goodness as a final cause. Things are good because God wills them, not vice versa: "Et Deus antecedenter vult omnes viatores juste vivere quia dat potentiam, intellectum, & affectum cum praecepto: nec ideo praecipit bona, quia bona sint, vel prohibet mala, quia mala sint: sed ideo haec bona sunt quia praecipiuntur: & mala, quia prohibentur [And God antecedently wills that all Christians live justly because he gives the power, the knowledge, and the disposition with

[11] John Duns Scotus, *Quaestiones in librum III sententiarum (Opus oxon.)* d 19 q un n 7, in *Opera omnia*, ed. Wadding, 14:718. Trans. in Allan B. Wolter, O.F.M., *Duns Scotus on the Will and Morality* (Washington, D.C.: Catholic Univ. of America Press, 1986), p. 16. Wolter emphasizes that this does not refer to natural or moral goodness, and thus does not exclude natural or moral law. God's will does not function arbitrarily. Already Alexander of Hales had emphasized that there is no final cause, properly speaking, to God's will, although the latter is not without *ratio*, following Anselm: "Item, quaeritur utrum suae voluntatis sit aliqua causa finalis. Quod autem non sit hoc verum, patet ex hoc quod causa finalis alicuius est melius eo cuius est causa; sed nihil est melius divina voluntate; ergo non habet causam finalem. Quod concedimus. Sed nec rationem habet; non tamen est praeter rationem, ne irrationabilis videatur eius voluntas, ut dicit Anselmus" (*Glossa* I d 45, 9 [1:42]).

[12] Pierre d'Ailly, *Quaestiones super libros Sententiarum cum quibusdam in fine adjunctis* (Strasbourg, 1490; repr. Frankfurt: Minerva, 1968), "Principium" (p. 42) and I d 45sq. See also Francis Oakley, *The Political Thought of Pierre d'Ailly: The Voluntarist Tradition* (New Haven: Yale Univ. Press, 1964), pp. 22–33. See also his discussion of God's will in *Omnipotence*, pp. 77–84; for a less "voluntarist" view see Oberman, *Harvest of Medieval Theology*, pp. 90–103, on God's "freedom from the law." Oberman quotes Biel (*Sent.* I d 43 a 1 cor 4): "Unde sola voluntas divina est prima regula omnis iustitie" (p. 96).

the precept. And he does not prescribe the good because it is good, or proscribe evil because it is evil: but things are good because they are prescribed, and evil because they are proscribed]" (p. 975).

The priority of God's will in determining good and evil does not preclude the possibility of moral or natural law, but here man's *merit* is certainly radically dependent on God's will. Divine will is not *necessarily* conditioned by goodness as a final cause (although in fact divine will tends to perform in an orderly and good way). The emphasis is on the will as a power prior to any determination by objects as final cause. God's will becomes an autonomous, originating power. The late scholastics would not admit that such a redefinition of God's will entails arbitrariness or willfulness,[13] but difficulties do arise out of this radicalization of the divine will, for it is projected onto the human will.

Although there is a general consensus preserving the freedom of human will in the Middle Ages, this "freedom" is often understood merely as efficient causation. In other words, man's will is free because the will can be the efficient cause of an event. This does not exclude God as a primary cause, nor does it exclude God's foreknowledge of an event. The will itself is also not free in the sense that it can choose or not choose any object, for it tends toward good objects, and knowledge of a good object leading to happiness entails willing it, although there is no "outside" constraint.[14] Similarly, the intellect is conceptually prior to the will, and can move it by presenting it with a good object.[15]

In the work of later scholastics, the will is often presented as axiomati-

---

[13] According to Scotus, God is always "ordinatissime volens" (quoted by Wolter, *Duns Scotus on the Will and Morality*, p. 19).

[14] If particular good objects have a demonstrated connection to beatitude, the will tends naturally and necessarily to them; if objects do not have this connection, the will is free to not tend toward them: "Sunt enim quaedam particularia bona, quae non habent necessariam connexionem ad beatitudinem, quia sine his potest aliquis esse beatus; et huiusmodi voluntas non de necessitate inhaeret. Sunt autem quaedam habentia necessariam connexionem ad beatitudinem, quibus scilicet homo Deo inhaeret, in quo solo vera beatitudo consistit. Sed tamen antequam per certitudinem divinae visionis necessitas huiusmodi connexionis demonstretur, voluntas non ex necessitate Deo inhaeret, nec his quae Dei sunt. Sed voluntas videntis Deum per essentiam de necessitate inhaeret Deo, sicut nunc ex necessitate volumus esse beati" (Aquinas, *Summa theologiae* I, 82 a 2 [1:502a–502b]).

[15] Aquinas distinguishes between temporal priority and priority in the "ordo naturae," in which the intellect is more perfect than the will: "Dicendum quod illud quod est prius generatione et tempore, est imperfectius; quia in uno eodemque potentia tempore praecedit actum, et imperfectio perfectionem. Sed illud quod est prius simpliciter et secundum naturae ordinem, est perfectius; sic enim actus est prior potentia. Et hoc modo intellectus est prior voluntate, sicut motivum mobili, et activum passivo; bonum enim intellectum movet voluntatem" (*Summa theologiae* I, 82 a 3 [1:503b]). On the final cause determining the will, see Klaus Riesenhuber, *Die Transzendenz der Freiheit zum Guten: Der Wille in der Anthropologie und Metaphysik des Thomas von Aquin* (Munich: Berchmannskolleg Verlag, 1971), pp. 45–47.

cally free—that is, to deny the freedom of the will is to contradict its definition and to go against an evident fact of experience. Scotus maintains
that the will "est libera per essentiam,"[16] and that in the case of contingent
events, "nihil aliud a voluntate potest esse totalis causa volitionis in voluntate secundum quod voluntas determinat se libere ad actum volendi cau-
sandum [nothing other than the will can be the total cause of volition in
the will according to which the will determines itself freely to an act of
willing]."[17] Gregory of Rimini, who is in other respects very traditional,
maintains that the will's freedom is something evidently demonstrated by
experience, and although Ockham accepts the evidence of experience, he
emphasizes that one cannot prove that the will is free.[18]

This very insistence on an essential, axiomatic, and unprovable free will
seems to be a projection of God's radically prior will onto human will. As
an unquestioned ability to choose to do otherwise, man's will is brought
closer, in the work of certain late scholastics, to that originating, autonomous divine will, free of object as final cause. This shift in emphasis makes
problematic the relationship between divine and human will, through the
so-called problem of future contingents (that is, of future events that are
not necessary but contingent). The problem is the following: When man
freely chooses an action, that choice is foreseen by God. Since it is foreseen,
it could not be otherwise. But free will is the ability to do otherwise. Therefore, man never freely chooses. The solution offered in varying forms by
Augustine, Boethius, Aquinas, and many others is to posit God's will in an
eternal "now," that is, outside of time. Thus God knows (and wills) certain
events contingently, that is, dependent on secondary causes such as human
will. He "knows" them in the sense that he knows which alternative is
chosen, but not strictly "before" it is chosen, as he exists in an eternal present.[19] Presumably, then, man can freely choose an alternative and God will
know what he has chosen.

[16] Quoted in Bonansea, *Man and His Approach to God*, p. 55.

[17] Quoted by Roy R. Effler, o.f.m., *John Duns Scotus and the Principle 'Omne quod movetur
ab alio movetur,'* p. 163 n. 212. This does not mean that the will is the total cause of volition,
in the sense that the intellect's knowledge of an object is a requirement, although in contrast
to the will, the intellect does not determine itself, but is caused naturally. Scotus argues
against Henry of Ghent, who held a more purely voluntaristic view, and against Godfrey of
Fontaines, who held the phantasm of the object to be the total cause of volition.

[18] See Gregory of Rimini, *Lectura super primum et secundum sententiarum* 6:2 (II d 24–25
q 1). Ockham: "Circa primum dico quod non potest probari per aliquam rationem, quia
omnis ratio hoc probans accipiet aeque ignotum cum conclusione vel ignotius. Potest tamen
evidenter cognosci per experientiam, per hoc quod homo experitur quod quantumcumque
ratio dictet aliquid, potest tamen voluntas hoc velle vel non velle vel nolle" (*Quodlibeta* I q 16
a 1; in *Opera theologica* 9:88), taking up Scotus's definition of will as the ability to will, to not
will, or to reject.

[19] A lucid formulation of the *nunc aeternitatis* of divine will (a characteristic of divine will
that distinguishes it essentially from human will) is found in Scotus, in answer to the question

A radical emphasis on will as a "self-determining power for opposites,"[20] and an insistence on God's absolute certainty regarding the disposition of his consequent will, combine to preclude any reconciliation of human free will and divine will in the writings of Ockham. For if the created (human) will's determination is necessary for the determination of God's will, then the latter cannot be *ab aeterno*, for God would not be able to know, before its choice, which of the alternatives will be chosen by the human will.[21] Yet we must not question God's knowledge of future contingent events: "Dico ad quaestionem quod indubitanter est tenendum quod Deus certitudinaliter et evidenter scit omnia futura contingentia [I say to the question that it is to be held without a doubt that God certainly and evidently knows all future contingents]."[22] The solution is simply that we cannot express how God knows what man will choose: "Sed hoc evidenter declarare et modum quo scit omnia futura contingentia exprimere est impossibile omni intellectui pro statu isto [But to declare this evidently and to express the way in which he knows all future contingents is impossible for all human understanding]" (ibid, pp. 583–84). We must rely on the authority of Scripture and of the Saints, and we simply cannot prove that God knows future contingents.

Once it is emphasized, then, that man's free will consists mainly of his

---

"Utrum praedestinatus possit damnari" (*Ordinatio* I d 40 q unica): "Ad primum argumentum dico quod procedit ex falsa imaginatione, cuius imaginationis intellectus iuvat ad intelligendum veritatem quaestionis propositae: si enim per impossibile intelligeremus Deum adhuc non determinasse voluntatem suam ad alteram partem, sed quasi deliberare utrum vellet istum praedestinare vel non, bene posset intellectus noster capere quod contingenter ipsum praedestinaret vel non praedestinaret, sicut apparet in actu voluntatis nostrae; sed quia semper recurrimus ad actum voluntatis divinae quasi praeteritum, ideo quasi non concipimus libertatem in voluntate illa ad actum quasi iam positum a voluntate. Sed ista imaginatio falsa est: illud enim 'nunc' aeternitatis, in quo est ille actus, semper praesens est; et ita intelligendum est de voluntate divina sive volitione eius ut est huius obiecti, sicut si per impossibile nunc inciperet Deus habere velle in isto 'nunc,'—et ita libere potest Deus in 'nunc' aeternitatis velle quod vult, sicut si ad nihil esset voluntas sua determinata" (in *Opera omnia*, ed. Balić, 6:311; see also *Opera omnia*, ed. Wadding, 10:681).

[20] This is the definition of will as conceived by Ockham given by Marilyn McCord Adams and Norman Kretzmann in their translation of Ockham's *Tractatus de praedestinatione et de praescientia Dei et de futuris contingentibus (Predestination, God's Foreknowledge, and Future Contingents)* (Indianapolis: Hackett, 1983), p. 18; see the introduction, pp. 12–19, for a useful summary of Ockham's arguments relevant to my discussion.

[21] "Si autem determinationem voluntatis divinae non necessario sequitur determinatio voluntatis creatae, igitur ad sciendum utrum effectus ponetur vel non ponetur, non sufficit determinatio voluntatis divinae, sed requiritur determinatio voluntatis creatae, quae non est adhuc vel non fuit ab aeterno. Igitur Deus ab aeterno non habuit certam notitiam futurorum contingentium propter determinationem voluntatis divinae" (Ockham, *Ordinatio* I d 38 q unica, in *Opera theologica* 4:582–83). See also the *Tractatus de praedestinatione et de praescientia Dei*, q 1, pp. 516–18.

[22] Ockham, *Ordinatio* I d 38 q unica, in *Opera theologica* 4:583.

real ability to do otherwise, and thus of an independence from the known object, God's foreknowledge is incompatible with man's free will. For if man chose merely according to the goodness of objects or their instrumentality in his happiness, presumably God would know these objects better than man, and would know the extent to which man was aware of their goodness. He would thus have no trouble foreknowing man's actual choice. The fact that showing this foreknowledge has become impossible for Ockham is a measure of the extent to which man's will has been emphasized in its autonomy from man's knowledge of objects. Man's will is increasingly, if unconsciously, defined as God's autonomous will. Man's and God's wills are not necessarily determined by *intellectus*, or by *bonitas*, as a final cause.

In turning to the novels of Rabelais I will be looking at the conflict between two different representations of decision or choice: one based on will as determined by knowledge of its object as final cause, and one based on will as independent of that knowledge. It seems that the latter notion is connected to a more "modern" representation of the individual, and implicitly to an *aporia* within literary representation itself in the Renaissance. These two condensed models of will are gleaned from scholastic discussions on the subject, and although no scholastic theologian would fully adhere to the second model, the tendency among late scholastics is to privilege the autonomy of the will.

Gargantua's Dilemma and Pantagruel's Choice of Panurge

In *Pantagruel*, Rabelais's first book, the father of Pantagruel is faced with a choice. His son has just been delivered and is alive and well, but Gargantua's wife has died while giving birth. He sees both son and wife and cannot decide whether to cry or to laugh, for his "sophistic" arguments *in modo et figura* do not permit him to resolve the question:

> Car, voyant d'ung cousté sa femme Badebec morte, et de l'aultre son filz Pantagruel né, tant beau et grand, il ne sçavoit que dire ny que faire. Et le doubte qui troubloit son entendement estoit, assavoir mon s'il debvoit pleurer pour le dueil de sa femme, ou rire pour la joye de son filz. D'ung costé et d'aultre il avoit d'argumens sophisticques qui le suffocquoient: car il les faisoit tresbien *in modo et figura*, mais il ne les povoit souldre. (3, pp. 20–21)[23]

[23] For a good discussion of this episode that takes up the problem of will and claims that Gargantua is inspired by grace to resolve the dilemma, see Weinberg, *The Wine and the Will*, pp. 139–41.

[For, seeing on the one hand his wife Badebec dead, and on the other his son Pantagruel born, so beautiful and big, he did not know what to say nor what to do. And the doubt that troubled his understanding was whether he should cry in mourning for his wife or laugh for joy because of his son. On one side and the other he had sophistic arguments that suffocated him, for he did them very well *in modo et figura* but he could not resolve them.]

The two objects are present beside him, and he cannot decide whether to cry for his wife or rejoice for his child. When he considers his wife, he cries, but when he remembers his son, he rejoices. The parody of scholastic argumentation in his deliberations is explicit, for the chapter is structured along the lines of a scholastic *quaestio*:

1. the question: *Utrum* . . . ("Pleureray je?")
2. the principal arguments
   a. for: *Quod sic: quia* . . . ("Ouy, car pourquoy? Ma bonne femme est morte . . .")
   b. against: *Quod non: quia* . . .
3. the *responsio* or *conclusio*: *Ad istam quaestionem dico* . . . ("il vault mieux pleurer moins, et boire davantaige").[24]

Gargantua cannot decide, for, as I am suggesting, his will is determined by the objects of his actions, and as soon as they are known or considered, they impose themselves. Thus, when contemplating his dead wife, he cries; but when perceiving or remembering his son, he rejoices. Alternating between sadness and joy, Gargantua is unable to act independently of perceived objects and becomes a veritable *mus in pice*. However, he does eventually decide:

Et, en ce disant, il ouyt la létanie et les *Mementos* des prebstres qui portoient sa femme en terre: dont laissa son bon propos, et tout soubdain fut ravy ailleurs, disant: "Jésus, fault il que je me contriste encores? Cela me fasche: le temps est dangereux, je pourray prendre quelque fièbvre, voy me là affollé. Foy de gentilhomme, il vault mieux pleurer moins, et boire davantaige. Ma femme est morte, et bien, par Dieu, je ne la resusciteray pas par mes pleurs." (p. 22)

[And, saying this, he heard the litany and the Mementos of the priests who lowered his wife into the ground: so he stopped what he was saying and all of

---

[24] As the reader can see, this schema does not fit perfectly, for, except in the conclusion, there are no arguments *contra*. This is, strictly speaking, a case of *electio* between two objects, and not a question of *velle/nolle* of one object (which is decided beforehand, for the wife will be mourned and the child celebrated). This situation constitutes a demonstration of the *liberum arbitrium* in Thomistic terms: "Proprium liberi arbitrii est electio: ex hoc enim liberi arbitrii esse dicimur, quod possumus unum recipere, alio recusato, quod est eligere" (Aquinas, *Summa theologiae* I q 83 a 3 [p. 509a]). There seems to be a confluence of different argumentative schemas here.

a sudden was ravished from elsewhere, saying: "Jesus, must I still be sad? That annoys me: times are dangerous, I could catch a fever, it's driving me crazy. By the faith of a gentleman, it is better to cry less and to drink more. My wife is dead, and well, by God, I will not resurrect her with my tears."]

Gargantua then goes on to describe her beatitude in heaven in a way that suggests rationalization rather than "objective" justification of his choice not to mourn. The turning point is "et tout soubdain fut ravy ailleurs." With this formulation Rabelais underlines certain aspects of Gargantua's decision: its suddenness, its force, and its "otherness," or rather, its seeming incongruity.[25] It is precisely *not* the result of argumentation; it does not follow from and does not cohere with any of the preceding deliberations. Deciding is something from *ailleurs*; it is irretrievable, outside of, irrelevant to what has preceded. It is also, more importantly, irrelevant to the objects present to the will. The closest motivation for Gargantua's choice is "cela me fasche." Deciding is irreducibly personal, and follows an inner counsel that is not revealed in argumentation or deliberation. We find here, then, the emergence of the individual will as autonomy vis-à-vis its objects.

Gargantua's autonomy is a development of the *voluntas* side in the dialectic between will and reason that constitutes man's *liberum arbitrium*, and is thus consonant with late scholastic thought. His decision is not, however, arbitrary. The reasons given for the decision are the will's *ratio*, although they do not *predetermine* the will, which is represented as being in essence inaccessible.

The Neoplatonic tone of Gargantua's "ravishment" suggests divine intervention: God's will is suddenly revealed to the giant, and he decides accordingly. Whether this is actually meant is not clear, for although the reasons for Gargantua's decision are not irreligious or unchristian, they are not explicitly *God's* will, either.[26] To the contrary: they are quite personal ("cela me fasche"). The specific conjunction of God's will and man's will is far from unproblematic, and Rabelais does not make divine will any more accessible than human will.[27]

[25] Other instances of the use of "ravy" in *Pantagruel*: the "grand clerc de Angleterre," Thaumaste, is "ravy en haulte contemplation" during his sign-language debate with Panurge (p. 111); the spectators in Pantagruel's judgment of the Baisecul-Humevesne dispute are "ravys en admiration de la prudence de Pantagruel plus que humaine" (p. 74). The glimpse of truth usually entails this semicomical "ravishment."

[26] See Gérard Defaux, *Pantagruel et les sophistes: Contribution à l'histoire de l'humanisme chrétien au XVIe siècle* (The Hague: M. Nijhoff, 1973), pp. 53–55, for an interpretation of this episode as divine intervention and the relativization of human reason.

[27] For an overview of possible Franciscan influences on Rabelais, including the Scotist definition of the will, see Krailsheimer, *Rabelais and the Franciscans*, pp. 195–208, 288–309. The

Rabelais does not say how and why Gargantua comes to his conclusion. This refusal to motivate the turning point seems to be an important feature of the autonomous will's narrative representation. Decision no longer depends entirely on knowledge of the object, but is conceived of as originating independently of knowledge. The *lack* of representation of Gargantua's motives for coming to a decision is a sign of this shift. Narrative representation of a decision is inherently a posteriori. The narrative breaks or signifies a disruption ("tout soubdain") and remotivates that disruption retroactively ("cela me fasche"). Individual decision is shown to have no *prior* constraints or determination by the very mode of its representation. The will is irreducibly individual and therefore unrepresentable, or rather, the representation depicts the will as something ultimately unrepresentable.

If Gargantua has trouble deciding between two equally rational alternatives, his son Pantagruel does not show the same hesitation. In a meeting the nature of which will determine much of the content of the following novels, Pantagruel selects Panurge as his friend for life. He encounters Panurge during one of his Socratic (or Christlike) strolls outside of the Paris walls, just as he had earlier encountered the pretentious student from Limoges. Whereas in that case he had simply collected information about the student's journey, and then, upon hearing his garbled Latin, punished him for his pretentiousness, Pantagruel decides in Panurge's case to love him *before* he collects specific information about him, and *in spite of* Panurge's unwillingness to provide that information to him. The meeting begins in the following way: Pantagruel is taking a walk with his servants and some students, and he sees a man "beau de stature et élégant en tous linéamens du corps, mais pitoyablement navré en divers lieux [handsome in stature and elegant in all features of his body, but pitifully wounded in several places]" (9, p. 207). Even from a great distance Pantagruel is able to distinguish his physiognomy from his bad experiences; Panurge must be a man "de riche et noble lignée," although "les adventures des gens curieulx le ont réduict en telle pénurie et indigence [the adventures of those who are curious have reduced him to such penury and indigence]." When Panurge is closer, Pantagruel addresses him:

> Mon amy, je vous prie que un peu vueillez icy arrester et me respondre à ce que vous demanderay, et vous ne vous en repentirez point, car j'ay affection très grande de vous donner ayde à mon povoir en la calamité où je vous voy, car vous me faictes grand pitié. Pour tant, mon amy, dictes-moy: Qui estes-vous? Dont venez-vous? Où allez-vous? Que quérez-vous? Et quel est vostre nom? (9, p. 207)[28]

---

specific problems evoked here are not really solved, because the will is not analyzed as a conceptual problem throughout scholasticism.

[28] Compare the beginning of the meeting with the student from Limoges: "Quelque jour,

[My friend, I beg of you to stop here and answer me, and you will not regret
it, for I have a great inclination to help you to the best of my power in the
calamity that I see you, for you make me feel great pity. Therefore, my friend,
tell me: Who are you? Where do you come from? Where are you going? What
do you seek? And what is your name?]

Pantagruel expresses his initial goodwill, his *voluntas antecedens*; he wants
to help someone in need. This initial goodwill is, however, quite specific,
since it is precisely Panurge, and not someone else, who benefits from this
good pleasure. In addition, Pantagruel announces to Panurge his good
intentions, rather than waiting for Panurge to present him with reasons to
like or dislike him, although the discrepancy between his physique and his
current appearance is a good sign for Pantagruel. All that is necessary for
Panurge to do is to respond to the few simple questions put to him.

This is precisely what Panurge refuses to do: in a bewildering and frus-
trating series of answers in foreign and imaginary languages, Panurge does
not give Pantagruel any information about himself, although he is perfectly
capable of doing so. He is not, on the surface, giving Pantagruel good
reasons to save him from his miserable state. Furthermore, he is acting
against his own interest, as the announced *voluntas antecedens* (Pantagruel
is the one who "vult omnes homines salvos fieri") is favorable to him. If
Pantagruel were to reject him, as he rejected the *écolier limousin*, his rejection could be seen as the causal result of the nature of the object, Panurge.
Panurge's vainglorious and self-destructive ostentation could very well be
a reason *not* to love him. Of course the exact opposite happens. Panurge's
behavior is in fact in no way related to the way Pantagruel reacts, in the
end, for the giant decides to love him forever. After the series of obfuscat-
ing languages, Panurge finally responds, in French, that he knows French,
that it is his native language, and that he was born in the Touraine. This
elicits Pantagruel's rejoinder, "Doncques (dist Pantagruel) racomptez-
nous quel est vostre nom et dont vous venez, car, par ma foy, je vous ay jà
prins en amour si grand que, si vous condescendez à mon vouloir, vous ne
bougerez jamais de ma compaignie, et vous et moy ferons un nouveau pair

---

que Pantagruel se pourmenoit après soupper avecques ses compaignons par la porte dont l'on
va à Paris, il rencontra ung eschollier tout jolliet, qui venoit par icelluy chemin; et, après qu'ilz
se furent saluez, luy demanda: 'Mon amy, dont viens tu à ceste heure?'" (6, pp. 31–32).
Pantagruel simply asks him where he is coming from, and has not decided that he will take
him into his affection; on the other hand, the student is well dressed and does not seem to be
in need of help. Pantagruel is not moved to charity or pity by the student's appearance. The
opposite reaction, open hostility, is the result of the student's pretentious responses; Pantagruel's will is thus determined by the object present before it. It is in the meeting with Panurge that the absolute priority of Pantagruel's (good)will is emphasized, and that Pantagruel
as a figure of will (and charity, which is close to being the same thing) comes into his own, as
it were.

d'amitié telle que feut entre Enée et Achates [So tell us your name and where you come from, for, by God, I already love you so much that, if you agree to my will, you will never leave my company, and you and I will make a new pair in friendship such as Aeneas and Achates]" (9, p. 212). Pantagruel wills to love Panurge in spite of the latter's obstreperousness, in a gesture that far exceeds any merit Panurge may have shown. He exercises the correlate to God's *voluntas consequens* in the most effective possible way. Pantagruel is demonstrating the absoluteness and the efficaciousness of his will precisely through its excessiveness and its lack of objective motivation.[29] The object does not determine Pantagruel's will; his choice to love Panurge eternally is a willful exercise of his charity. Panurge's behavior is irrelevant to his selection by Pantagruel, his patron. At the same time Pantagruel's choice becomes through its very willfulness mysterious; the priority of his will has effectively removed the giant from coherent literary motivation.

Panurge's Dilemma

Rabelais's *Tiers livre* (1546) is the first in a series of books (two or three, depending on the authenticity of the *Cinquième livre*) describing Panurge's quest for an answer to the questions: Should he marry? If he marries, will his wife be unfaithful, steal from him, and beat him? In the *Tiers livre* we have the most elaborate discussion of the problem, as various ways of obtaining an answer are tried out, from the "sorts virgilianes" and the interpretation of dreams to consultation with theologians and physicians. The book is divided into chapters that correspond to the diverse authorities consulted. Throughout these consultations the will is a theme, for it is a matter of willing or refusing to be married, a *velle/nolle* situation.[30]

[29] As literary critics our need for coherence at any price makes us distrust such statements of *non*motivation and makes us seek out some implicit or symbolic motivation to patch things up. If this need for motivation is a critical presupposition it becomes well-nigh impossible for the writer to present anything as being *without* reason, even if, paradoxically, it makes *sense* for some actions to be beyond motivation, or simply incoherent. To say that Pantagruel loves Panurge in eternal friendship because Panurge is, say, intelligent, funny, and so on is to ignore the fact that this is not the way Rabelais has set it up in his text. It is important, then, that we ask ourselves why we cannot precisely say how Pantagruel's choice of Panurge is motivated. Or, to state it more strongly, it is *important* that we are not able to motivate this choice. See my discussion of Montaigne's choice of La Boëtie, Chapter Five ("Sovereign Friendship").

[30] According to Gregory of Rimini, this precise situation is an example of an action not caused by the object as its immediate cause, but by the will, for the wish to take a wife is not merely an object in the world, nor is it merely a series of signs, but it is instead a statement signifying the relationship between signs and objects (a *complexe significabile*) and thus cannot be an immediate cause: "Actus potest libere elici circa aliquod volibile complexum seu tantum complexe significabile, sicut patet, cum quis vult non cenare vel ducere uxorem. Cum ergo

In chapter 9 ("Comment Panurge se conseille à Pantagruel, pour sçavoir s'il se doibt marier [How Panurge asks Pantagruel's advice, in order to know if he should get married]") we find an exposition of the problem through a dialogue between Panurge and Pantagruel. Panurge had announced in the previous chapter that he wanted to get married ("Je me veulx marier"), and he now asks for Pantagruel's advice:

> Je vous supply, par l'amour que si long temps m'avez porté, dictez m'en vostre advis. —Puis (respondit Pantagruel) qu'une foys en avez jecté le dez et ainsi l'avez decreté et prins en ferme deliberation, plus parler n'en fault, reste seulement la mettre à execution. —Voyre mais (dist Panurge) je ne la vouldrois executer sans vostre conseil et bon advis. —J'en suis (respondit Pantagruel) d'advis, et vous le conseille.[31]

> [I beg you, by the love which so long you have felt for me, tell me your opinion. —Since (replied Pantagruel) you have thrown the dice and have decreed it and taken it in firm deliberation, don't talk about it anymore; the only thing left is to execute it. —But (said Panurge) I would not want to execute it without your counsel and good opinion. —I agree (replied Panurge) with you, and advise you to go ahead.]

Pantagruel assumes that Panurge's will has led to a decision to marry, that is, that Panurge is precisely beyond the turning point of Gargantua ("tout soubdain . . ."). Any advice for or against is in some sense irrelevant to the decision itself, so Pantagruel is content to affirm what he takes to be a decision. However, he finds out quickly that Panurge's will is *not* transcendent to the sum total of reasons. Panurge continues: "Mais (dist Panurge) si vous congnoissiez que mon meilleur feust tel que je suys demeurer, sans entreprendre cas de nouvelleté, j'aymerois mieulx ne me marier poinct. —Poinct doncques ne vous mariez, respondit Pantagruel [But (said Panurge) if you knew that it would be best for me to stay the way I am, without attempting anything new, I would rather not get married. —So don't get married, replied Pantagruel]" (ibid.). Panurge is here requiring knowledge of future events (si vous *congnoissiez*) to determine his will, or rather, the

---

talia complexe tantum significabilia non sint aliquae entitates . . . sequitur quod nullius actus possint esse causae effectivae" (*Lectura* II d 24–25 q 1 [6:13]). See Gordon Leff, *Gregory of Rimini: Tradition and Innovation in Fourteenth-Century Thought* (Manchester: Univ. of Manchester Press, 1961), pp. 57–58, 167, for an explanation of this passage. For a general but somewhat imprecise discussion of uses of "vouloir" in Rabelais, see Verdun-L. Saulnier, *Rabelais*, vol. 1, *Rabelais dans son enquête* (Paris: SEDES, 1983), "Rabelais Maître de Volonté," pp. 57–64.

[31] Rabelais, *Le tiers livre*, pp. 75–76. Screech notes that the language Pantagruel uses (jecté le dez, decreté) is Erasmian, from the adage *Omnem iacere aleam* (p. 75n). See also Screech, *The Rabelaisian Marriage. Aspects of Rabelais's Religion, Ethics and Comic Philosophy* (London: Arnold, 1958), for a discussion of the evangelical-Stoic sources of these chapters.

decision is conceived of as being entailed by its object. When the latter is not present, as it cannot be, the will is essentially incomplete, and therefore cannot tend one way or another. Panurge represents an extreme version of the "intellectualistic" side of scholastic definitions of the will, whereas Pantagruel represents the "voluntaristic" side, simply put. The giant ends up giving him the only advice he can, namely, to make up his mind. This advice is inherently no help to Panurge: "Aussi (respondit Pantagruel), en vos propositions tant y a de Si et de Mais, que je n'y sçaurois rien fonder ne rien resouldre. N'estez vous asceuré de vostre vouloir? Le poinct principal y gist: tout le reste est fortuit et dependent des fatales dispositions du Ciel [Also (replied Pantagruel) in your propositions there are so many Ifs and Buts that I would not know how to establish or resolve anything. Are you not sure of your will? The main point is there—all the rest is fortuitous and depends on the fatal dispositions of the heavens]" (p. 80).[32] The narrative function of these two figures of will is also illustrated in the exchange. Pantagruel keeps telling him to marry or not to marry, based on the presentation of future events by Panurge. Strictly speaking, he is telling him *nothing*, that is, he is not adding information, and he is not conveying certainty about future events. What Pantagruel seems to be demonstrating is the *irrelevance* to will of reasons, advice, and projections of future events. Will is something entirely other to objects outside of itself. What is talked about or represented are the objects of will, never will itself. Pantagruel's "advice" is semantically redundant to each of Panurge's copious complaints. Will does not reside in meaning but somehow escapes, is tangential to, semantic representation.

A further example of the will's status outside of, or beyond, representation in Pantagruel's sense is the way in which the giant deals perceptively with Panurge's basic impulse, which really *is* to get married. In the following chapters, whenever a counsel or prediction is to be interpreted, Panta-

[32] Although there are Stoic and evangelical reminiscences here, this is also compatible with a scholastic conception of God's will. As we have seen, God's antecedent *voluntas beneplaciti* allows for man's will to determine contingent events; once his disposing consequent will is in effect, it is precisely a "fatale disposition" in the sense that it is unimpedable. There is a confluence of many traditions here; the scholastic is not, however, excluded. Pantagruel of course repeats these kinds of statements, for example, "Il se y convient mettre à l'adventure, les oeilz bandez, baissant la teste, baisant la terre, et se recommandant à Dieu au demourant, *puys qu'une foys l'on se y veult mettre*" (10, p. 81; italics mine), and "en l'entreprinse de mariage chascun doibt estre arbitre de ses propres pensées et de soy mesmes conseil prendre" (29, p. 204). For a Stoic interpretation of the problem of will in the portrayal of Panurge, see Nash, "Rabelais and Stoic Portrayal." His reading is based on the Stoic concept of "active virtue," which includes the "primacy of reason . . . when reaching a decision" (p. 71). The problem, I am suggesting, is that in the end, for Rabelais, decisions have to be nonrational, as one cannot have sufficient information about future contingent events: this is why will has to *precede* understanding.

gruel chooses the (more obvious) pessimistic interpretation, whereas Panurge persistently interprets information in his own favor. Panurge really *wants* to get married, and wants to believe that his wife will be faithful and neither rob nor beat him. Of course, he still cannot *will* to marry. In their first exchange on the subject Pantagruel announces his own pessimism when Panurge mentions the subject of cuckoldry. He likes cuckolds (the implication being that he has undoubtedly caused that state of affairs himself), but he does not wish to be one. Pantagruel uses a maxim of Seneca to show Panurge that he will be one, too:

> J'ayme bien les coquz [says Panurge], et me semblent gens de bien, et les hante voluntiers, mais pour mourir je ne le vouldroys estre. C'est un poinct qui trop me poingt. —Poinct doncques ne vous mariez (respondit Pantagruel), car la sentence de Senecque est veritable hors toute exception: ce qu'à aultruy tu auras faict, soys certain qu'aultruy te fera. —Dictez vous (demanda Panurge) cela sans exception? —Sans exception il le dict, respondit Pantagruel. —Ho, ho (dist Panurge), de par le petit diable! Il entend en ce monde, ou en l'aultre. (p. 77)

> [I like cuckolds, and they seem to me to be good people, and I like to hang around them, but I would never ever want to be one of them. That's a point that is too troublesome for me. —So don't get married (replied Pantagruel), for the maxim of Seneca is true without any exception: what you will have done to others, be sure that they will do to you. —Do you (asked Panurge) say that without exception? —Without exception he says it, replied Pantagruel. —Ho, ho (said Panurge), by the little devil! He means in this world, or in the next?]

In asserting that whatever one has done to another will be done to him, Pantagruel is for once giving Panurge a substantive declaration concerning his future situation. Presumably Seneca's maxim is incontrovertible, that is, it is *not* contingent. The maxim should, then, determine precisely Panurge's decision, as his will is dependent on its objects for its orientation. Panurge, however, needs a further confirmation, and asks Pantagruel if he (Pantagruel) says this without exception ("Dictez vous . . . cela sans exception?"). In fact that is what Pantagruel did say: "La sentence de Senecque est veritable hors toute exception." Yet in responding to Panurge's question, Pantagruel slips away by saying that *Seneca* says it without exception: "Sans exception *il* le dict." Panurge continues to use the third person pronoun in his reply. The shift from the *vous* to the *il* is significant, because even though Panurge addresses the question to Pantagruel himself, the giant at the last moment refuses to identify himself totally with Seneca's assertion.[33] Pantagruel has once again escaped; he has once again said *noth-*

---

[33] Pantagruel has shifted from an *assertio* to a *recitatio*, in scholastic terminology (from being

ing. However, that is perhaps because he cannot say anything, for the will as autonomous power is irrelevant to reasons and advice as efficient causes. The transmission of a turning point, an *ailleurs*, is beyond the scope of linguistic communication.[34]

By now my analyses should have made clear that I am not claiming the influence of scholastic sources on Rabelais, except in a general way. Rather, a central problem of Rabelais's novels, the conflicting avatars of the will, is elucidated with great rigor among the scholastics, and their distinctions provide a conceptual, structural key to understanding how Rabelais was able to represent individuality, and, for that matter, how will and individuality are sometimes connected in Renaissance literature. For, as opposed to both Neoplatonic and Stoic accounts of the will, we have seen that the late scholastic treatment of divine will deals succinctly with the priority of the will over knowledge, that is, with the nonrational and inaccessible feature of coming to a decision that is part of the early modern literary imagination. Although the identification of scholastic and especially Franciscan topics is valuable in demonstrating the influence of Rabelais's education and the extent to which theological concepts were current,[35] topical analysis is distinct from the focus of my study, which deals more with the presence and function of cultural structural models concerning the relationship of the divine to the human, and specifically, the representation of the creature's effective action.

In the most obviously theological of Panurge's consultations, in chapter 30 of the *Tiers livre*, he seeks advice from Hippothadée, a soft-spoken theologian. This character has been identified diversely, either as Lefèvre d'Etaples or as Philip Melanchthon,[36] and his theology as Erasmian-evangelical, although in essence he uses scholastic distinctions, and his irrelevance to Panurge's problem is clearly seen through those distinctions. Panurge finds him to be of no help, either, for even though the theologian

---

an author asserting something to being a compiler reciting something someone else asserts). This distinction allowed the inclusion of pagan sayings in Christian treatises. See Minnis, *Medieval Theory of Authorship*, pp. 193–94.

[34] This conclusion is partially consonant with Gérard Defaux's interpretation of Christian humanism as containing an implicit critique of language as such (see, other than *Le curieux, le glorieux, et la sagesse du monde dans la première moitié du XVIe siècle: L'exemple de Panurge (Ulysse, Démosthène, Empédocle)* [Lexington, Ky.: French Forum, 1982], "Clément Marot: Une poétique du silence," in *Pre-Pléiade Poetry*, ed. Jerry C. Nash, [Lexington, Ky.: French Forum, 1985], pp. 44–64). The scholastic tradition of discussion of the will provides a structurally more intricate background to Rabelais's narrative strategies than Christian humanism, although the explicit links to evangelism certainly are evident in Rabelais's work. I suspect that in some regards Christian humanism is intellectually more derivative of post-Thomist scholasticism than the humanists themselves would have been willing to admit.

[35] See the studies by Krailsheimer, and Etienne Gilson, "Notes médiévales au *Tiers livre* de Pantagruel," pp. 72–88.

[36] See Screech, *Rabelaisian Marriage*, pp. 67–68.

counsels marriage to those who burn with the fires of concupiscence, he cannot answer a question concerning future contingents:

> Seray je poinct coqu? [asks Panurge] —Nenny dea, mon amy (respondit Hippothadée), si Dieu plaist. —O, la vertus de Dieu (s'escria Panurge) nous soit en ayde! Où me renvoyez-vous, bonnes gens? Aux conditionales, les quelles en Dialectique reçoivent toutes contradictions et impossibilitez. Si mon mulet Transalpin voloit, mon mulet Transalpin auroit aesles. Si Dieu plaist, je ne seray poinct coqu; je seray coqu si Dieu plaist. Dea, si feust condition à laquelle je peusse obvier, je ne me desespererois du tout; mais vous me remettez au conseil privé de Dieu, en la chambre de ses menuz plaisirs. (pp. 210–11)

> [Will I be a cuckold? —Not at all, my friend (replied Hippothadée), if it pleases God. —Oh (Panurge cried out), may God's strength help us! Where do you send me, good people? To the conditionals, which in Dialectic allow all sorts of contradictions and impossibilities. If my transalpine mule flew, my transalpine mule would have wings. If it pleases God, I will not be a cuckold; I will be a cuckold if it pleases God. If it were a condition which I could avoid, I would not despair at all; but you send me back to the private counsel of God, into the chamber of his little pleasures.]

Hippothadée's answer to Panurge's question involves God's *voluntas beneplaciti consequens*, that is, his actual disposing of events taking into consideration what man has chosen to do. God's *pleasure* ("si Dieu plaist"), his *beneplacitum*,[37] is precisely his inner counsel that, since it involves future events contingent on man's choices, is not revealed in advance to man. Hippothadée goes on to explain that one can find out more about God's will by reading the Bible and following his commandments, and by choosing a wife who will follow them, too. Strictly speaking, he is shifting the grounds of the discussion, for as he recites the advantages of reading the Scriptures and describes the ensuing conjugal fidelity, he is speaking about God's *voluntas signi*, that is, his revealed will. This revealed will does not and cannot answer a question such as "Seray je poinct coqu?" For the answer to the question depends on a choice made by Panurge, and on the response of God's *voluntas beneplaciti consequens*, not his *voluntas signi*. The answer is, then, still a conditional sentence: If you observe the revealed will of God, and if your spouse does so too, then you will not be a cuckold. Of course this is more or less a tautology, for since in divine law "est rigoureusement defendu adultere [adultery is rigorously prohibited]" (p. 213),

---

37 In *L'évangélisme de Rabelais: Aspects de la satire religieuse au XVIe siècle* (Geneva: Droz, 1959), Michael Andrew Screech devotes a chapter to the "conseil privé de Dieu" and shows that the *bon plaisir* of God, his *beneplacitum*, is part of the evangelical vocabulary of the period (see pp. 57–76). In this case, as in the case of the distinction between revealed and internal will, Screech does not mention the long tradition of scholastic commentaries which precedes the evangelical usage and must have been familiar to anyone trained as a Franciscan.

a wife who observes God's revealed will, by the same token, will be faithful. Hippothadée in that respect *is* preserving the ultimate inaccessibility of God's pleasure, and is also not giving Panurge the answer he wants. Thus we find an exchange similar to the initial dialogue between Panurge and Pantagruel: the giant will not and cannot provide what is necessary for Panurge to decide. The radical conditionality of Hippothadée's statements demonstrates the irrelevance of advice to an autonomous will, and the permanent gap between the autonomous will of Pantagruel and the dependent will of Panurge.

The essential irrelevance of advice given to Panurge by his friends contrasts with the paradoxical relevance of advice given to the mad king Picrochole by his counselors in the earlier *Gargantua*. Much of the novel's narrative is propelled by the *guerre picrocholine*, as much of the *Tiers livre* is propelled by Panurge's quest for certainty. Of course, whereas Panurge has trouble deciding whether or not to marry, Picrochole has no trouble whatsoever in deciding to wage war against Gargantua's peasants. Picrochole's overt problem is, on the ethical plane, a complete lack of prudence, and on the religious plane, the fact that God has left him to his own devices. Grandgousier offers the latter explanation for Picrochole's foolhardy aggression: "Dieu eternel l'a laissé au gouvernail de son franc arbitre et propre sens, qui ne peut estre que meschant sy par grace divine n'est continuellement guydé [Eternal God has left him under the direction of his free will and his own sense, which can only be evil if it is not continually guided by divine grace]" (27, p. 181). This explanation is certainly consonant with medieval and evangelical anti-Pelagianism, but it masks what goes on in the exchange between Picrochole and his advisors. After having rejected Grandgousier's peace initiatives, they begin planning their imperialist exploits. One part of their army will defeat Grandgousier's forces, the other will launch a glorious expedition against Spain and Portugal, crossing the straits of Gibraltar and subduing North Africa. These deeds are described in the future tense, but the present tense begins to intrude, representing events as already having happened: "Voicy Barberousse, qui se rend vostre esclave [Here is Barberousse, who is offering himself as your slave]," "Le pouvre Monsieur du Pape meurt desjà de peur [The poor Pope already is dying of fear]" (31, p. 195), and so on. Picrochole's advisors are obviously speaking about future events that are contingent. These events depend among other things on Picrochole's decisions, and yet they are presented as no longer being either future or conditional. This is *relevant* advice, false and deluded as it may be, for it provides a way of avoiding the annoyance of future contingents. Picrochole can decide to act because his actions are represented as already having been accomplished. In other words, Panurge's quandary has been eliminated, for Picrochole has been given that which Panurge so insistently seeks, "certainty" about future contingent events. Picrochole, then, is a figure of a comically anachronistic, dependent will functioning in a utopian absence of future contingents.

This is precisely what Panurge's situation is *not*, for the advice offered to him by his entourage is never a representation of the future as already having happened. In spite of all predictions and counsels, a basic conditionality is always preserved. This conditionality is what prevents Panurge's will from carrying out its function. This permanent gap is, of course, the source and driving force of Panurge's quest, and, one may argue, of the Rabelaisian quest.[38] For Panurge's will entails an endless accumulation of information and yet never precisely that which is necessary. In this sense Panurge, the *homo logos*,[39] or rather *loquax*, is both an anachronism and, paradoxically, that which still *can* be represented.[40] His search for certainty and his dependence on "external" reasons are the very material with which individuality can be rendered. Panurge's problem is, at least in part, the need to define that which has become in essence beyond definition. Pantagruel is the figure of the autonomous yet subservient will, and he poses a fundamental problem to literary representation as it is conceived in the early modern period, for he points beyond the representation of the individual as more or less determined by the *intellectus* in its important moments to an individual constituted as such by his irrelevance to reason.

Panurge and Picrochole are anachronistic figures determined by a dependent will; are the residents of Thélème, then, *a contrario*, examples of an autonomous θέλημα? Clearly the description of the abbey's inhabitants underlines the role of their will in fashioning Thélème's life-style: "Toute leur vie estoit employée non par loix, statutz ou reigles, mais scelon leur vouloir et franc arbitre. Se levoient du lict quand bon leur sembloit, beuvoient, mangeoient, travailloient, dormoient quand le desir leurs venoit. Nul ne les esveilloit, nul ne les parforceoyt ny à boyre, ny à manger, ny à faire chose aultre quelconques. [Their whole life was organized not by laws, statutes, or rules, but according to their will and free choice. They got up when it seemed good to them, drank, ate, worked, slept when the desire came to them; no one woke them, no one forced them to drink, to eat, nor to do anything else]" (55, pp. 301–2). The "vouloir et franc arbitre" of the Thelemites is prior to any outside constraint.[41] Their private

---

[38] The continuing debate over the authenticity of the fifth book is in some ways emblematic of this very problem; the "resolution" at the end of the fifth book is the sort of epistemic shift that removes the difference of wills and at the same time removes the cause of writing.

[39] The expression is Alice Fiola Berry's (*Rabelais: Homo Logos* [Chapel Hill: Dept. of Romance Languages of the Univ. of North Carolina, 1978]).

[40] Panurge is possibly an example of "creative" anachronism in the sense of Thomas M. Greene, *The Vulnerable Text: Essays on Renaissance Literature* (New York: Columbia Univ. Press, 1986), especially "History and Anachronism," pp. 218–35.

[41] On freedom as lack of constraint in Rabelais, see Wayne A. Rebhorn, "The Burdens and

pleasure, their *voluntas beneplaciti* ("quand bon leur sembloit"), determines when they will get up, eat, and so forth. Of course this does not imply anarchy, for aristocratic courtly culture guarantees the Thelemites' pursuit of honor and prevents them from choosing vice. The emphasis on lack of constraint, however, highlights their power *ad oppositum*, even though they make little use of it. So in all these ways their lives are guided by will as an autonomous, original faculty.

Yet Thélème is a remarkably nonindividual place. None of its inhabitants are named; they all do the same things and dress the same way. The episode is completely without narrative interest in its static, architectural quality. The blandness of the inhabitants is perhaps related to the impossibility of representing the will inasmuch as it is autonomous. Pantagruel's semantic redundancy in answering Panurge's questions is a linguistic mirror of the peculiar sameness of the Thelemites, for a certain conception of individuality and the will leads to this conundrum: to the extent that the will is free from constraint and conditions it is nonindividual in its very individuality. It does not add anything one can talk about. If will were constrained and conditioned, it would be representable and thus representable *as* different from other individual wills. Being essentially prior and autonomous, however, it is not representable as a substantial difference, for it would then be both accessible and conditioned. This is an important feature of the distinction between *voluntas beneplaciti* and *voluntas signi*, which, as a distinction concerning God's will, is a projection of difficulties concerning the conceptualization of human will and human individuality. Rabelais's utopian abbey of will in its very lack of interest is an incarnation of divine will in human individuals.

Joys of Freedom: An Interpretation of the Five Books of Rabelais," *Etudes rabelaisiennes* 9 (1971): 71–90, esp. pp. 72–77 on Thélème.

FIVE

THE FREE POET: SOVEREIGNTY AND THE

SATIRIST

Ce qui me contraint n'est pas moi.
(Valéry, *Monsieur Teste*)

His idem propositum fuit quod regibus, ut ne qua re egerent,
ne cui parerent, libertate uterentur, cuius proprium est sic
vivere, ut velis.
(Cicero, *De officiis*)

Eyn Christen mensch ist eyn freyer herr ueber alle ding und
niemandt unterthan. Eyn Christen mensch ist eyn dienstpar
Knecht aller ding und yderman unterthan.
(Luther, *Von der Freyheyt eynisz Christen menschen*)[1]

Du Bellay's Refusal

JOACHIM DU BELLAY begins his satiric and nostalgic sonnet collection *Les regrets et autres oeuvres poëtiques* (1558) with a gesture of
refusal, reiterated anaphorically throughout the sonnet and accentu-
ated by the reinforced negation *point*:

> Je ne veulx point fouiller au seing de la nature,
> Je ne veulx point chercher l'esprit de l'univers,
> Je ne veulx point sonder les abysmes couvers,
> Ny desseigner du ciel la belle architecture.[2]

[I do not want to dig in nature's breast; I do not want to search for the spirit
of the universe; I do not want to investigate covered depths; Nor do I want
to sketch the beautiful architecture of the sky.]

---

[1] Valèry: "What constrains me is not I"; Cicero, "Such men have had the same aims as
kings—to suffer no want, to be subject to no authority, to enjoy their liberty, that is, in its
essence, to live just as they please"; (trans. Walter Miller); Luther, "A Christian is a free master
over all things and is no one's subject. A Christian is a docile servant of everything and is
subject to everyone." Unless indicated otherwise, all translations are my own.

[2] All quotations from the *Regrets* are from the Jolliffe and Screech edition. On Du Bellay's
negative poetics, see François Rigolot, "Du Bellay et la poésie du refus," *Bibliothèque
d'humanisme et Renaissance* 36 (1974): 489–502.

In scholastic terminology, he is exercising his *voluntas libera* by willing not to act. The satiric enterprise, at least as it is conceived by Du Bellay, is linked to a demonstration of the poet's freedom, a freedom that here relates to the choice of themes and genres. Du Bellay's freedom consists also, more profoundly, in the refusal of Rome, the wish to separate himself from the decadent conditions he perceives there in his position as *intendant* of the cardinal Jean Du Bellay. Finally, his freedom is also the ability to see what is no longer in what is. I will attempt to define the basic form of freedom as manifested in Du Bellay's initial gesture of the will by looking at "extreme cases" of freedom in the Renaissance. These extreme cases will involve utopian discourse, conceptions of political sovereignty, and divine absolute power. I will argue that freedom can be understood here as the positing of an origin prior to any constraint, or as the necessity of an unnecessary origin of a system, or as the irrecoverability by the system of its own origin. These formulations are deliberately general, but also deliberately specific in suggesting that freedom and its derivates are not a priori invariable concepts, nor the convenient termini ad quem of analysis, but must be examined historically through literature and other cultural discourses. In the following pages, before returning to the text of the *Regrets*, I suggest ways in which Du Bellay's willful gesture of freedom can be understood in political and theological terms.

If Du Bellay's refusal to write like his predecessors or his contemporaries is typical of the satiric tradition, his willful gesture is also linked to utopian discourse, as the negative moment that will become the occasion for the construction of an alternative.[3] That alternative is at the same time for Du Bellay an idealized France and an idealized ancient Rome, and is as sketchy as it is nostalgic. To the extent, then, that the alternatives to present conditions are irremediably past, and entirely unsystematic, Du Bellay's satiric poetry never becomes truly utopian.

However, the demonstration of freedom is an important initial gesture shared by the satirist and the utopian thinker. In More's *Utopia* (1516), Raphael Hythlodaeus, through whom the narrator More learns of the island Utopia, must demonstrate at the outset that he is not a courtier, and that he is free: "As it is, I now live as I please."[4] Rabelais's utopian abbey of Thélème has as its device "Faictz ce que vouldras," and the Rabelaisian narrator emphasizes the freedom of its inhabitants, although, similarly to

---

[3] See Verdun-L. Saulnier, "L'utopie en France: Morus et Rabelais," in *Les utopies à la Renaissance* (Paris: Presses univ. de France, 1963), pp. 137–62: "De l'utopie, la première valeur est donc négative. L'utopie est le contraire de quelque chose de réel. . . . Sa valeur d'impulsion satirique (négative, mais tonique), suffit d'ailleurs à distinguer la tentation utopique des autres rêves. Elle se veut le contraire de quelque chose, elle va vers un contraire construit" (p. 142).

[4] Thomas More, *Utopia*, ed. and trans. Edward Surtz, s.j. (New Haven: Yale Univ. Press, 1964), p. 17. This is, according to Surtz, Cicero's definition of liberty (*sic vivere, ut velis*).

More's utopia, the actual activities in the abbey end up being highly regimented.[5]

The utopian gesture of freedom, that is, the demonstration of free "will" and "pleasure,"[6] is linked to the idea of conventionality. Through a free decision one sets conventions. This is particularly apparent in the area of language; More's *Utopia* includes a set of characters used on the island, and in Geofroy Tory's *Champ Fleury* (1529), they are described as follows: "Ie vous ay aussi en oultre adiouxte les Lettres Utopiques que iappelle Uto-piques pource que Morus Langlois les a baillees & figurees en son Livre quil a faict & intitule. Insula Utopia. Lisle Utopique. Ce sont Lettres que pouvons appeler Lettres *voluntaires /& faictes a plaisir* [I have also added for you letters which I call utopian because More the Englishman has given and figured them in his book entitled 'Insula Utopica,' 'The Utopian Isle.' They are letters that we can call voluntary and done by our plea-sure]."[7] The voluntary, deliberate choice of letters can extend to the rela-tionship between words and things. Words are the result of man's free will, according to Charles de Bovelles, in his *Liber de differentia vulgarium lin-guarum et Gallici sermonis varietate* (1533). The semantic field of the free decision that institutionalizes and systematizes includes *arbitrium* and *ar-bitratus*. God freely grants free will to Adam, who then freely chooses names for things:

Primum, quod doceat stetisse in primo parente, & munere dei, primae totius mundi linguae voluntariae institutionis arbitrium, ut qui sua singulis animan-tibus, iubente deo, nomina posuerit. Secundum, quod testetur donatum à deo hominem esse libero arbitrio, impensumque illi hunc honorem, ut singulas mundi substantias, propter hominem factas arbitrariis nominibus imbueret. Sicut enim ab arbitrio dei, libera & spontanea substantiarum omnium origo pependit, ita nimirum voluit sanxitque deus, omnium nominum, vocum, & appellationum originem ab hominis (nempe à primi parentis) arbitratu profi-cisci debere.[8]

---

[5] See Rabelais, *Gargantua*, chaps. 54–55, and above, Chapter Four.

[6] The Latin original of Raphael's statement is "sic vivo ut volo," so the English "please" is slightly misleading, although one finds in the 1551 translation by Ralph Robynson "after myn owne mynde and pleasure"; here "pleasure" is undoubtedly closer to the Latin *placitum*, that is, resolution, that which is found to be agreeable to oneself.

[7] Geofroy Tory, *Champ Fleury. Auquel est contenu lart & science de la deue & vraye proportion des lettres attiques . . .* (Paris: G. de Gourmont, 1529; repr. Paris: C. Bosse, 1931, ed. Gustave Cohen), f. 73 vᵒ; italics mine. Saulnier ("L'utopie en France") notes that this is the first use in French of *utopique*.

[8] Charles de Bovelles, *Liber de differentia vulgarium linguarum et Gallici sermonis varietate*, ed. and trans. Colette Dumont-Demaizière (Paris: Klincksieck, 1973), p. 46. This is obvi-ously not a purely "conventional" view of language, since the Adamic origin is incompatible with a purely "arbitrary" relationship between sign and referent. For a discussion of various

[The first (mystery) that teaches that the decision to institute voluntarily the first language of the world was in our first father and by the gift of God, for this man, on the order of God, gave names to all living beings; the second that shows that man received from God free will and that this honor was given to him: to attribute to all substances of the earth, made for man, the names of his choice. Just as the free and spontaneous origin of all substances depended on a decision of God, so God has undoubtedly willed and prescribed that the origin of all names, words, and appellations should come from the decision of man (of the first man, of course).]

In his *Dialogo delle lingue* (1542), Sperone Speroni similarly attributes the strength of languages to human will and decision, although the Adamic theme is not explicitly central to his argument. Languages are not produced by nature, but "fatte & regolate dallo artificio delle persone à beneplacito loro [made and regulated by human artifice and through their good pleasure]." In addition, "ogni loro vertu nasce al mondo dal voler de mortali [all their quality arises from the willing of mortals]," and "tutto consista nello arbitrio delle persone [everything consists in the decision of humans]."⁹ These passages are familiar to Du Bellay, who in his *Deffence et illustration de la langue francoise* (1549) uses Speroni's dialogue to praise the function of the human will in creating languages that are lexically adequate. Languages are not born out of themselves, like plants, but rather, translating Speroni, "toute leur vertu est née au monde du vouloir & arbitre des mortelz."¹⁰ So when Du Bellay begins his sonnet collection by a reiterated act of will, "Je ne veulx point," his rhetorical display of originality is also a gesture connoting the exercise of man's free will in establishing imaginary and real social conventions. That free will is connected, in the Renaissance, to terms such as *beneplacitum*, *arbitrium*, and *voluntas*, all of which are far-ranging in their connotations.

But the linguistic and utopian senses of will are not precise, in that the texts using them do not focus on the meaning of these terms, as they are being used to delimit other concepts that are more important to their subjects. In addition, there is a fluctuation between individual will (such as Adam's) and the will of man, in general. The single will is, paradigmatically, the sovereign's or God's. It is especially political theory and theology that tend to focus on what it means for an individual will to be free, and these are the areas I will turn to briefly for a more concise definition. I will

---

views of language in the sixteenth century, especially in relation to the myth of Babel, see Claude-Gilbert Dubois, *Mythe et langage au seizième siècle* (Bordeaux: Ducros, 1970).

⁹ Sperone Speroni, *Dialogo delle lingue*, ed. and trans. Helene Harth (Munich: W. Fink, 1975), pp. 116, 118. Harth's edition is based on the 1740 edition of the *Dialogo*.

¹⁰ Joachim Du Bellay, *La deffence et illustration de la langue francoise*, ed. Henri Chamard (Paris: Didier, 1948), p. 12. See his notes to pp. 12 and 13.

argue that the pertinent definition of freedom underlying its use is the absence of (prior) constraint, and that this is in a dialectical relationship to another, often dominant, definition. This other meaning is something like the inner ability to do something in accordance with principles that transcend the individual but that he can draw on in himself.[11] I will focus on the absence of constraint as a criterion for freedom, because I believe it is more pertinent to what is of most interest in Renaissance individualism. Freedom is demonstrated most dramatically by the most visibly powerful individual of Renaissance culture, the sovereign. The question of sovereignty is related at heart to the ability of the sovereign to act in a way that is not determined by those who are subject to him. Similarly, freedom as sovereignty in Christian culture is intimately connected to the question of God's power to act independently of his creation. In both of these instances a certain model of freedom tends to become important in the early modern period, namely, the idea of the sovereign or God as prior to or above the constraints or laws he may set down. In the end, the theological seems to be primary, since by imagining God man thinks out the most extreme example of freedom and power. In other words, the theological allows a kind of logical reduction that goes a long way in establishing conceptual limits and categories for *human* freedom and power. It is a commonplace to assert that in the Renaissance divinity is more and more attributable to the human creature—let us now see what that actually means.[12]

The Sovereign as the Unbound: The Huguenots and Bodin

In 1573 the Huguenot jurist François Hotman published a treatise advocating a limited monarchy, based on a tradition of Franco-Gallic liberty, against the Roman-influenced tendencies of royal absolutism. The *Francogallia* maintains that under the medieval French dynasties the welfare of the people always constituted the supreme law, and that the public council effectively counterweighed the power of the king. The attitude Hotman was attacking found its justification in Roman law, in the *Digest*, and was called the *lex regia*, which Hotman describes in a 1576 addition to his treatise: "Nor can I be sufficiently astonished at the ignorance of those men who had some elementary acquaintance with Roman Law and derived the opinion from our records that under the *lex regia* the people of the Roman

---

[11] This is the general argument of Erich Fromm in *Escape from Freedom*, which is a rather diffuse and inexact treatment of these issues in the Christian West. In spite of many reservations one may have, this is still an important and valuable thesis.

[12] For a fine, extensive discussion of the interpenetration of humanist and theological thought in Italy, see Trinkaus, *In Our Image and Likeness*.

empire conceded all its authority and power, and who approve of a perpetual, free and unlimited power in all kings, which they call by the barbarous and inappropriate word 'absolute' [. . . continuo *liberam* quandam et *infinitam* Regum omnium *potestatem* commenti sunt, quam Absolutam barbaro et inepto nomine appellant]" (italics mine).[13] The absolute power of the sovereign is linked to his freedom and to the absence of limits or boundaries. In another passage of the *Francogallia*, there is a more direct echo of the text of Roman law: "We believe, therefore, that it has been sufficiently shown that a boundless and unlimited power was not allowed the kings of Francogallia by their subjects, and they cannot be described as free from all laws. Rather they were restrained by defined laws and compacts [Satis igitur demonstratum esse arbitramur, Regibus Francogalliae non immensam atque infinitam potestatem a suis civibus permissam fuisse, *ut legibus omnibus soluti dici possint*, sed eos certis legibus et pactionibus obligatos esse]" (pp. 458–59; italics mine). The allusion is to *Digesta* 1 3.31, "Princeps legibus solutus est," the well-known formula for the legislator's sovereignty.[14] To be "absolved" of the laws one has set down is of course a sign of one's power and freedom, a sign of the fact that one is not "obliged" or tied or bound (ob-*ligatus*).[15] In Roman law a counterweight could be found to the *lex regia*, one that ensured the sovereign's obligation to his own laws. This was called the *lex digna*, and made it part of a ruler's dignity to profess himself to be bound by the laws: "Digna vox maiestate regnantis legibus alligatum se principem profiteri [It is a sentence worthy of majesty that the prince declare himself bound by the laws in force]" (*Codex* 1 14.4). Once again the notion of ties or bonds (ad-*ligare*) is essential here, a complement to the notion of freedom as the absence of these constraints. The *lex digna* was of course invoked by the Huguenots as prior to or more important than the *lex regia*.[16]

[13] François Hotman, *Francogallia*, Ed. Ralph E. Giesey, trans. J.H.M. Salmon (Cambridge: Cambridge Univ. Press, 1972), pp. 414, 415.

[14] See Brian Tierney, " 'The Prince Is Not Bound by the Laws.' Accursius and the Origins of the Modern State," *Comparative Studies in Society and History* 5 (1963): 378–400, and the somewhat spotty survey by A. Esmein, "La maxime *Princeps legibus solutus est* dans l'ancien droit public français," in *Essays in Legal History*, ed. Paul Vinogradoff (London: Oxford Univ. Press, 1913), pp. 201–14.

[15] The definition of an obligation in Roman law makes this sense of necessary tie or bond even clearer: "Obligatio est iuris vinculum quo necessitate adstringimur alicuius solvendae rei secundum nostrae civitatis iura" (*Inst.* 3, 13) (in *Corpus iuris civilis*, ed. Paul Krueger and Theodor Mommsen [Berlin: Weidmann, 1954], vol. 1). See also Hans-Peter Schramm, "Zur Geschichte des Wortes 'obligatio' von der Antike bis Thomas von Aquin," *Archiv für Begriffsgeschichte* 11 (1967), 119–47.

[16] The *Vindiciae contra tyrannos* by "Junius Brutus" (Hubert Languet?) quotes the *lex digna* as an epigraph. In the French translation (1581) we read: "C'est une chose bien seante à la Maiesté d'un qui domine sur les autres, de declairer qu'il est Prince lié aux loix" (ed. Henri Weber et al. [Geneva: Droz, 1979], p. 3). The *Vindiciae*, as other Huguenot political treatises,

Huguenot insistence on the *lex digna* is nothing new: in medieval and early Renaissance political theory such an emphasis is commonplace. A good example of the relative familiarity of the *lex regia–lex digna* complementarity is their presence in handbook-sized compilations printed at the beginning of the sixteenth century, called *Flores legum*. Thus, on the one hand, *princeps legibus solutus est*, but, on the other, *princeps quamvis legibus sit solutus attamen secundum leges vivere vult* [although the prince is absolved of the laws nevertheless he wishes to live according to the laws].[17] Even the allegedly preabsolutist Guillaume Budé uses this principle in defining the limitations on the monarch—"C'est parolle digne de Prince, que de se dire & maintenir estre subiect à la Loy"[18]—and he is merely repeating what medieval theorists such as John of Salisbury have said before him.[19]

Another antidote to the *lex regia* and the concurrent absolute power of the sovereign was Hotman's philological analysis of expressions of royal power. The most obvious example of royal whim was the formula "Car tel

---

end up stressing the sovereign's obligation to divine law, rather than simply affirming the power of the people. See J. W. Allen, *A History of Political Thought in the Sixteenth Century* (New York: The Dial Press, 1928; repr. London: Methuen, 1960), pp. 302–31, for a standard summary of Huguenot resistance theory, and the selections in Julian H. Franklin, *Constitutionalism and Resistance in the Sixteenth Century: Three Treatises by Hotman, Beza, and Mornay* (New York: Pegasus, 1969).

[17] See *Flores legum* (Paris: Jean Petit, 1513), no pagination. This little compendium exists in various editions, available at the Bibliothèque nationale in Paris.

[18] Guillaume Budé, *De l'institution du prince* (Paris: Nicole, 1547), p. 137. Cf. Claude de Seyssel, *La monarchie de France* (1519), 1.12: "Et sont les rois beaucoup plus à louer et priser de ce qu'ils veulent en si grand autorité et puissance être sujets à leurs propres lois et vivre selon icelles, que s'ils pouvaient à leur volonté user de puissance absolue" (ed. Jacques Poujol [Paris: Librairie d'Argences, 1961], p. 120). In his notes to the English translation of Seyssel's *Monarchy*, Donald R. Kelley lists Aristotle's *Politics* and John Fortescue as sources of the passage (New Haven: Yale Univ. Press, 1981), p. 57 n. 26. The correlation between *princeps legibus solutus* and the *lex digna* is also affirmed by Budé in his commentary on the *Digests*, where in discussing the former principle and its various uses in classical times, he alludes to the latter principle. Quoting Plutarch (who is quoting Pindar): "Quis igitur principi princeps erit? nempe lex, quae omnium regina est mortalium atque immortalium ut inquit Pindarus. Quae verba consentanea esse videntur cum lege Digna vox. Cod. de legibus." This is to be understood not as the prince's subordination to written, external law, but his observance of an inner sense of the law: "Lex (inquit [Plutarch]) principis imperatrix erit: non illa quidem aut in libris extrinsecus scripta, aut in tabulis. Sed animata intus in ipso ratio, semper cum eo conservans, eiusdémque observatrix" (*Annotationes . . . in quatuor & viginti Pandectarum libros*, p. 92).

[19] "C'est digne voiz que personne se die et afferme en magesté regnant estre prince lié et obligié aus loys," *Le Policraticus de Jean de Salisbury traduit par Denis Foulechat* (1372), bk. 4, ed. Charles Brücker (Nancy: Presses univ. de Nancy, 1985), p. 7. On the fortunes of Roman law in the Middle Ages, see Walter Ullmann, *Law and Politics in the Middle Ages: An Introduction to the Sources of Medieval Political Ideas* (Ithaca: Cornell Univ. Press, 1975), pp. 51–116 (on the *lex regia*, pp. 56–57), and the fundamental discussion in Kantorowicz, *The King's Two Bodies*, esp. pp. 95–97, 102–7.

est nostre plaisir [For such is our pleasure]." The Latin original, "Quia tale est nostrum placitum," does not necessarily contain the sense of "pleasure" (or "fancy"); according to Hotman, a *placitum* is simply a "counsel" or "common decision." In fact, the idea of consultation is contained within the very word *placitum*. Such is the meaning of the Roman phrase *placere senatui*.[20] Hotman then goes on to suggest that the royal clerks began to translate *placitum* as the vernacular *plaisir*, thus transforming what was rational, deliberate, and consultative into an expression of the monarch's absolute power.[21] The complaint against linking the king's sovereignty to his "pleasure" is also not original with Hotman, but arises out of a long tradition of attempts to moderate or limit royal power. Again, a quite explicit example of a critique of this association is found in John of Salisbury's *Policraticus*. He complains that flatterers of the king will claim that (in Foulechat's translation) "le prince n'est point sougiet à la loy. Et tout ce qui plait au prince si a force et vertu [the prince is not subject to the law. And everything that pleases the prince has force and virtue]." Thus, whatever pleases the prince has "vigueur de loy [strength of law]," and these flatterers make the king into someone "franc des liens de la loy [free from the ties of the law]." John of Salisbury maintains, however, that kings cannot command or prohibit "simplement selon leur pur plaisir [simply according to their mere pleasure]."[22] The link between whim, pleasure, and freedom

[20] Hotman, *Francogallia*, pp. 342–44. In Old French, by the way, *placitum* becomes *plaid*. Before Hotman, Guillaume Budé had already laid out the definition of *placitum* as *arestum* (French *arrêt*), in the *Forensia*: "Senatui placere dicebant ut apud Ciceronem quinta & nona Philip. pro eo quod Graeci dicunt δοκεῖν. Unde Dogmata, id est decreta dicta. Ita Curiae placere dici hodie potest, praesertim in his decretis quae auctoritate & potestate legibus soluta magis quam legum antiquarum praescripto constant. Quanquam ipsa curiae decreta, Aresta videri possunt esse dicta, quasi curiae placita. Aresta enim a Graecis dicuntur, quae placent & probantur" [Paris: Robert Estienne, 1548], p. 14). The problematic connection between *placitum* and sovereignty is thus already pointed out in Budé's commentary. In the same edition, the useful glossary by Jean Du Luc lists *placitum* as *arrest* (p. 124).

[21] Hotman, *Francogallia*, pp. 344–46. Protestant attacks against this formula are frequent. See, for example, Agrippa d'Aubigné, *Les tragiques*: "Ainsi l'embrasement des masures de France / Humilie le peuple, esleve l'arrogance / Du tyran, car au pris que l'impuissance naist, / Au pris peut-il pour loy prononcer: *Il me plaist*" ("Les fers," 985–88, in *Oeuvres*, p. 174). In a note to these lines the editors refer to the *Miroir des François* (bk. 1, dialogue 5) which contains similar criticisms.

[22] Salisbury, *Policraticus*, pp. 59–60 (chap. 7). On the principle of *Quidquid principi placuit, legis vigorem habet* (*Dig.* 1 4.1), see André Bossuat, "The Maxim 'The King Is Emperor in His Kingdom': Its Use in the Fifteenth Century before the Parlement of Paris," in *The Recovery of France in the Fifteenth Century*, ed. P. S. Lewis (London: Macmillan, 1971), pp. 185–95, esp. 191; and Ullmann, *Law and Politics*, pp. 56–57. It is important to distinguish the *lex animata* (the emperor's will is the law) from the concept of no superior appeal, that is, there is no one to whom one can appeal a judgment of the sovereign, and no one to judge the sovereign if he does break the law (he is *capable* of breaking the law). See Tierney, "The Prince Is Not Bound." The tyrant at least attempts to acquire the former power.

from the ties of the law is obvious, and it will be a constant in descriptions of the bad prince or tyrant in political theory as well as in courtly literature.[23]

In some ways critiques of unlimited royal power are conceptually the most interesting, as the negative image tends to incarnate what one fears about the exercise of power as such, and thus represents a *cas limite*. However, the most famous apologist for absolute royal power in the sixteenth century, and its most radical proponent before Hobbes, Jean Bodin, does discuss sovereignty in a way that makes clear the importance of lack of constraint in the definition of freedom and will of the sovereign. In the *Six livres de la Republique* 1, 8 ("De la souveraineté"), Bodin purports to do what no one else has done before him and actually define what sovereignty *is*. In Bodin, true sovereignty is understood not so much as an accumulation of powers through history as an analytic necessity. If one analyzes the concept of sovereignty itself, one arrives at conclusions that affirm its absoluteness.[24] For example, sovereignty has to be both absolute and perpetual; otherwise the ruler would be in some way subject to the ones he ruled, which would mean that he would not be sovereign.[25] Bodin insists on the *unconditional* transferral of the people's power to the sovereign, thus extending the *lex regia*, so that the transferral of power is a "pure and simple" *gift*. It thus has to be perpetual and cannot be retracted (pp. 88–89). This is all implied by the concept of sovereignty itself.

Similarly, Bodin defends the Roman principle *princeps legibus solutus est* by making it an analytic necessity. The sovereign could not be bound by his own laws, because it is impossible to bind oneself with something that depends on one's own will. It is worth quoting most of this passage here, as Bodin touches on all the points discussed above:

> On peut bien recevoir loy d'autruy, mais il est impossible par nature de se donner loy, non plus que commander à soy mesme chose qui depende de sa volonté, comme dit la loy, *Nulla obligatio consistere potest, quae à voluntate promittentis statum capit*: qui est une raison necessaire, qui monstre evidemment que le Roy ne peut estre subiect à ses loix. . . . Le Prince souverain ne se peut lier les mains, quand ores il voudroit. Aussi voyons nous à la fin des edicts & ordonnances ces mots: CAR TEL EST NOSTRE PLAISIR, pour faire entendre que les loix du Prince souverain, ores qu'elles fussent fondees en bonnes & vives

[23] The most famous example is found in Castiglione's *Libro del cortegiano*; see above, Chapter Two.

[24] Julian H. Franklin states, in *Jean Bodin and the Rise of Absolutist Theory* (Cambridge: Cambridge Univ. Press, 1973), p. 53, that for Bodin, "absolute authority was an analytic implication of supremacy."

[25] Jean Bodin, *Les six livres de la Republique* (1576), rev. ed. (Lyons: Jacques du Puys, 1580), p. 85.

raisons, neantmoins qu'elles ne dependent que de sa pure & franche volonté. (p. 92)[26]

[One can well receive a law from someone else, but it is by nature impossible to give oneself a law, or to command oneself something that depends on one's own will, as the law says, *No obligation can exist which derives its conditions of being from the will of the promising party*: which is a necessary reason that shows obviously that the king cannot be subject to his laws. . . . The sovereign cannot tie his own hands, even if he wanted to. So we see at the end of edicts and ordinances these words: FOR SUCH IS OUR PLEASURE, to show that the laws of the sovereign, although they may be based on good and substantial reasons, nevertheless only depend on his pure and free will.]

In the margins of this passage Bodin indicates the sources of his reasoning, with reference to two fragments from the *Digests*.[27] The principle enunciated in the first fragment referred to is "Nulla promissio potest consistere, quae ex voluntate promittentis statum capit [No promise can exist which takes its conditions of being from the will of the promising party]" (*Dig.* 45 1.108). In this fragment the example given is the following: "If someone marries me, do you promise to give me as her dowry ten? [Si qua mihi nupserit, decem dotis eius nomine dare spondes?]. If by the protasis is meant "For anyone who marries me . . . ," and if I do marry someone, the person who has promised me to pay her dowry is indeed bound by the promise, in spite of the fact that the future spouse is unknown when the promise is made. If it were within the promising person's power to nullify the promise once a choice of spouse had been made, then the promise would have been a pure product of that person's will: it is this situation that is not a promise. Thus a promise cannot depend on the will of the person promising, but must depend on conditions external to the person, and those conditions are obliging.[28] Since a promise to oneself depends on

---

[26] It should be noted that for Bodin princes are subject to divine and natural law, and are bound to contracts they make, although the extent to which the sovereign can more easily revoke the contract for good cause is not clear: "Il ne faut donc pas confondre la loy & le contract: car la loy depend de celuy qui a la souveraineté, qui peut obliger tous ses subiects, & ne s'y peut obliger soy mesme: & la convention est mutuelle entre le Prince & les subiects, qui oblige les deux parties reciproquement, & ne peut l'une des parties y contrevenir au preiudice, & sans le consentement de l'autre: & le Prince en ce cas n'a rien par dessus le subiect" (p. 94). See also Franklin, *Jean Bodin*, pp. 55–61, on oaths and promises of the sovereign. Compare with God's *promissio*, in late medieval theology, below, "God's Sovereignty."

[27] The reference is "1. à Titio.§.nulla. de verb. obli. 1. Si quis in princio. de legat.," which I take to be, respectively, *Dig.* 45 "De verborum obligationibus" 1.108 "A Titio stipulatus . . . ," and *Dig.* 32 "De legatis et fideicommissis" 22 "Si quis in principio testamenti adscripserit. . . ."

[28] Cf. *Dig.* 44 7.8: "Sub hac condicione 'si volam' nulla fit obligatio: pro non dicto enim

one's will—that is, there are no factors outside of oneself that can be obliging—such a statement cannot be considered a promise. Bodin must consider this analogous to the sovereign promising to follow laws he himself has laid down: laws are a product of the sovereign's will, and to promise to follow them would make no sense, as one would merely be promising to follow one's own will, which cannot be a promise. The very nature of sovereignty excludes the sovereign from any obligations to that which sovereignty enables him to do.

The second reference is to a principle in testamentary law: "Nemo enim eam sibi potest legem dicere, ut a priore ei recedere non liceat" (*Dig.* 32 22). No one can give himself a law such that he would not be permitted to withdraw from an earlier expression of his will. That is, one cannot oblige oneself in such a way that changing one's mind would be prohibited (since no one and nothing other than the writer of the testament can determine its elements). The analogy is now between the sovereign's laws and a person's testament: there is nothing external to the sovereign that would prevent him from changing his mind about a law he himself had previously set down. In other words, the sovereign's laws are not laws when applied to himself.

In both cases the justification of the sovereign's absoluteness implies that the freedom *to* determine is somehow analytically related to the freedom *from* determination. The sovereign is only truly free *to* legislate if he is free *from* legislation. There must be a hypothetical instance from which everything is determined but which itself necessarily escapes determination. Or, if there is obligation, there must be something radically outside of obligation. Obligation and determination make no sense if there is no essential freedom from obligation or determination.

Bodin goes on to say that even if the sovereign wanted to bind himself, he would not be able to do so ("le Prince ne se peut lier les mains, quand ores il voudroit"). The unboundness of the sovereign is a logical rather than a historical fact. It is contained within the very definition of *promissio* or *legatum*. It is also a *limit* to his will—even if he willed to do so, he could not be less than absolved of obligation to his own laws. The sovereign could not will himself to be less powerful, because that would involve a contradiction. This reasoning is very close to that which characterizes discussions of the power of God: the only limit to God's absolute power is usually taken to be the law of noncontradiction. Thus God cannot do anything that is contrary to his own nature, such as limit his own power.[29] For

---

est, quod dare nisi velis cogi non possis: nam nec heres promissoris 'eius, qui numquam dare voluerit,' tenetur, quia haec condicio in ipsum promissorem numquam exstitit."

[29] Cf. Bodin, *Les six livres*, pp. 149–50: "Or tout ainsi que ce grand Dieu souverain ne peut faire un Dieu pareil à luy, attendu qu'il est infini, & qu'il ne se peut faire qu'il y ayt deux choses infinies, par demonstration necessaire: aussi pouvons nous dire que le Prince que nous

the very act of doing so would demonstrate that he was able to do everything; thus he would not in fact have limited his power. Following his own order makes God more powerful, not less.

Actually following one's own laws is, then, a demonstration not of the *iuris vinculum* but of one's sovereignty or will, for one is never *bound* to follow them by something external to oneself.[30] In this sense being "above" the law is not negated by following the law; in some cases one may argue that following one's own laws, for a sovereign, implies greater power than willfully disobeying or disregarding them.[31] The sovereign's orderly behavior, as it were, is a product of will, not of necessity or obligation (except for obligation to divine and natural law).

Although, as was pointed out by Hotman, the original sense of *principi placuit* or *placitum* was not pure and simple "pleasure" of the sovereign, the sign of the sovereign's unboundness, "Tel est nostre plaisir," was often taken to mean just that. Even if it was claimed that the connection between *placitum* and *plaisir* was merely a courtier's flattery, the semantic overlap was unavoidable, especially as the sense of "counsel" or "agreeableness" becomes less obvious in the vernacular. The mark of sovereign "pleasure" is, then, freedom, in the sense of freedom from prior constraint, and the mark of freedom is pleasure. Even if what one ends up doing is equal to what one would do if obliged to, the fact that one is not *obliged* to do it constitutes the crucial difference.

As medieval critics of the sovereign's absolute power had already suggested, the (false) equation of the king's *placitum* and his pleasure or whim was a product of courtly flattery and courtly power in general. In a poem by the most well known of court poets, Pierre de Ronsard, we find a little summary of the political-legal problems engendered by the sovereignty of the prince. Ronsard assiduously flattered important patrons in hopes of obtaining a benefice or other rewards, and in many cases he was more successful than Du Bellay, but in others he was not.[32] One of his great disap-

---

avons posé comme l'image de Dieu, ne peut faire un subiect egal à luy, que sa puissance ne soit aneantie." On these questions, see below, "God's Sovereignty," and Francis Oakley, *Omnipotence*.

[30] Cf. James I: "A good king will frame all his actions to be according to the Law; yet is he not bound thereto but of his good will, and for good example-giving to his subiects" (*The Trew Law of Free Monarchies* [1598], in *The Political Works of James I*, ed. Charles H. McIlwain [New York: Russell and Russell, 1965], p. 63). See James Daly, "The Idea of Absolute Monarchy in Seventeenth-Century England," *The Historical Journal* 21 (1978): 227–50, on various definitions of "absolute" in this context.

[31] This voluntarist version of the *lex digna* seems related at least structurally to the concept of Christian liberty, as Luther defines it (see epigraph), that is, power is the will to follow laws just as faith enables the Christian to submit to all contingencies and laws.

[32] See Isidore Silver, "Pierre de Ronsard: Panegyrist, Pensioner, and Satirist of the French Court," *Romanic Review* 45 (1954): 89–108. For an assessment of the relationship between

pointments was the indifference shown to him by someone Ronsard celebrated persistently, the Cardinal of Lorraine. Eventually the poet gave up,
and published a poem displaying his annoyance, "Le proces" (1565). The
poem is more or less a plea by the accuser, Ronsard, who lists his various
services to the cardinal and deplores his lack of reward. The poet then
imagines what the cardinal's defense would be, and renders a judgment
favorable to himself. The whole trial is of course problematic, as, strictly
speaking, the defendant is not obliged by the services rendered to him by
the poet. This is expressed in the exordium by Ronsard's insistence on the
priority of the cardinal's pleasure or whim:

> J'ay proces, Monseigneur, contre vostre grandeur,
> Vous estes defendeur, & je suis demandeur:
> J'ay pour mon advocat Calliope, & pour juge
> Phebus qui vous cognoist, & qui est mon refuge:
> Et pour vostre advocat vous avez seulement
> Il me plaist, je le veux, c'est mon commandement.[33]

[I bring suit, Monseigneur, against your greatness; you are the defendant, and
I am the accuser: I have as my lawyer Calliope, and as a judge Phoebus, who
knows you, and who is my protection. And as your lawyer you have only "it
pleases me," "I want it," "that is my order."]

Ronsard can be successful in his "suit" only if he can deprive Charles de
Lorraine of his status as prince, cardinal, or Ronsard's "master" and have
him considered a "personne privée," which would make the contract binding. There is, however, no way of forcing the cardinal to become a private
person; all Ronsard can do is exhort him to do so, and to "think of himself"
as one:

> Or devant que plaider il ne faut penser estre
> Prince ny Cardinal, Monseigneur, ny mon maistre,
> Issu de Charlemagne, & de ce Godeffroy
> Qui par armes se feit de Palestine Roy,
>
> . . . .
>
> Mais il faut penser estre un d'entre le vulgaire,
> Et personne privée: autrement mon affaire
> Auroit mauvaise issue, & sans heureux succes
> Je serois en danger de perdre mon proces.
>
> (pp. 17–18, 7–10, 15–18)

---

his role as a courtier and his "personal" poetry, see Ullrich Langer, "A Courtier's Problematic
Defense: Ronsard's 'Responce aux injures,'" *Bibliothèque d'humanisme et Renaissance* 46
(1984): 343–55.

[33] Pierre de Ronsard, "Le proces," in *Oeuvres complètes* 13:17, 1–6.

[Now before pleading you should not think of yourself as prince or cardinal, Monseigneur, nor as my master, descendant of Charlemagne, and of that Godfrey who through arms made himself king of Palestine. . . . But you should think of yourself as one of the people, and as a private person: otherwise my case would have a bad end, and without success I would be in danger of losing my suit.]

The courtier is in fact flattering the cardinal into allowing himself to be bound by a contract, as a private person, as if there were no prior or external constraints to the "master." This unequal situation is emphasized by the fact that there is no superior instance of appeal, no one who could force the sovereign to keep his promise. If the cardinal is "annoyed" by being vanquished in a trial, the courtier can only appeal to the cardinal's "goodness," not to a superior agency: "Et si vous ennuyez de vous voir surmonté / J'appelle à mon secours vous & vostre bonté" (pp. 18–19, 33–34). Finally, Ronsard appeals implicitly to the *lex digna*, by which it is of greater "honor" to not deceive the less powerful by broken promises: "Peu d'honneur est receu / Quand par le grand seigneur le petit est deceu" (p. 19, 41–42). All ties are *internal* to the sovereign: it is his decision to become a *personne privée*, his decision to receive greater "honor" by keeping his promises.

At the end of the poem Ronsard does invoke "l'equité" as a principle that should oblige the cardinal: "Il faut que l'amendiez [i.e., that you pay amends to the poet], autrement l'equité / Ne seroit qu'un nom feinct, sans nulle authorité" (p. 28, 263–64). The fact that the poet again gives the cardinal the alternative—pay me or else equity is a word without authority—seems to suggest that equity is a matter of the conscious choice of the powerful, not something with unquestioned prior authority.[34] The courtly situation radicalizes the unboundness contained for Bodin in the idea of sovereignty: the *princeps*-patron is truly *legibus solutus*.

God's Sovereignty

The various terms defining the king's sovereignty in early modern political theory are closely duplicated in theological discourse of the Middle Ages and early Renaissance. *Placitum, obligatio, alligatio, promissio, absolutus,* and

[34] This poem can be read as a surreptitious self-aggrandizement of the poet as well: Ronsard attributes great eloquence to Charles de Lorraine, who must be kept from speaking too long by Phoebus, lest he win his case. Of course, Ronsard's epideictic eloquence is what made him deserving of reward in the first place, so in the end he is like the cardinal, or rather, puts himself into the place of the cardinal. Flattery of the sovereign often contains such an implicit arrogation of sovereignty to oneself, a desire to be in a position to exercise one's whim. This structural reversal is similarly contained in Du Bellay's *Regrets*, as I will show below.

voluntas are to be found in discussions of royal as well as divine power. The reason is partly historical and terminological. In addition, I think, there is a basic similarity in conceiving the relationship between the powerful and the less powerful.

Historically, the common influence of Roman law seems the strongest reason for this terminological overlap. In Western Christianity the most important common source of theological and political thought was the Bible; the Vulgate was suffused with Roman legal terminology simply because of the Roman legal culture of the early Christian scholars. Tertullian, Cyprian, Lactantius, Jerome, and Ambrose were all formed in that culture and used terms derived from Roman law.[35] The combination of Roman legal terminology and Christian theology was, of course, far from unproblematic,[36] but perhaps simply for lack of alternatives the overlapping terminology persists. This results in conceptual parallels too striking to be dismissed.[37] In the specific question of sovereignty the theoretical problems just discussed are mirrored in theological discussions of God's power to do whatever he pleases.

The most convenient way of defining God's sovereignty might lead through the problem of man's merit.[38] God appears to have promised us that he will reward us, on certain conditions, with grace and salvation.[39] Given, then, that we have, with the help of God, fulfilled those conditions, does God *owe* us salvation? Is God our debtor (*debitor*)? In spite of his anti-Pelagian arguments, Augustine seems to allow for a certain usage of *debitor*. God does not owe us anything in return for something we have given him (for we cannot give him anything he does not already have). He "owes" us a reward because he has freely promised that he would reward us, or because it pleased him to promise us: "Debitor enim factus est, non aliquid a nobis accipiendo, sed quod ei placuit promittendo."[40] God was not constrained by anyone to promise this to us, and he will hold his promise not because he is constrained by anything outside of himself, but by his very nature, that is, his truthfulness, goodness, and faithfulness. So, strictly

---

[35] See Ullmann, *Law and Politics*, pp. 32–50, and Hamm, *Promissio*, pp. 462–66.

[36] See Hamm, *Promissio*, pp. 53–56, for Cardinal Laborans's critique of civil law terminology in theological discussion.

[37] See Kantorowicz, *The King's Two Bodies*, pp. 87–192, for many such parallels; Kantorowicz is especially concerned with the distinction between the public and private person; see also Oakley, *Omnipotence*, esp. pp. 93–122, on sovereignty.

[38] See above, Chapter Two, for a fuller discussion of *meritum de congruo* and *meritum de condigno*. I am interested here in what concerns God, not man.

[39] Such as in Zech. 1:3: "Convertimini ad me, ait Dominus exercituum, Et convertar ad vos," and 2 Tim. 4:8: "In reliquo reposita est mihi corona iustitiae, quam reddet mihi Dominus in illa die iustus iudex: non solum autem mihi, sed et iis, qui diligunt adventum eius."

[40] *Sermo* 158.2.2, in *Patrologiae cursus completus*, ed. J.-P. Migne (Paris: L. Migne, 1845), 38:863. See the discussion of this passage in Hamm, *Promissio*, pp. 8–11.

speaking, he does not depend on *us* in any way. He is only a *debitor* because he himself has promised freely and not because he was occasioned to promise in return for some human deed or other necessity. The decision to promise, and thus bind himself, is a sign of his sovereignty, for he was not obliged to do so—it pleased him.

All of this sounds familiar, for the secular sovereign's decision to bind himself to his own laws must, under absolutist theory, be similarly free, since otherwise he would not be sovereign. However, the difficulties posed by Bodin's legal analysis of *princeps legibus solutus est* are not resolved here. First, no one can "promise" anything if the promise is merely to follow one's own will, that is, if it is allowable for one to change one's mind. There must be conditions not subject to one's will that are binding. Second, no one can impose a law upon himself such that he cannot revoke it at a later date (such as in a testament). Since God's promise to reward man's behavior allows of no conditions outside of himself (he is the one infusing man with the capacity to please him, by his *gratia creata*), he cannot "promise," according to the first problem. Furthermore, since the "promise" is a free and unrequired one, there is nothing prior to it or outside of it that would prevent God from changing his mind. Can God, in other words, be *obliged* by his promise?

The implications of Roman law conflict with the conviction held by anti-Pelagian Christian theologians that God is essentially sovereign and free, for under Roman law any contract or promise is a kind of bind or tie, whereas it is of the essence of many medieval views of God that he be free of any ties, by virtue of his omnipotence. Medieval theologians are aware of this problem and protest against the implications of the terminology they are using.[41] The Franciscans, especially, reject any strict *obligation* of God by insisting on a distinction between the two powers of God or, more precisely speaking, the two ways in which his power may be perceived. *De potentia absoluta* God is not bound to his promise, that is, he could have chosen a different order of salvation than he did, and hypothetically he could change the current order. In this sense he is *legibus solutus* and consistently sovereign. He is also not tied or obliged by anything external to himself to fulfill any promise he may have made. He could save undeserving people and not save even those who possess the habit of grace. However, *de potentia ordinata*, he has committed himself to a certain order, and although the latter is contingent, it is contingent upon God, who is reliable and truthful. This is the basic argument of Duns Scotus, as he discusses the question "Utrum in anima viatoris sit necesse ponere charitatem creatam

---

[41] See Hamm, *Promissio*, on Cardinal Laborans (above, note 36), and Peter Lombard, *Sent.* I d 43 c unicum: "Sed, ut mihi videtur, hoc verbum debet venenum habet. Multiplicem enim et involutam tenet intelligentiam, nec Deo proprie competit, qui non est debitor nobis, nisi forte ex promisso, nos vero ei debitores sumus ex commisso" (vol. 1, pt. 2, p. 300).

formaliter inhaerentem? [Is it necessary to posit in the soul of the Christian wayfarer a formally inherent habit of grace?]"; it is worth reproducing the entire passage, which is central in defining God's sovereignty:

> Dico quod sicuti in Deo ponitur duplex potentia, scilicet ordinata et absoluta, ita et duplex necessitas ei correspondens. Deus autem de potentia absoluta non necessitatur ut infundat charitatem informantem animam, ad hoc ut justificet impium, et acceptet ipsum ad vitam aeternam, *quia potentiam suam non alligavit Sacramentis*, nec forte alicui formae creatae, quando immediate possit per se, quidquid potest cum causa secunda, quae non est essentia rei, potentia tamen sua ordinata non justificat aliquem, nisi conferendo sibi charitatem, qua acceptatur ab ipso; quae potentia dicitur ordinata, non secundum propria principia practica, quia illa sunt necessaria, sed secundum suas leges quas statuit, contra quas potest de potentia absoluta, quod si alias statueret, et illae etiam leges essent rectae.[42]

> [I say that as in God one finds a double power, namely, ordained and absolute, so also is there a double corresponding necessity. God is not necessitated, by virtue of his absolute power, to infuse charity (i.e., grace) into the soul, such that he might justify the impious and accept him in eternal life, for he has not bound his power to sacraments, and not to any created form, as he can do immediately by himself whatever he can do by a secondary cause which is not the essence of the thing; however his ordained power does not justify someone except by conferring onto him charity, through which he is accepted by God; this power is called ordained, not according to his inner principles, for these are necessary, but according to his laws which he has set down, against which he is able to act by virtue of his absolute power, because if he laid down different ones, these laws would also be just.]

God cannot be tied by the sacraments; he can do things immediately that normally are done through secondary causes. The only limit to his absolute power is the principle of noncontradiction. Thus God's absolute power is a way of avoiding saying that he can be obliged.

The idea that as author of laws God cannot be obliged by those laws is already suggested by Geoffroy de Poitiers ("Cum enim auctor sit legum,

---

[42] John Duns Scotus, *Reportata parisiensia* I d 17 q 1 (in *Opera omnia*, ed. Wadding, 22:206; italics mine). See the discussion by Hamm on the term *promissio*, in *Promissio*, pp. 410–14. On the distinction between absolute and ordained powers, see Oakley, *Omnipotence*, pp. 42–65; Bannach, *Die Lehre von der doppelten Macht Gottes*; and McGrath, *Iustitia Dei* 1:119–28. See also Altensteig, *Vocabularius theologie*: "Potentia Dei est duplex, scilicet, absoluta & ordinata. Potentia ordinata est, quae leges sequitur à divina voluntate positas. Absoluta est quae abstrahit ab illis legibus" (pp. 715–16); and John Major, *In primum sententiarum* I d 43 q unica: "Potentia absoluta dei se extendit ad illa quae contradictionem non implicant. . . . Alia est potentia dei ordinata: et est illa quae est conformis legi ordinate quae nobis constat per Scripturam vel revelationem" (Paris: I. Badius, 1519, f. c col. ii).

nulla lege potest obligari [As he is verily the author of the laws, he cannot be obliged by any law]").[43] The principle that no one can impose a law on himself is also brought into this question by a contemporary of Scotus, Petrus Paludanus ("Ergo ex hoc ipse non obligatur nec etiam ex promisso, quia nemo potest sibi legem imponere, a qua non liceat sibi recedere [Therefore he himself is not obliged by this, nor even by a promise, because no one can impose a law on himself, from which it would not be permitted to him to withdraw]").[44] The tradition of divine sovereignty is summed up, finally, by Ockham: "Deus autem nulli tenetur nec obligatur tamquam debitor [God is held by nothing nor is obliged as debtor]."[45] God's sovereignty is conceived of as an absolute freedom from external constraints or ties, on the one hand, and the voluntary decision to bind himself, on the other. Especially the Franciscan tradition emphasizes this sovereignty, and the dialectic between the two powers of God. As we have seen, this dialectic is mirrored in the dual nature of the secular sovereign's power, the *lex regia* and the *lex digna*.[46]

I will summarize and generalize by reiterating some more or less equivalent principles which run through the political and theological discussions. I take these statements to characterize a certain ideology, that of an early modern individualism. This individualism is by no means dominant in the Renaissance, for in many ways individual persons tend to choose and act according to social patterns that preclude any real notion of the individual as essentially preceding constraints.[47] Nevertheless, the following statements seem to structurally unite the political, the theological, and the literary, or at least aspects of Renaissance poetics put into practice.

—The author of a system is never bound by that system, absolutely speaking.
—The existence of a system implies an origin that is outside of the system. "Outside" means inaccessible to the system.
—If the author of a system binds himself, it is in a paradoxical gesture that

[43] Quoted by Hamm, *Promissio*, p. 126 n. 56.

[44] Quoted by Hamm, *Promissio*, p. 413 n. 132.

[45] Ockham, *Sent.* II d 19 H. Quoted by Hamm, *Promissio*, p. 420.

[46] On the possible connection between Scotist "voluntarism" and Bodin's absolutism, see Margherita Isnardi Parente, "Le volontarisme de Jean Bodin: Maïmonide ou Duns Scot?" in *Jean Bodin: Verhandlungen der internationalen Bodin Tagung in München*, ed. Horst Denzer (Munich: C. H. Beck, 1973), pp. 39–51.

[47] See the suggestive discussion of the epistemological makeup of Renaissance culture in Timothy J. Reiss, *The Discourse of Modernism* (Ithaca: Cornell Univ. Press, 1982). To use his own terms, if anything, I am tracing the emergence of an "analytico-referential" discourse presupposing the notion of a transcendent subject, by focusing on the extreme conceptual experiments that are theological discussion of God's freedom and political discussion of the notion of absolutism itself. It should be clear from the outset that I am *assuming* that intellectual culture of the period is still primarily collectively "patterned."

always recalls an initially unbound state, for, logically, such a gesture is impossible.

—The recalling of the unbound state is essential to the author's status as author.

Du Bellay and the Voluntary

What, if anything, do these statements have to do with Du Bellay's writing? On the face of it, very little. Du Bellay seems more like the irremediably *bound* person. He has no power; he is poor; he must do boring work; he is relatively uneducated; he lacks support from a patron; he is in a place that he would rather not be in. "Le malheur me poursuit, & tousjours m'importune [Misfortune pursues me, and always torments me]" (43, 11); "Je suis . . . serviteur inutile [I am a useless servant]" (46, 14); "Moy qui suis moins que rien [I who am less than nothing]" (49, 9): there are hardly any sonnets in the *Regrets* that do not point out in some way the poet's oppressed condition.[48] The most dramatic image of oppression is undoubtedly contained in the opening of sonnet 21:

> Conte [Nicolas Denisot], qui ne fis onc compte de la grandeur,
> Ton Du Bellay n'est plus. Ce n'est plus qu'une souche
> Qui dessus un ruisseau d'un doz courbé se couche.
>
> (1–3)

[Count, you who never insisted on grandeur, your Du Bellay is no longer. It is only a tree trunk which lies above a creek with a bent back.]

The poet refers to himself in the third person, he is nothing but a lifeless object occupying little space, in a perfect figuration of melancholy.

Du Bellay has been abandoned by the Muse and, more importantly, by royal favor. Other poets, such as Ronsard, enjoy the court's attention and its generosity, but he, Du Bellay, is "absent des raiz de [s]on Soleil [absent from the sun's rays]" (8 , 9) and is not inspired by its warmth. In a sonnet that repeats conventions of Neoplatonic poetic inspiration, Du Bellay recalls a period when his works were read by the court and he composed poetry with a "fureur d'esprit." But now that has changed:

[48] Du Bellay likes to *list* his misfortunes, for example, in sonnet 79: "Je n'escris point d'amour, n'estant point amoureux, / Je n'escris de beauté, n'aiant belle maistresse, / Je n'escris de douceur, n'esprouvant que rudesse, / Je n'escris de plaisir, me trouvant douloureux," etc. Each line indicates a personal misfortune or a complaint about his Roman "exile." The anaphoric "Je n'escris" is slightly ironic, given that he ends up writing a sonnet about what he does not write about. On Du Bellay's writing as purifying itself through obstacle and misfortune, see Floyd Gray, *La poétique de Du Bellay* (Paris: Nizet, 1978), esp. pp. 59–110 ("Sermo pedestris").

Ores je suis muet, comme on voit la Prophete
Ne sentant plus le Dieu, qui la tenoit sujette,
Perdre soudainement la fureur & la voix.
Et qui ne prend plaisir qu'un Prince luy commande?
L'honneur nourrit les arts, & la Muse demande
Le theatre du peuple, & la faveur des Roys.

(7, 9–14)

[Now I am mute, as one sees the Prophetess, no longer feeling the God who held her, suddenly lose furor and voice. And who does not take pleasure in receiving a prince's order? Honor nourishes the arts, and the Muse demands the audience of the people, and the favor of kings.]

The poet is no longer "subject" to the sibyl, he is no longer "commanded" by a prince. The kind of poetry written at the court is perhaps simply a *poésie de commande*; one's subjection to the Muse is occasioned by one's subjection to the king. This is all positive, and inspiration, the patron's favor and power, and one's own pleasure go together. The conventional vocabulary of pleasant subjection and bondage characterizes Du Bellay's description of inspired poetry, especially in the prefatory poem to D'Avanson:

Leur chant flatteur [of the nine Muses] a trompé mes esprits,
Et les appaz aux quels elles m'ont pris,
D'un doulx lien ont englué mes aelles.
Non autrement que d'une doulce force
D'Ulysse estoient les compagnons liez.

(46–49)

[Their flattering song has deceived my spirits, and the traps in which they have caught me, with a sweet bind, have limed my wings. Not otherwise, but by a sweet force the companions of Ulysses were bound.]

Yet this longing for pleasant and profitable subjection is bad faith. When Du Bellay describes what *he* is doing now, he describes a kind of writing he has voluntarily adopted, by refusing to write like those who are in favor at the court and who are inspired by a divine *afflamen*. Du Bellay's suffering is a suffering he has chosen, which allows him to be insubstantial, without ties or obligation. The only "ties" might be his own verses, recording his every whim; in their very fragmentariness and contingency they are signs of his will. In the introductory sonnet, after repeated proclamations of what he does *not* want to do ("Je ne veulx point"), Du Bellay ends up telling the reader what he does want:

Je ne peins mes tableaux de si riche peinture,
Et si hauts argumens ne recherche à mes vers,

Mais suivant de ce lieu les accidents divers
Soit de bien, soit de mal, j'escris à l'adventure.
Je me plains à mes vers, si j'ay quelque regret,
Je me ris avec eulx, je leur dy mon secret,
Comme estans de mon coeur les plus seurs secretaires.

(1, 5–11)

[I do not paint my paintings so richly, and I do not seek out such lofty ideas
for my verse, but following of this place the diverse accidents, either good or
bad, I write at random. I complain to my verse, if I have a sorrow, I laugh with
them, I tell them my secret, as they are the surest secretaries of my heart.]

The flexibility and easy movement of his verse is deceiving, for anyone
attempting to imitate the poet will be working in vain, as the next sonnet
emphasizes: "En vain travaillera, me voulant imiter [He who wants to imitate me works in vain]" (2, 14). Du Bellay demonstrates his *choice* of subjects first, and then shows how unforeseeable his writing will be, since in
effect his writing depends precisely on his (changeable) whims ("j'escris à
l'adventure") and the diverse events of his own situation ("les accidents
divers"). This sort of poetry wants to be unconventional; it displays its own
privateness and inaccessibility as it goes through the motions of choosing
to write again and again. This display of authorial privacy belongs to the
satiric genre as such, especially to "Horatian" satire, but the reiterated use
of such conventions of unconventionality must be understood as a more
general cultural gesture. I am suggesting that poetic or satiric sovereignty
takes on a meaning in the context of other contemporary discussions of
sovereignty that is not simply summarized by its place in a genre. Du Bellay
is being a satiric poet here, and his satiric sovereignty is demonstrated in
opposition to other genres or modes of inspiration, such as epic or lyric.
But he is also participating in a more general structure of sovereignty, of
which he seems aware, and which in turn informs his writing.

Du Bellay's vision of poetic sovereignty is expressed most coherently
when the poet finds himself in the most desperate state. In a poem addressed to "Vineus" (probably Jérôme de la Rovère), he complains first
that "[de] tous les chetifs le plus chetif je suis [of all the lowly I am the
lowliest]" and exclaims, "O que je suis comblé de regrets, & d'ennuis! [Oh
how I am filled with regrets and annoyances!]" (42, 2, 7). He goes on to
sketch out a state of poetic bliss in which he would be a satiric poet like
Pasquin or Marphore, who were able to write what pleased them:

Pleust à Dieu que je fusse un Pasquin ou Marphore,
Je n'aurois sentiment du malheur qui me poingt,
Ma plume seroit libre, & si ne craindrois point
Qu'un plus grand contre moy peust exercer son ire.

Assure toy Vineus que celuy seul est Roy,
A qui mesmes les Roys ne peuvent donner loy,
Et qui peult d'un chacun à son plaisir escrire.

(8–14)

[Were I only a Pasquin or Marphore, I would not feel the misfortune that torments me; my pen would be free, and so I would not fear that a more powerful person could exercise his wrath against me. Be sure, Vineus, that only he is king, on whom even the kings cannot impose a law, and who can write at his pleasure about everyone.]

The sovereign satirist is above his own misfortune, that is, he is not obliged to himself, as he is not obliged to others, whose ire he does not fear. He is also the last instance of judgment or appeal, since no one can impose a law on him, whereas he is free to write anything he wants to about anyone, "à son plaisir."[49]

The ideal of the personal sovereignty of the satirist participates, in Du Bellay's poetry, in at least two cultural traditions: the legal-political and the ethical-Stoic. The former clearly influences the choice of terms in sonnet 42, and the latter determines the ideal of sovereignty expressed in another poem, addressed to Du Bellay's friend, J.-A. de Simiane, seigneur de Gordes. His friend complains that Du Bellay is becoming arrogant, against which the poet protests, emphasizing not only his integrity but especially his ignorance of the ambitious courtier life:

Tu dis que Dubellay tient reputation,
Et que de ses amis il ne tient plus de compte:
Si ne suis-je Seigneur, Prince, Marquis, ou Conte,
Et n'ay changé d'estat ny de condition.
Jusqu'icy je ne sçay que c'est d'ambition,
Et pour ne me voir grand ne rougis point de honte,
Aussi ma qualité ne baisse ny ne monte,
Car je ne suis subject qu'à ma complexion.
Je ne sçay comme il fault entretenir son maistre,
Comme il fault courtiser, & moins quel il fault estre
Pour vivre entre les grands, comme on vid aujourdhuy.
J'honnore tout le monde, & ne fasche personne,
Qui me donne un salut, quatre je luy en donne,
Qui ne fait cas de moy je ne fais cas de luy.

(74)

---

[49] Cf. sonnet 48: "O combien est heureux, qui n'est contreint de feindre / Ce que la verité le contreint de penser, / Et à qui le respect d'un qu'on n'ose offenser, / Ne peult la liberté de sa plume contreindre!" (1–4). The free poet is here only under the constraint of truth, and free from external constraints. God and the poet are, of course, *veraces*.

[You say that Du Bellay has a name now, and that he no longer is concerned with his friends: but I am neither Sir, Prince, Marquis, or Count, and have changed neither my status nor my condition. Up till now I do not know what ambition is, and because I am not great I do not blush with shame; my quality neither lowers nor rises, for I am subject only to my own temperament. I don't know how to entertain a master, how to be a courtier, and less how one must be in order to live among the powerful, as one lives nowadays. I honor everyone, and annoy no one; whoever gives me a coin, I give him four back. Whoever is not interested in me does not interest me either.]

Contrary to the politically powerful, who have no obligation to their friends and forget them, the poet does not neglect his friends, although he too is free of "subjection" to anyone but himself. Underlying this serene integrity is undoubtedly a Stoic detachment from external things.[50] In addition, the private person exercises generosity, as he gives four *saluts* to those who give him one. The ethical realm of private contracts and exchanges allows for a constancy of "quality," that is, a freedom from the vicissitudes of favor and disfavor, and for the absence of subjection to anything but one's own nature. The orderly private life is, then, the free life in that it is an order that one chooses. The free inner realm is simply an absence of external "subjection" or constraints. If one is constrained, the constraint comes from within and is exercised by one's own equity and integrity.

Clearly, however, this ethical, Stoic vision of private sovereignty is incompatible with the ideal of satiric writing *à son plaisir*; one has only to look at any one of the various sonnets satirizing life in papal Rome to see that Du Bellay can hardly claim, "J'honnore tout le monde, & ne fasche personne" (12). The wish to be essentially free from *any* obligation is already hinted at in the praise of his own generosity, his *liberalitas* (13). If in fact he rewards to excess those who have given him something, he is exercising an essentially royal or divine privilege. What is suggested is the wish to be in a position to be royally generous. The critical impulse of satire undermines the Stoic vision of personal serenity; the desire to be authentically sovereign, essentially unbound, remains at the heart of the poet's Stoic private disguises. The wish to be free from constraints has a seemingly inherent tendency to absolutize itself.

This desire is expressed again and again through Du Bellay's insistence

[50] For example, "Libertas est animum superponere iniuriis et eum facere se, ex quo solo sibi gaudenda veniant, exteriora diducere a se, ne inquieta agenda sit vita omnium risus, omnium linguas timenti" (Seneca the Younger, *De constantia* 19.2). The ideal of personal equity is expressed similarly to Du Bellay by Guillaume Du Vair; justice can be divided into three parts, according to what it incites us to do: "L'une, à vivre honnêtement, sans violer les lois de Dieu et du pays; l'autre, à n'offenser personne ne de fait ne de parole; la troisième, à rendre à chacun ce qui lui appartient" (*De la sainte philosophie*, p. 46).

on his will. We have seen this insistence in the opening sonnet ("Je ne veulx point"), where anaphora highlights the poet's refusal to write like others. Similar instances of the poet's initial willfulness characterize his statements concerning the composition of the *Regrets*: "Je ne veulx pour un vers alonger, / M'accoursir le cerveau [I do not want to shorten my brain in order to lengthen a verse]" (2, 4–5); "Je ne veulx fueilleter les exemplaires Grecs [I do not want to leaf through Greek books]" (4, 1); "Je ne veulx point Juppiter assommer [I do not want to assault Jupiter]" (188, 1); "Aveques la vertu je veulx au ciel monter [With virtue I want to climb to heaven]" (189, 13). Poetry is a way of imagining a state of unconstrainedness in a life oppressed by obligations and troubles; it allows the projection of a state of pure priority through the exercise of one's will.

To do things "à son plaisir" (42, 14) is to duplicate the non-economy of the sovereign. It is a way of not being attached to the system of exchanges governing beings obliged by and subject to the law. This non-economy (or, perhaps, a quasi-theological gift economy) means in addition that one's product, the poem, is not a part of the system of reward or price that governs other products. For one is at the same time *hors prix* and *gratuit*, as poets before Du Bellay, such as Clément Marot, have complained. In sonnet 153 Du Bellay describes various other professions that enjoy material rewards, rewards that the poet cannot expect: "Car quel loyer veuls-tu avoir de ton plaisir, / Puis que le plaisir mesme en est la recompense? [For what reward do you want for your pleasure, since pleasure itself is the reward?]" (13–14). "Ton plaisir" is evidently equivalent to one's *own* pleasure in writing poetry; the second "plaisir," one's "recompense," can be taken to refer again to one's own pleasure, or to the pleasure created in the reader or the listener. In the former case, the poet's reward is his own pleasure in composing poetry, so the poet writes for himself, or in an exchange with himself, rather than in exchange for something else. The poet does not oblige and is not obliged by anything external (he gives to himself, as it were); he is as God or the sovereign in respect to his writing. Neither God nor the sovereign exchange, absolutely speaking, with others; they act autonomously. If one takes the second "plaisir" to refer to the listener's pleasure as well, then poetry becomes part of a courtly system of pleasure. The paradigmatic listener is the prince, and poetry is oriented toward his pleasure or favor. This pleasure, as the rest of the sonnet makes clear, is far from lucrative, and remains just that—that is, is not converted into material reward. So pleasure is simply outside of the economic sphere, and sets the person experiencing it apart from the rest of society. It is the sign of autonomy, of doing what one wills, even if one is poor.

Poverty is also the implied subject of the final sonnet, a whimsical plea for reward that compares divine and royal power:

Sire, celuy qui est, a formé toute essence
De ce qui n'estoit rien. C'est l'oeuvre du Seigneur:
Aussi tout honneur doit flechir à son honneur,
Et tout autre pouvoir ceder à sa puissance.
On voit beaucoup de Roys, qui sont grands d'apparence,
Mais nul, tant soit il grand, n'aura jamais tant d'heur
De pouvoir à la vostre egaler sa grandeur:
Car rien n'est apres Dieu si grand qu'un Roy de France.
Puis donc que Dieu peult tout, & ne se trouve lieu
Lequel ne soit encloz sous le pouvoir de Dieu,
Vous, de qui la grandeur de Dieu seul est enclose,
Elargissez encor sur moy vostre pouvoir,
Sur moy, qui ne suis rien: à fin de faire voir,
Que de rien un grand Roy peult faire quelque chose.

(191)

[Sire, he who is, has formed all essences from what was nothing. That is the work of the Lord: thus all worldly honor must bend down before his honor, and all other power cede to his power. One sees many kings who are great in appearance, but no one, as great as he may be, will ever have so much fortune to be able to equal your greatness: for nothing after God is as great as a king of France. Since, therefore, God can do everything and there is no place that is not enclosed by God's power, you, whose greatness is enclosed only by God, extend your power also to me, who am nothing, so as to show that out of nothing a great king can make something.]

The final sonnet of the *Regrets* evokes God's creation ex nihilo and God's omnipotence, then describes royal power in similar terms, as limited, *enclose*, only by God himself. Since God can do anything ("Puis donc que Dieu peult tout"), the king ought to be able to imitate him even in his powers of creation, and make something out of nothing, that is, "reward" the poet. This reward is not really inherent in the poet's work; perhaps the only motivation the king has is to display ("faire voir") his power. The rewarding of the poet is thus a gratuitous act in the same sense that the creation of the universe was a free act of God. When the king "rewards" the poet, he is not, strictly speaking, fulfilling any obligation, since the poet is "nothing"; rather, he is demonstrating his sovereignty, his *lack* of obligation to anyone except God.

As whimsical as this exhortation—or rather, supplication—may seem, it does present a secular version of free creation, for a creation ex nihilo is precisely not constrained by any necessity outside of the creator.[51] The ter-

---

[51] See above, Chapter Three, on the distinction between *creator* and *artifex* in medieval theology.

minology is not quite consistent, for the expression "formé toute essence / De ce qui n'estoit rien" seems to suppose some sort of material that was there before and "formed" by God. Similarly, the poet cannot literally be *rien*—only *peu de chose*, if one will—except that his poetry is, as we have seen, outside of any economic measure. But, as especially the Latin version shows,[52] divine and royal sovereignty is defined as free creation, as a lack of prior constraints. Thus the sonnet collection ends with the same vision of autonomy that it started with. The initial voluntary gesture is mirrored in the final acknowledgment of divine and royal sovereignty. The poetic gesture cannot be measured; it is as inaccessible as the divine and royal decisions to create something out of nothing.

Negative Sovereignty

The author of the rhetoric *Ad C. Herennium* lists, as an example of *commutatio*, a saying attributed to Aristarchus of Samothrace by Porphyry: "Ea re poëmata non facio, quia cuiusmodi volo non possum, cuiusmodi possum nolo [I do not write poems, because I cannot write the sort I wish, and I do not wish to write the sort I can]" (trans. H. Caplan) (4.28.39). The example of Aristarchus, whose philological and critical severity prevents him from writing, or rather, causes him to choose not to write, is a commonplace.[53] The chiasmus-like structure of Aristarchus's sentence emblematizes the negative voluntaristic posture of the lucid satiric poet: What I will do I cannot; what I can do I will not. The impotence of the writer is here a precise reflection of his excessive will; "volo" . . . "nolo" embraces "(non) possum." This willfulness of negation confers, however, a sovereignty on the critic: if he does not write, it is because, strictly speaking, he wills or chooses not to. He is thus free from criticism by others and therefore inaccessible, guarded by his choice.

[52] A rough Latin version of this sonnet figures as the *first* poem of Du Bellay's *Epigrammata*, as Screech points out, and here the *creatio ex nihilo* is even more explicit: "Esse dedit cunctis, solus qui dicitur esse, / Omnia qui solus fecit, & ex nihilo" (1–2) and "Omnipotens igitur cum sit, qui cuncta creavit" (9) (*Poésies françaises et latines*, ed. Ernest Courbet [Paris: Garnier, 1919], 1:454).

[53] Aristarchus, editor of Homer, is the figure of the (sometimes overly) severe critic and grammarian in texts as widely ranging as Lucian, *Vera historia* 2.20; Ovid, *Ex Ponto* 3.9.23–24; Horace, *Epistula ad Pisones* 450; Quintilian, *Institutio oratoria* 1.4.20, and 10.1.54 and 59; Sextus Empiricus, *Adversus mathematicos* 1.44; Tertullian, *Apologeticum*, 3.7; Ronsard, *Abbregé de l'art poëtique françois*, ed. Laumonier, 14:20, 332; Montaigne, *Les essais* III, 13, p. 1075; Agrippa d'Aubigné, *Confession du sieur de Sancy* 2.2 (ed. Weber, p. 632). Du Bellay himself refers a few times to Aristarchus: *Deffence et illustration* 2.2 (p. 97); *L'olive*, "Au lecteur" (ed. E. Caldarini, [Geneva: Droz, 1974], p. 48); see also below.

Du Bellay uses the example of Aristarchus to describe, in the *Regrets*, the authority of the (pedantic) critic in terms of royal sovereignty:

> Ne t'esmerveille point que chacun il mesprise,
> Qu'il dedaigne un chacun, qu'il n'estime que soy,
> Qu'aux ouvrages d'autruy il veuille donner loy,
> Et comme un Aristarq' luymesme s'auctorise.
> Paschal, c'est un pedant': & quoy qu'il se deguise,
> Sera tousjours pedant'. Un pedant' & un roy
> Ne te semblent-ilz pas avoir je ne sçay quoy
> De semblable, & que l'un à l'autre symbolise?

(66, 1–8)

[Don't be surprised that he looks down on everyone, that he has esteem only for himself, that he wants to impose laws on the works of others, and that as an Aristarchus he is his own authority. Paschal: he is a pedant, and however he disguises himself, he will always be a pedant. A pedant and a king—don't they seem to you to have something in common, and to be in accord with each other?]

The king and the pedant are further comparable in that the king has his subjects and his kingdom, just as the pedant schoolmaster has his pupils and his school, according to the subsequent tercet. The sovereignty of Aristarchus is expressed by the fact that he constrains others, but himself remains unconstrained. He derives his authority not from outside, but from himself. His sovereignty is coextensive with his perfectly negative attitude: he criticizes everyone but himself, just as he sets down laws for everyone except himself.[54] Aristarchus is the perfect satirist in this precise sense: he is able to do whatever he pleases, and he is able not to do whenever he pleases, just as the king and as God. Everything depends on his willful decision.

The negative aspects of the *lex regia*, without the counterbalancing *lex digna*, become clear in the final lines of the sonnet, where the pedant is compared explicitly to a classical example of tyranny, the spectre of absolute power gone awry:

> Et c'est pourquoy jadis le Syracusain [Dionysus the Younger],
> Ayant perdu le nom de roy Sicilien,
> Voulut estre pedant', ne pouvant estre prince.

[54] The independence of the pedant is a theme of anticourt writing; see Philibert de Vienne, *Le philosophe de court*: "Vous les [the 'curieux' who investigate the arts and sciences] verriez à la Court plus mornes, plus tristes, plus melancholiques, ilz ne mengent que à leurs heures, ilz ne parlent sinon quand il leur plait, ilz ne riroient pas pour le Pape, ilz ne veulent estre subietz à Prince ne seigneur tant grand soit il, ilz trouvent mauvais tout ce que les autres sont, brief ilz ne plaisent à personne" (p. 47).

[And that is why the Syracusan, having lost the name of King of Sicily, wanted to be a pedant, not being able to be a prince].

The figure of the person who constitutes his own authority—pedant/critic, king, satirist—traverses the poetry of Du Bellay, and is structured by the concept of political and divine sovereignty, as I have defined it above.

In his ironic manual of instruction to prospective court poets, "Le poëte courtisan" (1559), Du Bellay again refers to Aristarchus. If the court poet follows only the judgment of those who are able to advance his interests, he will be thought of as a king among the erudite: "Tu tiendras le lieu d'un Aristarque / Et entre les sçavants seras comme un Monarque."[55] Just prior to this reference to the grammarian, Du Bellay advises the prospective courtier not to write anything, lest he be criticized by envious peers:

> Et à la verité, la ruse coustumiere,
> Et la meilleure, c'est rien ne mettre en lumiere:
> Ains jugeant librement des oeuvres d'un chascun,
> Ne se rendre subject au jugement d'aulcun.
>
> (121–24)

[And in truth the usual, and the best, ruse is not to produce anything; rather, judging freely the works of everyone else, you do not render yourself subject to the judgment of others.]

Du Bellay has transposed the willful refusal of Aristarchus into the court situation, where the freedom of the courtier depends on his ability to remain inaccessible to others while criticizing them. This sovereignty is of course an inversion of royal sovereignty, but it nevertheless is structurally identical to the lack of obligation essential to royal power. It is, as it were, the *lex regia* of the courtier. The successful courtier must be invisible. His being "nothing" is as much a measure of his power as the opposite is a measure of the king's power. This invisibility also implies an absence of constraint; the successful courtier must be able to choose freely to whom he will be obliged, that is, he must enjoy the freedom to be obliged to a prince but not to his peers or inferiors.

The "Poëte courtisan" takes up a by that time banal opposition between the courtier and the truly learned man who patiently studies the classical authors. The courtier follows only the court: "La court est mon autheur, mon exemple & ma guide" (p. 130, 10). This is equivalent to saying that the courtier-poet follows nature rather than art:

> Ce procés tant mené, & qui encore dure,
> Lequel des deux vault mieulx, ou l'art, ou la Nature,

---

[55] Joachim Du Bellay, *Oeuvres poétiques*, ed. Henri Chamard, 6 vols. (Paris: Droz, 1931), 6:137, 141–42.

En matiere de vers, à la court est vuidé:
Car il suffit icy que tu soyes guidé
Par le seul naturel, sans art & sans doctrine,
Fors cet art qui apprend à faire bonne mine.

(p. 132, 45–50)

[This question, debated for so long, and which still endures—which of the following is worth more in poetry, art or nature—is solved at the court; for it is sufficient here that you be guided by your natural inclination only, without art or knowledge, except for this art that teaches you to put on a good appearance.]

The following of nature is an element of the courtier's freedom; he is unconstrained by the study of poetic technique and the reading of ancients to be imitated. Following his "naturel" also means producing short, insubstantial poetry, such as *sonnets*, *dixains*, *chansons*, *rondeaux*, and *ballades*, rather than an epic (pp. 132–33, 51–54).[56] Of course, the best thing may be not to write at all, but only to judge others' writing, and it is with the figure of Aristarchus criticizing all and producing nothing that the poem ends.

The more successful the courtier becomes, then, the less he will write and publish, for his writings are means by which he can be bound and subjected. The vanishing point of the ideal courtier is the divine paradox of omnipresence and yet actual absence. God is everywhere, yet nowhere in a definable or limited sense. This is, as I have suggested, equally a feature of the king's absolute power.

If the courtier participates in the problem of sovereignty, what can be said about the poet's writing his ironic instruction manual to court life? In the exordium to his "Poëte courtisan" Du Bellay uses an extensive negative definition of his *propositio* that recalls the anaphoric refusals of the initial sonnets of his *Regrets*. This technique is also, of course, a kind of *praeteritio*, in that by showing what he chooses not to do, he also shows what he might have been able to do:

Je ne veulx point icy du maistre d'Alexandre
Touchant l'art poëtiq' les preceptes t'apprendre:
Tu n'apprendras de moy comment joüer il fault
Les miseres des Roys dessus un eschafault:
Je ne t'enseigne l'art de l'humble comoedie,
Ny du Mëonien la Muse plus hardie.

(pp. 129–30, 1–6)

---

[56] The court is bored with long works: "La longueur sur tout il convient que je fuye, / Car de tout long ouvraige à la court on s'ennuye" (p. 130, 13–14).

[I do not wish to teach you the precepts of the teacher of Alexander concerning the art of poetry: you will not learn from me how to represent the sufferings of kings on a stage: I do not teach you the art of humble comedy, nor the braver Muse of the Maeonian.]

Du Bellay similarly advises against the study of books: "Je ne veulx que long temps à l'estude il pallisse, / Je ne veulx que resveur sur le livre il vieillisse [I do not wish that he become pale through long study; I do not wish that he age by dreaming over a book]" (p. 131, 21–22). The injunctions against the study of Aristotle's *Poetics*, tragedy, comedy, and epic are introduced as a consequence of Du Bellay's willful refusal; the same rhetorical procedure is used to define what sort of poetry he will not write himself in the *Regrets*. The injunctions addressed to the courtier are meant to be ironic, but that irony is undercut by Du Bellay's own refusal to write epic, Apollo-inspired poetry.[57]

The underlying (but denied) identification with the courtier-poet is furthermore evident in Du Bellay's discussion of a rival poet arriving at the court. If Du Bellay's protégé encounters a newcomer to the court, he should resist his own feelings of envy and appear to welcome him. He should even introduce him to the king and serve as his guide to the court:

> Ainsi tenant tousjours ce pauvre homme soubz bride,
> Tu te feras valoir, en luy servant de guide:
> Et combien que tu soys d'envie époinçonné,
> Tu ne seras pour tel toutefois soubsonné.
>
> (p. 135, 92–96)

[So, always holding the poor man's bridle, you will make yourself seem worthy, by serving as his guide: and even though you may be consumed by envy, you will, however, not be suspected of it.]

Du Bellay's courtier-poet is thus able to constrain his rival ("tenant . . . ce pauvre homme soubz bride") while seeming to be free from envy himself. The rival is dependent on him, not vice versa. This is exactly the rhetorical situation of the poem as a whole, for Du Bellay is ironically offering, with

---

[57] There are other instances of parallels between what Du Bellay is doing in the *Regrets* and what he satirizes in the "Poëte courtisan": the Horatian "Pour un vers allonger ses ongles il ne ronge" (p. 131, 29) used to satirize the court poet is part of Du Bellay's own project in the *Regrets*: "Je ne veulx, pour un vers allonger, / M'accoursir le cerveau: ny pour polir ma ryme, / Me consumer l'esprit d'une songneuse lime, / Frapper dessus ma table ou mes ongles ronger" (2, 5–8). The exhortation to the courtier to follow his "seul naturel" ("Poëte courtisan," p. 132, 49) is quite close to Du Bellay's own "simple" writing in the *Regrets*: "J'escry naïvement tout ce qu'au coeur me touche" (21, 6). This is a frequent theme in Du Bellay's poetry; see, for example, his "Elegie amoureuse": "Me contentant de vous dire / Ce que je puis de mon amour escrire / Naïvement, sans art & fiction, / Comme sans art est mon affection" (*Divers jeux rustiques* 33 [1558], in *Oeuvres poétiques*, 5:134, 17–20).

his "Poëte courtisan," to guide a young rival through the labyrinth of courtly politics to the king's favor. Du Bellay projects himself into the (conventional) role of the old, successful courtier who is able to deal with rivals in a magnanimous way that preserves his own sovereignty.

The irony of the "Poëte courtisan" is a complicated matter. The very satire that Du Bellay is attempting, one that preserves his negative sovereignty, is what is necessary in order to be a successful courtier, who, in turn, is attacked through the satire itself. The author of such a self-contradictory—or, more precisely, self-suspending—writing becomes completely evanescent, as no determined position can be attributed to him. The dream of inaccessibility, of invisibility, underlies this self-effacing writing and is rendered explicit in a sonnet of the posthumously published *Amours* (1568). The poet announces his unwillingness to become, as Jupiter (and as Ronsard), a golden rain shower in order to seduce his beloved. Rather, he would prefer to possess the legendary ring of Gyges:

> Je souhaitte plustost pour voir ce beau visage
> Où le ciel a posé son plus parfaict ouvrage,
> L'anneau qui feit en Roy transformer un Berger.[58]

[I wish, rather, in order to see this beautiful face, where the heavens have put their most perfect work, to possess the ring that transformed a shepherd into a king.]

The royal invisibility conferred upon the poet is analogous to the inaccessibility required to maintain a perfectly "free" and powerful courtly position. The "nothing," the *rien* that is the poet in the final sonnet of the *Regrets*, is structurally equivalent to the absolute power of the king, and is an imitation of the power of the ultimate author, God.[59]

A well-known satiric poem from the *Divers jeux rustiques* (1558), "Contre les Petrarquistes" (first version published in 1553), will serve as a final example of satiric negative sovereignty. It is a poem that lists commonplaces of the Petrarchan but also of the Neoplatonic and generally classically inspired traditions of love poetry. It assumes, taking up a presumably contrary "Gallic" and medieval anticourtly position, that love poems

---

[58] In *Oeuvres poétiques*, rev. ed., ed. Chamard (Paris: Didier, 1970), 2:246, 20, 9–11. The legend is recounted by Plato (*Republic*, 359d–360b). See also, on this sonnet, the analysis of François Rigolot, in *Le texte de la Renaissance: Des rhétoriqueurs à Montaigne* (Geneva: Droz, 1982), pp. 207–12; he sees these phenomena in psychological, rather than ideological, terms.

[59] See the ending of Du Bellay's "Discours au roy sur la poësie" (composed ca. 1558, ed. 1560), which foreseeably claims that poetry, along with history, renders the king immortal through its praise. But the poet, as opposed to the historian, has the special quality of imitating God: "Cestuy-la [the poet] toutefois est trop plus admirable, / Et son oeuvre n'est moins que l'histoire durable, / Pource qu'en imitant l'autheur de l'univers, / Toute essence et idee il comprend en ses vers" (in *Oeuvres poétiques* 6:166, 113–16).

are always only expressions of physical desire. The poet denounces the Petrarchan and Platonic commonplaces as mere masks for the real intention of poets, sexual seduction. In doing this, he sets up an opposition between the artifice of conventional lyric and the more authentic self, which, when allowed to act in *franchise*, will pursue only physical pleasure. This opposition on the erotic plane is similar to the one encountered in the *Regrets* between the servile courtier and the ethical-Stoic man of personal liberty. In the end, however, there is no consistent way of defining that opposition; the poet's *franchise* cannot be defined as an ethical alternative, but is structured precisely as the negative sovereignty we have encountered elsewhere.

Du Bellay announces in the opening lines that he has forgotten the art of imitating Petrarch and will speak freely about love:

> J'ay oublié l'art de Petrarquizer,
> Je veulx d'Amour franchement deviser,
> Sans vous flatter, & sans me deguizer.[60]

The greater part of the poem, nevertheless, is a list of Petrarchan and general love poetry commonplaces that shows how insincere his rivals are, and that Du Bellay will not write this sort of poetry, although he could if he chose to. For example, the poet could describe his own suffering in conventionally hyperbolic terms:

> Si pour sembler autre que je ne suis,
> Je me plaisois à masquer mes ennuis,
> J'irois au fond des eternelles nuictz
> Plein d'horreur inhumaine:
> Là d'un Sisyphe, & là d'un Ixion
> J'esprouverois toute l'affliction.

> (p. 71, 41–46)

[If, in order to seem different from what I am, I amused myself by choosing to mask my troubles, full of inhuman horror I would go into the eternal nights; there I would suffer like Sisyphus and Ixion.]

This kind of writing is a matter of the writer's pleasure or whim ("Si . . . je me *plaisois* à masquer mes ennuis"), not a necessity. Du Bellay is showing that, after all, he *could* write conventional poetry, while at the same time he is criticizing it.

What, then, is his *true* nature? If he refuses to be like others, what is he in himself? There is rather little to go on here. Of the twenty-six stanzas that make up the poem, only two really describe the poet in his *franchise* in an affirmative way:

---

[60] In *Oeuvres poétiques* (Paris: Hachette, 1923), 5:69, 1–3.

Mais quant à moy, sans feindre ny pleurer,
Touchant ce poinct, je vous puis asseurer,
Que je veulx sain & dispos demeurer,
Pour vous faire service.
De voz beautez je diray seulement,
Que si mon oeil ne juge folement,
Vostre beauté est joincte egalement
A vostre bonne grace:
De mon amour, que mon affection
Est arrivee à la perfection
De ce qu'on peult avoir de passion
Pour une belle face.

(pp. 76–77, 189–200)

[As far as I am concerned, without disguising myself or crying, on this point I can assure you that I want to remain healthy and able, so as to serve you. Of your beauty I will only say that unless my eye completely misjudges, your beauty is joined with your grace; of my love, that my affection is as much passion as one can have for a pretty face.]

Du Bellay's "sincere" statement of desire is at the same time perfectly bland and couched in various conditions: *concerning* his health, he can tell her this and that; *if* his eye judges correctly, then she is beautiful; his love is great *relative* to expectations. His *franchise* is strangely insubstantial and, if anything, rather less than autonomous, for it contains a very conditional desire. Rather than encountering a Stoic independence from external conditions, we find, simply, a vague statement of *relative* desire.

The final stanza confirms this relativity of Du Bellay's *franchise*. If the lady prefers Petrarch to his honest desire after all, he is ready to write Petrarchan love lyric once again: "Si toutefois Petrarque vous plaist mieux, / Je reprendray mon chant melodieux" (p. 77, 201–2). His *franchise* has not gone so far as to cause him to refuse a return to "masks," if the lady is more easily seduced, or pleased, by his masks. In retrospect his "sincere" statements become as much a means to an end as the conventional poetry he so vehemently derides. If changing to insincere writing is such an easy decision, one wonders about "sincere" writing, which now is also determined by its functionality in seduction. The final stanza shows that Du Bellay's *franchise* is not an ethical stance, as it is subject to the same pragmatic end as its presumably unethical alternative, and can be rejected by reason of that end. Something else is in play here.

One of the rhetorical devices of this kind of satire is the complicity between reader and author in exposing the corruption of others. Thus Du Bellay establishes a complicity between himself as honest lover and his lady, who is allowed a glimpse of the malicious intentions of fellow love poets. Once she has understood the hypocrisy of Petrarchan poetry, she will be disabused enough not to require Du Bellay to write insincere verses, too. How could she then prefer Petrarchan poetry in the end, as is suggested in the final stanza? Or, to put it in different terms, why would the poet insist on presenting her with a choice? Clearly the rhetorical situation is not dialogic: the poet is more concerned with demonstrating his own virtuosity than with genuine seduction, on the one hand, or genuine self-representation, on the other. If the lady demands Petrarchan writing in spite of its insincerity, she will be requiring a technical exercise of the poet, and enjoying it as such. So the *choice* of styles is what matters, and it is in that choice that the flexible poet-lover establishes his *franchise*. Far from being an ethical stance, Du Bellay's freedom is one that allows him to do *anything*, dependent only on *plaisir*—his own ("si je me plaisois à . . .") or his lady's ("si toutefois Petrarque vous plaist mieux . . .").

The Proteus of styles remains as inaccessible in his prolixity as Aristarchus in his lack of production; neither produces what is *his*, neither renders the law governing himself accessible to others. The Protean lover, then, participates in the same structure of negative sovereignty as the critic-pedant and the courtier. That negative sovereignty is an ideological construct most evidently demonstrated in the maxim *princeps legibus solutus est*: for *princeps*, substitute *deus*, *poeta*, and *curialis*.

Sovereign Friendship: Montaigne and La Boëtie

Du Bellay cultivates inaccessibility as a mark of his power. This inaccessibility, I have suggested, can be understood through contemporary political and theological discourses on the sovereign. I wish to conclude this chapter by reflecting on an essay of Montaigne, the subject of which apparently runs counter to the insistence on lack of constraint as a sign of personal sovereignty. "De l'amitié [Of Friendship]" (I, 28) is an homage to Estienne de La Boëtie, a jurist, political writer, and poet, who died in 1563 and is remembered by the essayist as the perfect friend. Montaigne had intended to publish the young La Boëtie's political work, the *Discours de la servitude volontaire* [*Discourse on Voluntary Servitude*], with this essay, but he changed his mind when his friend's text was used in Huguenot polemics. "Voluntary servitude" is also precisely *friendship*, for it is a relationship that in a positive way combines two seemingly irreconcilable qualities: it is both purely voluntary (as opposed to obligatory, as are familial and marital relationships) and perfectly binding.

Friendship is a frequent subject of praise and analysis in antiquity, and Montaigne indeed takes his inspiration and various examples from dialogues and treatises dealing in part or entirely with friendship by Aristotle,

Cicero, Plutarch, Lucian, and Plato.[61] In the Renaissance these works not only were widely available and translated, but also served as a basis for a discourse on friendship that reflected humanist aspirations and imitation of classical values. An example of this discourse is the work of Montaigne's contemporary, the editor, translator, and Neoplatonic hermetic philosopher Blaise de Vigenère, who published together three dialogues on friendship (Plato's *Lysis*, Cicero's *De amicitia*, and Lucian's *Toxaris*), which he translated and to which he added his own preface and an introduction culled from Marsilio Ficino's commentary on Plato.[62] Vigenère's preface is in fact a "letter" to his friend Jean Andreossi in which he praises their friendship and adds his own reflections on its nature and degree of intensity. The etiology of their friendship is clear to him: they were of the same age, and Andreossi had an excellent reputation:

> La moindre ondee de vos vertus & merites m'a donné un desir de vous accoster & cognoistre: Ce desir apport une frequentation: La frequentation une mutuelle benevolence; & ceste cy une Amitié ferme & indissoluble à jamais; comme estant establie sur la vertu, son principal & plus asseuré fondement sur tous autres. [p. ii]

> [The least wave of your virtues and merits gave me a desire to meet and know you; this desire leads to frequentation; frequentation to mutual goodwill; the latter to a firm and indissoluble, eternal friendship, as it is based on virtue, its most important and most certain foundation among all others.]

Vigenère represents the origin of friendship in a perfectly conventional way. The reputation of virtue and merit precedes the actual meeting, which leads to greater knowledge and goodwill, which in turn produces an eternal friendship based on virtue.[63] Friendship is elaborately *motivated*, first

---

[61] For a discussion of friendship in the *Essais* in general, see the suggestive study by Barry L. Weller, "The Rhetoric of Friendship in Montaigne's *Essais*," *New Literary History* 9 (1977–1978): 503–23.

[62] Blaise de Vigenère, trans. *Trois dialogues de l'amitié: Le Lysis de Platon, et le Laelius de Ciceron; contenans plusieurs beaux preceptes, & discours philosophiques sur ce subject: Et le Toxaris de Lucian; ou sont amenez quelques rares exemples de ce que les amis ont fait autresfois l'un pour l'autre* (Paris: Nicolas Chesneau, 1579). For a brief introduction to Vigenère, see Marc Fumaroli, "Blaise de Vigenère et les débuts de la prose d'art française: Sa doctrine d'après ses Préfaces," in *L'automne de la Renaissance 1580–1630*, ed. Jean Lafond and André Stegmann, (Paris: Vrin, 1981), pp. 31–51.

[63] The gradual nature of the birth of friendship is emphasized also by Aristotle: "Further, such friendship [perfect friendship based on excellence] requires time and familiarity; as the proverb says, men cannot know each other till they have 'eaten salt together'; nor can they admit each other to friendship or be friends till each has been found lovable and been trusted by each. Those who quickly show the marks of friendship to each other wish to be friends, but are not friends unless they both are lovable and know the fact; for a wish for friendship

because each stage is explained and justified, and second because in its origin and its "foundation," friendship is dependent on virtue. Although Vigenère claims that Plato is the most important source, this is an essentially Ciceronian view. Friendship is "the most complete agreement in policy, in pursuits, and in opinions": "voluntatum, studiorum, sententiarum summa consensio."[64] It can exist only among good men (". . . sentio, nisi in bonis amicitiam esse non posse," 5.18), and it is impossible without virtue ("haec ipsa virtus amicitiam et gignit et continet nec sine virtute amicitia esse ullo pacto potest [but this virtue is the parent and preserver of friendship and without virtue friendship cannot exist at all]") (6.20).[65] The resemblance of virtuous men can lead to a friendship in which the friend is like another self: "Est enim is [amicus], qui est tamquam alter idem" (21.80).[66]

Thus, although friendship is not a utilitarian relationship of exchange of services (Cicero, *Laelius* 8.26–32), and in this sense is autonomous, it is nevertheless a relationship in the end dependent on the virtuousness of the friends. This is an important aspect of classical views of friendship, for the personal relationship is understood here as an ethically motivated gesture, a gesture that is *civic*, in that it is accessible and repeatable. Friendship is inserted into a network of values that provides its foundation and its explanation. Vigenère's own version of friendship imitates this classical ideal, and in so doing repeats another classical aspect of the discourse on friendship, namely, the comparison of exemplary friendships among each other, or to one's own friendship.[67]

---

may arise quickly, but friendship does not" (*Nicomachean Ethics*, 1156b 25–32). This is, as we will see, quite different from Montaigne's *sudden* friendship with La Boëtie.

[64] Cicero, *Laelius de amicitia* 4.15; in *Cicero's Works*, ed. and trans. William A. Falconer (Cambridge, Mass.: Harvard Univ. Press, 1933), vol. 20.

[65] See also Cicero, *Laelius* 27.100: "Virtus, virtus, inquam, . . . et conciliat amicitias et conservat. In ea est enim convenentia rerum, in ea stabilitas, in ea constantia; quae cum se extulit et ostendit suum lumen et idem aspexit agnovitque in alio, ad id se admovet vicissimque accipit illud, quod in altero est; ex quo exardescit sive amor sive amicitia." See also Aristotle, *Nicomachean Ethics* 1170a 13: "A virtuous friend seems to be naturally desirable for a virtuous man."

[66] This formula is found in Aristotle's *Nicomachean Ethics* 1166a 31 and 1170b 6, and in a somewhat different version in Diogenes Laertius's account of Aristotle's philosophy: a friend is "a single soul dwelling in two bodies" (*Lives of Eminent Philosophers*, ed. and trans. R. D. Hicks [Cambridge, Mass.: Harvard Univ. Press, 1925], 1.5.20). See also Jonathan's friendship with David, in 1 Sam. 18:1: "Anima Ionathae conglutinata est animae David, et dilexit eum Ionathas quasi animam suam"; similar expressions are in 1 Sam. 18:3 and 1 Sam. 20:17. In Plato's inconclusive dialogue, however, this resemblance of good men is problematized, for the perfectly good is self-sufficient and does not desire, thus does not love, a friend (*Lysis* 214d–215c). Aristotle responds to this argument by saying that friends are the greatest of external goods, and that to do good is better than to receive benefits, so the good man needs friends to whom he can do good, *qua* his goodness (*Nicomachean Ethics* 1169b 3–21).

[67] In Lucian's dialogue *Toxaris*, a Scyth and a Greek compare exemplary friendships in a

Montaigne's essay on friendship superficially follows conventional lines, but in fact it signals a departure from classical ethical discourse, and in this departure reproduces the private sovereignty discussed throughout this chapter. The first few pages of the essay are devoted, however, to a definition of friendship in opposition to other forms of affection or love (filial, paternal, fraternal, conjugal, homosexual, and heterosexual desire). Friendship is characterized by its autotelic nature—that is, there is no goal outside of friendship that determines it. Friendship has itself as its goal:

> Il n'est rien à quoy il semble que nature nous aye plus acheminé qu'à la societé. Et dit Aristote que les bons legislateurs ont eu plus de soing de l'amitié que de la justice. Or le dernier point de sa perfection est cetuy-cy. Car, en général, toutes celles que la volupté ou le profit, le besoin publique ou privé forge et nourrit, en sont d'autant moins belles et genereuses, et d'autant moins amitiez, qu'elles meslent autre cause et but et fruit en l'amitié, qu'elle mesme. (p. 184)[68]

> [There is nothing to which nature seems to have inclined us more than to society. And Aristotle says that good legislators have had more care for friendship than for justice. Now the ultimate point in the perfection of society is this. For in general, all associations that are forged and nourished by pleasure or profit, by public or private needs, are the less beautiful and noble, and the less friendships, insofar as they mix into friendship another cause and object and reward than friendship itself.] (p. 136)

Friendship is the natural perfection of social relationships, and this natural perfection is beyond any calculation of profit.[69] Montaigne also insists on the voluntary aspect of friendship, a condition sine qua non, which allows him to exclude familial and conjugal relationships from this category: "Et puis, à mesure que ce sont amitiez que la loy et l'obligation naturelle nous commande, il y a d'autant moins de nostre chois et liberté volontaire. Et nostre liberté volontaire n'a point de production qui soit plus proprement sienne que celle de l'affection et amitié" (p. 185) [And then, the more they

---

competition that is left without judgment, but that ends in a vow of friendship between the two competitors.

[68] All quotations are from the *Essais*, ed. Villey, rev. ed., ed. Saulnier. Translations are from *The Complete Essays of Montaigne*, trans. Frame. On the autotelic nature of friendship, see also Augustine's distinction between enjoyment (*fruitio*) and use (*usus*); the former is properly directed towards God, while the latter characterizes human relationships. On *fruitio*: "Frui autem est amore inhaerere alicui rei propter se ipsam [To enjoy something is to cling to it with love for its own sake]" (*On Christian Doctrine*, trans. D. W. Robertson, Jr. [Indianapolis: Bobbs-Merrill, 1958], 1, 3). Peter Lombard devotes the first distinction of his *Sentences* to this question (d 1 c 1–3). See below, note 74.

[69] Cf. Cicero: "Quapropter a natura mihi videtur potius quam ab indigentia orta amicitia, adplicatione magis animi cum quodam sensu amandi, quam cogitatione quantum illa res utilitatis esset habitura" (*Laelius* 8.27).

are friendships which law and natural obligation impose on us, the less of our choice and free will there is in them. And our free will has no product more properly its own than affection and friendship (p. 137)].[70] Similarly, Cicero insists on the truthful and "voluntary" nature of friendship.[71] In all of these senses Montaigne sets out a conventional, classical view of friendship.

But when the essayist concentrates on his friend La Boëtie, something else enters into the picture. Rather than depict their relationship as a voluntary, social gesture, Montaigne removes from it any motivation or explanation. Friendship is here a force beyond reason and choice, and is not necessarily dependent on virtue: "En l'amitié dequoy je parle, elles [our souls] se meslent et confondent l'une en l'autre, d'un melange si universel, qu'elles effacent et ne retrouvent plus la couture qui les a jointes. Si on me presse de dire pourquoy je l'aymois, je sens que cela ne se peut exprimer, qu'en respondant: Par ce que c'estoit luy; par ce que c'estoit moy" (p. 188) [In the friendship I speak of, our souls mingle and blend with each other so completely that they efface the seam that joined them, and cannot find it again. If you press me to tell why I loved him, I feel that this cannot be expressed, except by answering: Because it was he, because it was I (p. 139)]. When Montaigne is pressed to explain his choice of friend, he feels that it cannot be expressed, except by a final, simple declarative. Note the progression of the introductory sentence: the apodosis "je sens que cela ne se peut exprimer" bears the weight of the response to "si on me presse de dire pourquoy je l'aymois." In fact, it *cannot* be expressed, except by saying precisely *nothing*: "Par ce que c'estoit luy; par ce que c'estoit moy." This sentence gives us no information about La Boëtie, and none about Montaigne. It simply identifies, designates "him" and "me." Montaigne does not, for example, say that he loved La Boëtie for his virtue or wisdom (something which, say, Cicero's Laelius does not hesitate to declare). The Attic, or perhaps even Longinian, simplicity[72] of these two declarative sentences is such that the friendship between Montaigne and La Boëtie remains ineffable and thus perfectly unconstrained and unrepeatable. In

---

[70] The absolute voluntariness of friendship is underlined even more by Pierre Charron, who takes much of his material from Montaigne's *Essais*. In his *Trois livres de la sagesse* (1601) he defines friendship as follows: "[Souls in perfect friendship are] [t]res-libres & basties par le pur choix & pure liberté de la volonté, sans aucune obligation, occasion ny cause estrangere. Il n'y a rien qui soit plus libre & volontaire que l'affection" (in *Oeuvres . . . reveues, corrigees, & augmentees* [Paris, 1635; repr. Geneva: Slatkine, 1970], vol. 1, bk. 3, p. 72). His discussion of sovereignty (bk. 1, chap. 49) takes up the problem of self-binding in the terms we encountered in Bodin's analysis (see esp. bk. 1, p. 174).

[71] "In amicitia autem nihil fictum est, nihil simulatum et, quidquid est, id est verum et voluntarium" (Cicero, *Laelius* 8.26).

[72] On Montaigne's brevity, see, most recently, Antoine Compagnon, "A Long Short Story: Montaigne's Brevity," *Yale French Studies* 64 (1983): 24–50.

other words, Montaigne has escaped any "pressure" of explanation by his apodictic nondefinition.

In the following paragraph the essayist insists on the providential, non-rational nature of their union. Montaigne seems here to have completely abandoned the ethical-voluntary view of friendship he espoused in the beginning of the essay:

Il y a, au delà de tout mon discours, et de ce que j'en puis dire particulierement, ne sçay quelle force inexplicable et fatale, mediatrice de cette union. Nous nous cherchions avant que de nous estre veus, et par des rapports que nous oyïons l'un de l'autre, qui faisoient en nostre affection plus d'effort que ne porte la raison des rapports, je croy par quelque ordonnance du ciel: nous nous embrassions par noz noms. (p. 188)

[Beyond all my understanding, beyond what I can say about this in particular, there was I know not what inexplicable and fateful force that was the mediator of this union. We sought each other before we met because of the reports we heard of each other, which had more effect on our affection than such reports would reasonably have; I think it was by some ordinance from heaven. We embraced each other by our names.] (p. 139)

Friendship in this passage appears to involve something totally *involuntary* and beyond any one individual's capacities to explain or understand it. Montaigne does take up the commonplace of prior reputation ("par des rapports que nous oyïons l'un de l'autre"), but those reputations were not sufficient to justify the force of attraction they felt for each other ("qui faisoient en nostre affection plus d'effort que ne porte la raison des rapports"). One can explain this force only by recourse to some celestial order ("je croy par quelque ordonnance du ciel"). This recourse does not, however, mean that La Boëtie and Montaigne were friends *in order to* accomplish something (such as justice and equity). The explanatory recourse to celestial fatality is both conditional ("je croy," "*quelque* ordonnance") and empty: it remains that this friendship really can be conceived of only in terms of itself. As Montaigne says further along, "Cette cy [this friendship] n'a point d'autre idée que d'elle mesme, et ne se peut rapporter qu'à soy" (p. 189) [Our friendship has no other model than itself, and can be compared only with itself (p. 139)]. "Fatality" and "providential determination" provide meanings for the particular event, meanings *outside* of the friendship itself. This is not at all the case with Montaigne and La Boëtie, however, for their relationship precisely excludes any external condition or model. In other words, the recourse to celestial determination is another way of saying that their friendship is inexplicable.

The two friends' first encounter takes place not by providential wisdom, but by chance, during festivities: "Et à nostre premiere rencontre, qui fut par hazard en une grande feste et compagnie de ville, nous nous trouvasmes si prins, si cognus, si obligez entre nous, que rien des lors ne nous fut si proche que l'un à l'autre" (p. 188) [And at our first meeting, which by chance came at a great feast and gathering in the city, we found ourselves so taken with each other, so well acquainted, so bound together, that from that time on nothing was so close to us as each other (p. 139)]. The chance encounter contrasts with its effect on the two, who are "si prins, si cognus, si obligez" that they are closer to each other than to anything else. If this ternary formula recalls the *veni, vidi, vici* of the triumphant general, in fact it expresses not triumph in an active sense, but sudden and total constraint: Montaigne and La Boëtie are "taken" and "bound" by their meeting. This boundness is elaborated further along, in contradistinction to other, "soft," friendships:

> Ce n'est pas une speciale consideration, ny deux, ny trois, ny quatre, ny mille: c'est je ne sçay quelle quinte essence de tout ce meslange, qui, ayant saisi toute ma volonté, l'amena se plonger et se perdre dans la sienne; qui, ayant saisi toute sa volonté, l'amena se plonger et se perdre en la mienne, d'une faim, d'une concurrence pareille. Je dis perdre, à la verité, ne nous reservant rien qui nous fut propre, ny qui fut ou sien ou mien. (p. 189)

> [It is not one special consideration, nor two, nor three, nor four, nor a thousand: it is I know not what quintessence of all this mixture, which, having seized my whole will, led it to plunge and lose itself in his; which, having seized his whole will, led it to plunge and lose itself in mine, with equal hunger, equal rivalry. I say lose, in truth, for neither of us reserved anything for himself, nor was anything either his or mine.] (p. 139)

The inexpressibility of their relationship continues to manifest itself in symmetrical declaratives: Montaigne's will is seized and led to plunge itself into La Boëtie's will, which in turn is identified totally with Montaigne's will. In other words, neither will has any content, and neither will is prior to the other. This is an elaborate way of saying that nothing, in substance, can be said. Furthermore, total constraint equals total power, for Montaigne's total submission to La Boëtie's will is nothing less than La Boëtie's total submission to Montaigne's will. We are at the paradoxical *degré zéro* of will.

The perfect mirroring of absolute submission and absolute power is, I suggest, the very core of the problem of self-binding, or of promise to oneself, that we encountered in both political and theological discussions of sovereignty. For how can the sovereign deity or the sovereign prince lay down and promise to follow an order to which he cannot be bound by anything outside of himself? There must be a condition or rule external to the sovereign to which he can be held, for otherwise a promise is inconceivable. And yet that promise is exactly what the sovereign, through his *potentia ordinata* or his dignity, seems to declare, in the very absence of external constraint or necessity. The "free" promise to oneself is, in essence, an *inexplicable* gesture of self-binding, for all acts of God or the secular sovereign to the "outside" (*ad extra*) are contingent and not necessary.

We have seen an analogous progression in Montaigne's reflections on friendship. The essayist insists on the "voluntary," unobliged nature of perfect friendship, but once the origin and motivation of his friendship with La Boëtie become the focus of his discussion, that very voluntariness removes any motivation or *content* from the gesture that unites the two friends. The gesture of self-binding is properly ineffable, beyond explanation and moreover absolute, in the sense that there is no remainder, no Montaigne outside of La Boëtie, and no La Boëtie outside of Montaigne: "Je dis perdre [the sense of self], à la verité, ne nous reservant rien qui nous fut propre, ny qui fut ou sien ou mien" (p. 189). "Losing" one's self and one's will is equivalent to saying that there is nothing outside of one's will and one's self. The one who thus binds himself is absolutely sovereign; there are no external conditions to the relationship one freely and inexplicably enters into.[73] Montaigne loves La Boëtie as God loves himself.[74]

Of course La Boëtie is dead. In a tragic, literal sense there is no "remainder," there is no La Boëtie outside of Montaigne's will. The binding is now literally to oneself, not to another. La Boëtie's works have been appropriated by others, and this is presumably the reason why Montaigne chooses not to reproduce the *Discours de la servitude volontaire*, and the reason why he omits his friend's sonnets in the final version he gives of the *Essais*: "Ces

---

[73] See p. 191: "L'unique et principale amitié descoust toutes autres obligations. Le secret que j'ay juré ne deceller à nul autre, je le puis, sans parjure, communiquer à celuy qui n'est autre: c'est moy."

[74] In this discussion I have not touched upon an important and fruitful area of inquiry linking late scholastic nominalist views of the creature's capacity for love with secular representations of love. Specifically, Montaigne seems to love La Boëtie the way the creature should love only his creator, that is, completely without regard for profit, and for itself (enjoyment, *fruitio*). The creature, according to early scholastics, loves other creatures only in view of something else, that is, profit, pleasure, or reward, or in view of the enjoyment of God (*usus*). In late scholasticism there is a suggestion that human beings can love other human beings for themselves, in the sense of *fruitio*. This is the case in Ockham's discussion of the distinction. See Arthur Stephen McGrade, "Ockham on Enjoyment: Towards an Understanding of Fourteenth-Century Philosophy and Psychology," *Review of Metaphysics* 34 (1981): 706–28; see also his "Enjoyment at Oxford after Ockham: Philosophy, Psychology, and the Love of God," in *From Ockham to Wyclif*, ed. Anne Hudson and Michael Wilks (Oxford: Basil Blackwell, 1987), pp. 63–88. Montaigne, however, seems to obliterate the creature/creator distinction: both he and La Boëtie act out divine paradoxes of love. See also Aristotle, *Nicomachean Ethics* 1155b 16–1156a 20.

vers se voient ailleurs" (p. 196) [These verses may be seen elsewhere (p. 145)]. Montaigne has also preserved the uniqueness of his friendship by not offering to his reader, in his essay on La Boëtie, anything belonging to La Boëtie and not belonging to Montaigne. So the bind that unites them continues to be unmotivated and inaccessible to others.

"De l'amitié" is an essay that reproduces the structures of sovereignty through a deification of the self in the gesture by which the self ties itself to another. What remains of greatest importance to Montaigne is the mystery of that gesture, and I would suggest that the paradox of self-binding is an essential element of what one calls the modern sense of the self. For Montaigne has not chosen to depict self-binding as a "natural" feature of social interaction, or as a form of service to virtue. The uniqueness of Montaigne's union with La Boëtie is not part of a rhetorical strategy intended to emulate the virtuous glory of his predecessors, or is only secondarily so. Montaigne's investigation of the paradoxes of self-binding turns out to reproduce the paradoxes of absolute power, paradoxes that are at the heart of political theory and nominalist theology. Self-binding is an unmotivated gesture only if one thinks of any motivation as prior constraint and necessity—in which case the self is conceived of, like God and the absolute sovereign, as radically prior, and above any laws it has set down.

EPILOGUE: WILL AND PERSPECTIVE

I N DISCUSSING the Renaissance conceptualization of will and freedom in the preceding chapters I have had frequent recourse to the
example of Rabelais's abbey of Thélème. In itself the episode borders
on the uninteresting. It is the most static and least funny set of chapters in
his novels. It is dominated by extensive description of objects: of the building, of the grounds, of the clothes that the happy few choose to wear. The
"freedom" of Thélème is, however, a precise analogue of the structure of
will and sovereignty that I described in the previous chapters. The exhortation "Faictz ce que vouldras" addresses the reader, offering a vantage
point or key to the utopian abbey. The reader belongs to Rabelais's utopia,
resembles the inhabitants, by exercising his or her will. The "rule" of Thélème is perfectly empty: it is not spelled out *what* one is enabled to do, but
just *that* one is free to do anything. Initially the reader-resident is free from
all constraints, as are the young inhabitants each morning when they wake
up.

That freedom from constraint is of course only the first instance of par-
ticipation in life at the abbey. It is then decided, pretty much by chance,
what to do. At that point *everyone* does the same thing. Everything is dependent on the point of view, as it were, that one can fix absolutely at will,
but once the point of view is fixed, all activities are precisely determined
and imitated. The difference between this abbey and, say, a traditional
monastery is the projection of that initial instance of freedom from constraint. How one gets from the priority of will to an actual, specific action
or activity is completely occulted. If the choice of activities were motivated,
then that motivation would constitute a constraint on the initial freedom.
So the passage from will to action is not a passage at all, but a hiatus, a
leap.

Political sovereignty involves, as we have seen, a similar projection of
freedom from constraint, as an analytic "necessity." The attempts to re-
motivate the sovereign's will through appeals to his dignity, and thus his
prior boundness to laws, are attacking a basic intuition of the unboundness
of the sovereign, and in many cases, of the tyrant. Again the system seems
to suppose the unsystematic as its authorizing origin; authority and origin
have to do with the ability to choose freely what comes after or is produced
by the author or the origin. In other words, the system can see itself only
as having been *chosen*, not as having arisen naturally or necessarily, and not
as having existed continuously.

I have argued further that a free God is a paradigm for these basic conceptions of willful organization. The nominalist God's *potentia absoluta* is a way of preserving the nonnecessary origin of any order, and the sense of continuing dependence on that origin. Once the point of view is fixed, ordained, one can be sure it will not vary. However, hypothetical alternatives are always present, and inform the way in which one reflects about the current order and its laws and necessities.

I am suggesting, of course, that all of these phenomena are interrelated in the French and Italian Renaissance. Although one rarely finds a statement as explicit as his, Leonardo da Vinci's remarks on the painter as God, in the so-called *Trattato della pittura*, emblematize the penetration of literary representation by the voluntary and the contingent. Throughout the comparison, Leonardo insists on the painter's *will*:

> Sel pittore *vol* vedere bellezze, che lo innamorino, egli n'è signore di generarle, et se *vol* vedere cose mostruose, che spaventino, o che sieno bufonesche, e risibili o veramente compassionevoli, ei n'è signore et dio (creatore). e se *vol* generare siti e deserti, . . . esso li figura. se *vol* valli . . . se *vole* delle alte cime de'monti scoprire gran campagne . . . egli n'è signore. (italics mine)[1]

> [If the painter wishes to see beauties who make him fall in love, he has the power to generate them, and if he wishes to see monstrous things, that scare him, or that are farcical, and laughable or truly pitiful, he is lord and God (creator) thereof. And if he wishes to generate inhabited places and deserts . . . if he wishes valleys . . . if he wishes from high mountaintops to discover great plains . . . he is lord to do so.]

Leonardo does not just say that when the painter paints he creates like God; instead, all depends on his will, and it is his will that makes him sovereign, *signore*.

Filippo Brunelleschi's first experimental demonstration of linear perspective is another such emblem, in the sense that it incarnates an organization of representation that can be read as the primacy of the voluntary. He painted a mirror image of the San Giovanni baptistery in Florence, as seen from the main portal of the facing cathedral, Santa Maria del Fiore, on a small panel which one could hold in one's hand in front of one's face. In the other hand the spectator held a mirror at arm's length, which he or

---

[1] Leonardo da Vinci, *Paragone: A Comparison of the Arts*, ed. and trans. Irma A. Richter (London: Oxford Univ. Press, 1949), p. 51. Translation and italics are my own. The concluding remarks of this fragment comparing the painter and God seem to refer to a *creatio ex nihilo*, although the terms are somewhat unclear: "Ciò, ch'è nel universo per essentia, presentia o' immaginatione, esso [the painter] l'ha prima nella mente, e poi nelle mani" (p. 52). Does this mean that things and forms precede their "creation" by the mind of the painter, which would suggest a fashioning of preexisting forms? Does the "prima" refer back to the things in the universe, or forward to "poi nelle mani"? The "immaginatione" is presumably the painter's, but again, this is not clear.

she could see through a small hole in the middle of the panel representing the baptistery. One thus looked at a reflection of the inversed painting of the baptistery, that is, at the representation of the way the baptistery actually looked. According to Brunelleschi's biographer, Manetti, the demonstration was completely convincing—the representation of the baptistery seemed identical to the real baptistery, seen from the same point of view.[2]

Brunelleschi's experiment rendered visually and objectively what was already contained in the technique of linear perspective: the point of view corresponded symmetrically to the vanishing point. The spectator, if he or she focused on the middle of the portal of the baptistery, could see his or her own eye reflected in the little hole that allowed the spectator to see the mirror in the first place. The representation was complete and "exact" only when one viewed the baptistery from a certain point of view, and the fixing of that point of view allowed the representation to exist, as the representational space was constructed as a reflection of the visual cone that emanated from the point of view. Once that point is fixed, all objects in the representational space depend on the point of view, or rather, they seem exact only if one occupies the point of view. Linear perspective, then, is perfectly objective only when it is perfectly subjective. It was when one saw one's eye reflected in the mirror of Brunelleschi's demonstration that one occupied the correct spot, and that the demonstration worked.

The world rendered in a perspectival painting, then, is "truthful," or seemingly identical to what one sees when looking around at the real world. At the same time this visual world of the representation is totally contingent; that is, it depends, as we have seen, on the position one occupies. In constructing the representation one can fix this position at will, but once it is fixed, all objects in the perspectival cone are also precisely fixed and outlined, according to their distance from the point of view one has chosen.

Once one chooses a point of view, one creates a visual world in which the relations between all objects are ipso facto determined, and in which in some sense one's own function is set once and for all. The deictic function of perspectival space works both ways, in that one sees and precisely determines, as spectator/creator, and yet one is seen and precisely determined at

---

[2] I have gleaned information on this experiment from John White, *The Birth and Rebirth of Pictorial Space* (London: Faber and Faber, 1967); Samuel Edgerton, *The Renaissance Rediscovery of Linear Perspective* (New York: Basic Books, 1975); and David C. Lindberg, *Theories of Vision from Al-Kindi to Kepler* (Chicago: Univ. of Chicago Press, 1976). For interesting interpretations of Brunelleschi's experiment and linear perspective in general, see Erwin Panofsky, "Die Perspektive als 'symbolische Form,' " in *Aufsätze zu Grundfragen der Kunstwissenschaft*, 2d ed. (Berlin: B. Hessling, 1974); Gottfried Böhm, *Studien zur Perspektivität: Philosophie und Kunst in der frühen Neuzeit* (Heidelberg: C. Winter, 1969); Hubert Damisch, *Théorie du nuage* (Paris: Seuil, 1972), pp. 157–58, 166–71; and Jean-Joseph Goux, "Descartes et la perspective," *L'esprit créateur* 25 (1985): 10–20.

the very same instant, through the vanishing point which is the mirrored point of view. One's freedom is pure priority, as it were: the spectator/creator has a choice, absolutely speaking, of where to situate the point of view, but once that point is chosen, all is determined. There is no necessity to locate the point of view here or there; it can be an arbitrary decision, depending on anything from chance to personal preference. There is no prior order in which the representation participates and which would determine its choice of point of view. The only order is mathematical or geometrical, and it inheres in the visual world one decides to create. This order does not tell one *what* to represent, just *how* to represent. Although the analogy should not be pushed too far, much of what has been discussed in the previous pages is contained in these speculations on Brunelleschi's little experiment, which is thus a fitting vanishing point for this book.

BIBLIOGRAPHY

PRIMARY SOURCES

Ailly, Pierre d'. *Quaestiones super libros sententiarum cum quibusdam in fine adjunctis.* Strasbourg, 1490. Repr. Frankfurt: Minerva, 1968.

Alexander of Hales. *Glossa in quatuor libros sententiarum.* Quaracchi: Collegium S. Bonaventura, 1951.

Altensteig, Johannes. *Vocabularius theologie complectens vocabulorum descriptiones, diffinitiones et significatus ad theologiam utilium: et alia quibus prudens et diligens lector multa abstrusa et obscura theologorum dicta et dissolvere et rationum et argumentorum difficiles nodos: et facile ea quae in ducem et principem sententiarum doctores scripserunt intelligere poterit magno cum labore et diligentia compilata a Joanne Altenstaig Mindelhaimensi sacre scripture vero amatore.* [Hagenau]: Henricus Gran, 1517.

———. *Compendium vocabularii theologici scholastici anno 1517. . . .* Rev. ed., ed. F. Thomas Beauxamis. Paris: Guillaume Chaudiere, 1567.

———. *Lexicon theologicum complectens vocabulorum descriptiones, diffinitiones & interpretationes, omnibus sacrae theologiae studiosis ac Divini verbi concionatoribus magno usui futurum, summo studio & labore concinnatum.* Antwerp: Petrus Bellerus, 1576.

———. *Lexicon theologicum* [1617]. Rev. ed., ed. Johannes Tytz. Repr. Hildesheim: G. Olms, 1974.

Ariosto, Ludovico. *Orlando furioso.* Ed. Lanfranco Caretti. Turin: Einaudi, 1966.

Aristotle. *The Complete Works of Aristotle.* Ed. Jonathan Barnes. 2 vols. Bollingen Series 71:2. Princeton: Princeton Univ. Press, 1984.

Aubigné, Agrippa d'. *Oeuvres.* Ed. Henri Weber, Jacques Bailbé, and Marguerite Soulié. Bibliothèque de la Pléiade. Paris: Gallimard, 1969.

Augustine, Saint. *City of God.* 3d ed. Ed. and trans. George E. McCracken. 7 vols. Repr. Cambridge, Mass.: Harvard Univ. Press, 1981.

———. *Confessions.* Ed. W.H.D. Rouse, trans. William Watts. 2 vols. Cambridge, Mass.: Harvard Univ. Press, 1912.

———. *On Christian Doctrine.* Trans. D. W. Robertson, Jr. Indianapolis: Bobbs-Merrill, 1958.

———. *Sermones.* In *Patrologiae cursus completus*, ed. J.-P. Migne, vol. 38. Paris: L. Migne, 1845.

Biel, Gabriel. *Collectorium super IV libros sententiarum.* Tübingen: Johann Otmar, 1501.

Boccaccio, Giovanni. *Il Decameron.* Ed. Charles Singleton. 2 vols. [Bari]: Laterza, 1966.

Bodin, Jean. *Les six livres de la Republique.* Rev. ed. Lyons: Jacques du Puys, 1580.

Boethius. *Boethii consolationis philosophiae libri quinque.* 3d ed. Ed. and Trans. Ernst Gegenschatz and Olof Gigon. Zürich: Artemis, 1981. Repr. Darmstadt: Wissenschaftliche Buchgesellschaft, 1984.

Bonaventure. *Opera omnia.* Quaracchi: Collegium S. Bonaventura, 1882.

Bovelles, Charles de. *Liber de differentia vulgarium linguarum et Gallici sermonis varietate*. Ed. and trans. Colette Dumont-Demaizière. Paris: Klincksieck, 1973.

Budé, Guillaume. *Annotationes . . . in quatuor & viginti Pandectarum libros*. Paris: R. Estienne, 1535.

———. *De l'institution du prince*. Paris: Nicole, 1547.

———. *Forensia*. Paris: R. Estienne, 1548. Includes Latin-French and French-Latin legal glossary by Jean Du Luc.

Castiglione, Baldassarre. *Il cortegiano del conte Baldesar Castiglione*. Ed. Vittorio Cian. Florence: Sansoni, 1894.

———. *The Book of the Courtier*. Trans. Charles S. Singleton. New York: Anchor, 1959.

Cervantes Saavedra, Miguel de. *The Adventures of Don Quixote*. Trans. J. M. Cohen. Harmondsworth: Penguin, 1950.

Chappuis, Claude. *Discours de la court*. Paris: A. Roffet, 1543.

Charron, Pierre. *Trois livres de la sagesse* [1601]. In *Oeuvres . . . reveues, corrigees, & augmentees* [Paris, 1635]; vol. 1. Repr. Geneva: Slatkine, 1970.

Chartularium universitatis parisiensis. Ed. H. Denifle and E. Chatelain. Vol. 1. Paris: Delalain, 1889.

Chrétien de Troyes. *Le chevalier au lion (Yvain)*. Vol. 4 of *Les romans de Chrétien de Troyes*. Ed. Mario Roques. Paris: Champion, 1971.

———. *Li contes del Graal (Perceval)*. Vol. 5 of *Les romans de Chrétien de Troyes*. Ed. Félix Lecoy. Paris: Champion, 1973.

Les chroniques gargantuines. Eds. Christiane Lauvergnat-Gagnière and Guy Demerson. Société des textes français modernes 186. Paris: Nizet, 1988.

Cicero, *Laelius de amicitia*. In *Cicero's Works*, ed. and trans. William A. Falconer, vol. 20. Cambridge, Mass.: Harvard Univ. Press, 1933.

Clichtove, Josse. *Le traicte de la vraye noblesse translate nouvellement de latin en francoys*. Paris: Jean Longis, 1529.

Corpus iuris civilis. Ed. Paul Krueger and Theodor Mommsen. 3 vols. Berlin: Weidmann, 1954.

Damian, Peter. *Pierre Damien: Lettre sur la toute-puissance divine [De divina omnipotentia]*. Ed. and trans. André Cantin. Paris: Editions du Cerf, 1972.

Dante. *La divina commedia*. Ed. Natalino Sapegno. La letteratura italiana: storia e testi 4. Milan: R. Ricciardi, 1957.

———. *Dantis Alagherii epistolae. The Letters of Dante*. Rev. ed., ed. C. G. Hardie. Trans. Paget Toynbee. Oxford: Clarendon, 1966.

Diogenes Laertius, *Lives of Eminent Philosophers*. Ed. and trans. R. D. Hicks. 2 vols. Cambridge, Mass.: Harvard Univ. Press, 1925.

Le disciple de Pantagruel (Les navigations de Panurge). Ed. Guy Demerson and Christiane Lauvergnat-Gagnière. Société des textes français modernes 175. Paris: Nizet, 1982.

Du Bartas, Guillaume Salluste. *La sepmaine*. Ed. Yvonne Bellenger. 2 vols. Paris: Nizet, 1981.

Du Bellay, Joachim. *Les regrets et autres oeuvres poëtiques*. Ed. Jean Jolliffe and M. A. Screech. Textes littéraires français 120. Geneva: Droz, 1966.

———. *La deffence et illustration de la langue francoise*. Ed. Henri Chamard. Paris: Didier, 1948.

———. *Poésies françaises et latines*. Ed. Ernest Courbet. Vol. 1. Paris: Garnier, 1919.

———. *L'olive*. Ed. E. Caldarini. Textes littéraires françaises 214. Geneva: Droz, 1974.

———. *Oeuvres poétiques*. Ed. Henri Chamard. 6 vols. Paris: Hachette, Droz, Didier, 1923–1931.

Duns Scotus, John. *Opera omnia*. Ed. Lucas Wadding. 26 vols. Paris: L. Vivès, 1891–1895.

———. *Opera omnia*. Ed. P. Carolus Balić et al. Vols. 1–7, 16–17. Vatican: Typis Polyglottis Vaticanis, 1950–1966.

Du Vair, Guillaume. *De la sainte philosophie*. Includes *La philosophie morale des stoïques*. Ed. Guy Michaut. Paris: Vrin, 1946.

Erasmus, Desiderius. *De libero arbitrio diatribe seu collatio*. In *Luther and Erasmus: Free Will and Salvation; Erasmus: De libero arbitrio; Luther: De servo arbitrio*, ed. and trans. E. Gordon Rupp, A. N. Marlow, Philip Watson and B. Drewery. Philadelphia: Westminster, 1969.

———. *Opera omnia*. 10 vols. Loudun: P. Vander Aa, 1703–1706.

Estienne, Henri. *Thesaurus graecae linguae*. Ed. Carolus Benedictus Hase. 8 vols. Paris: Firmin Didot, 1831–1865.

Flores legum. Paris: Jean Petit, 1513.

Gerhard, Johann. *Loci theologie*. . . . Jena: T. Steinmann, 1610.

Gregory of Rimini. *Lectura super primum et secundum sententiarum*. Ed. A. Damasus Trapp Osa and Venicio Marcolino. Berlin: Walter de Gruyter, 1981.

Guazzo, Stefano. *La civil conversatione*. Trans. George Pettie [1581]. Repr. London: Constable, 1925.

Guevara, Antonio de. *Aviso de favoriti et dottrina de cortegiani*. Trans. Vicenzo Bondi. Venice: [M. Tramezino], 1544.

———. *Le favori de court*. Trans. Jaques de Rochemore. Anvers: C. Plantin, 1557.

Herberay des Essarts, Nicolas de, trans. *Amadis de Gaule*. Bk. 1. Ed. Hugues Vaganay and Yves Giraud. 2 vols. Paris: Nizet, 1986.

Hotman, François. *Francogallia*. Ed. Ralph E. Giesey, trans. J.H.M. Salmon. Cambridge: Cambridge Univ. Press, 1972.

James I. *The Political Works of James I*. Ed. Charles H. McIlwain. New York: Russell and Russell, 1965.

John of Salisbury. *Le Policraticus de Jean de Salisbury traduit par Denis Foulechat*. Ed. Charles Brücker. Nancy: Presses univ. de Nancy, 1985.

La Boëtie, Estienne de. *De la servitude volontaire*. Ed. Malcolm Smith. Geneva: Droz, 1987.

Le Caron, Louis. *Les dialogues*. Ed. Joan A. Buhlmann and Donald Gilman. Textes littéraires français 337. Geneva: Droz, 1986.

Lefèvre d'Etaples, Jacques. *Epistres et evangiles pour les cinquante et deux dimenches de l'an*. Text of the edition Pierre de Vingle [1531–1532]. Ed. Guy Bedouelle and Franco Giacone. Leiden: E. J. Brill, 1976.

Leonardo da Vinci. *Paragone: A Comparison of the Arts*. Ed. and trans. Irma A. Richter. London: Oxford Univ. Press, 1949.

Lucian. *How to Write History*. Ed. and trans. K. Kilburn. In *Lucian's Works*, vol. 6. Cambridge, Mass.: Harvard Univ. Press, 1959.

Luther, Martin. *De servo arbitrio*. In *Luther and Erasmus: Free Will and Salvation; Erasmus: De libero arbitrio; Luther: De servo arbitrio*, ed. and trans. E. Gordon Rupp, A. N. Marlow, Philip Watson, and B. Drewery. Philadelphia: Westminster, 1969.

———. *Werke. Kritische Gesammtausgabe*. Vol. 1. Weimar: H. Böhlau, 1883.

Major, John [Jean Mair]. *In primum sententiarum*. Paris: I. Badius, 1519.

Marguerite de Navarre. *L'Heptaméron*. Ed. Michel François. Paris: Garnier, 1967.

Marot, Clément. *Les épîtres*. Vol. 1 of *Oeuvres complètes*, ed. C. A. Mayer. Paris: Nizet, 1977.

Melanchthon, Philip. *Werke*. 2d ed. Ed. Hans Engelland and Robert Stupperich. Vol. 2, pt. 1. Gütersloh: G. Mohn, 1978.

Montaigne, Michel de. *Les essais*. 3d ed., ed. Pierre Villey, revised by Verdun-L. Saulnier. 2 vols. Paris: Presses univ. de France, 1978.

———. *The Complete Essays of Montaigne*. Trans. Donald M. Frame. Stanford: Stanford Univ. Press, 1957.

More, Thomas. *Utopia*. Ed. and trans. Edward Surtz, s.j. New Haven: Yale Univ. Press, 1964.

Ockham, William of. *Opera philosophica et theologica (Opera theologica)*. Ed. G. I. Etzkorn, Gedeon Gal, F. E. Kelley, Joseph C. Wey, c.s.b., and Carolus A. Grassi. 10 vols. St. Bonaventure, N.Y.: Franciscan Institute, 1967–1986.

———. *Tractatus de praedestinatione et de praescientia Dei et de futuris contingentibus (Predestination, God's Foreknowledge, and Future Contingents)*. Trans. Marilyn McCord Adams and Norman Kretzmann. Indianapolis: Hackett, 1983.

Ovid. *The Art of Love, and Other Poems*. 2d ed., ed. G. P. Goold, trans. J. H. Mozley. Cambridge, Mass.: Harvard Univ. Press, 1979.

Peter Lombard. *Sententiae in IV libris distinctae*. 3d ed. 2 vols. Grottoferrata: Collegium S. Bonaventura, 1971–1981.

Philibert de Vienne. *Le philosophe de court*. Lyons: Jean de Tournes, 1547.

Piccolomini, Eneo Silvio (Pope Pius II). *De curialium miseriis*. Ed. Wilfred P. Mustard. Baltimore: Johns Hopkins Univ. Press, 1928.

Pomponazzi, Pietro. *Libri quinque de fato, de libero arbitrio et de praedestinatione*. Ed. Richard Lemay. Lungano: Thesaurus Mundi, 1957.

Pulci, Luigi. *Il Morgante*. Ed. Franca Ageno. La letteratura italiana: storia e testi 17. Milan: R. Ricciardi, 1955.

Quintilian. *The Institutio oratoria*. Ed. and trans. H. E. Butler. 4 vols. Cambridge, Mass.: Harvard Univ. Press, 1922.

Rabelais, François. *Pantagruel*. Ed. Verdun-L. Saulnier. Textes littéraires français 2. Geneva: Droz, 1965.

———. *Gargantua*. Ed. Ruth Calder and M. A. Screech. Textes littéraires français 163. Geneva: Droz, 1970.

————. *Le tiers livre*. Ed. M. A. Screech. Textes littéraires français 102. Geneva: Droz, 1974.

————. *Le quart livre*. Ed. Robert Marichal. Textes littéraires français 10. Geneva: Droz, 1947.

Ronsard, Pierre de. *Oeuvres complètes*. Ed. Paul Laumonier, Isidore Silver and Raymond Lebègue. 20 vols. Paris: Hachette, Didier, Droz. Repr. Paris: Nizet, 1914–1983.

Sale, Antoine de la. *Jehan de Saintré*. Ed. Jean Misrahi and Charles A. Knudson. Textes littéraires français 117. Geneva: Droz, 1967.

Sansovino, Francesco. *Propositioni, overo considerationi in materia di cose di stato*. Vinegia: A. Salicato, 1583.

Seyssel, Claude de. *La monarchie de France*. Ed. Jacques Poujol. Paris: Librairie d'Argences, 1961.

————. *The Monarchy of France*. Trans. Donald R. Kelley. New Haven: Yale Univ. Press, 1981.

Speroni, Sperone. *Dialogo delle lingue*. Ed. and trans. Helene Harth. Munich: W. Fink, 1975.

Tasso, Torquato. *Gerusalemme liberata*. Ed. Luigi de Vendittis. Parnaso italiano 6. Turin: Einaudi, 1961.

Thomas Aquinas, Saint. *Opera omnia*. 25 vols. Parma: P. Fiaccadori, 1856–1873. Repr. New York: Musurgia, 1948–1950.

————. *Concerning Being and Essence [De ente et essentia]*. Trans. George G. Leckie. New York: Appleton-Century-Crofts, 1937.

————. *Summa theologiae*. 5 vols. Ottawa: Medieval Studies Institute, 1941–1945.

Tory, Geofroy. *Champ Fleury. Auquel est contenu lart & science de la deue & vraye proportion des lettres attiques*. . . . Text of the edition of G. de Gourmont, 1529. Ed. Gustave Cohen. Repr. Paris: C. Bosse, 1931.

Valla, Lorenzo. *On Free Will [De libero arbitrio]*. Trans. Charles Trinkaus. In *The Renaissance Philosophy of Man*, ed. Paul Oskar Kristeller, Ernst Cassirer and John Herman Randall, Jr., 155–82. Chicago: Univ. of Chicago Press, 1948.

————. *Elegantiae*. In *Opera*. Basel: H. Petrus, 1540. Repr. Torino: Bottega d'Erasmo, 1962.

Vida, Marco Girolamo. *De arte poetica*. Ed. and trans. Ralph G. Williams. New York: Columbia Univ. Press, 1976.

Vigenère, Blaise de, trans. *Trois dialogues de l'amitié: Le Lysis de Platon, et le Laelius de Ciceron; contenans plusieurs beaux preceptes, & discours philosophiques sur ce subject: Et le Toxaris de Lucian; ou sont amenez quelques rares exemples de ce que les amis ont fait autresfois l'un pour l'autre*. Paris: Nicolas Chesneau, 1579.

Vindiciae contra tyrannos. [Hubert Languet?] French trans. 1581. Ed. A. Jouanna, J. Perrin, M. Soulié, A. Tournon, and H. Weber. Geneva: Droz, 1979.

SECONDARY SOURCES

Adorno, Theodor W., and Max Horkheimer. *Die Dialektik der Aufklärung*. Amsterdam: Querido, 1947. Repr. Frankfurt: S. Fischer, 1969.

Allen, J. W. *A History of Political Thought in the Sixteenth Century*. New York: The Dial Press, 1928. Repr. London: Methuen, 1960.

Antoniotti, Louise-Marie, O.P. "La volonté divine antécédente et conséquente selon Saint Jean Damascène et Saint Thomas d'Aquin." *Revue thomiste* 65 (1965): 52–77.

Ascoli, Albert Russell. *Ariosto's Bitter Harmony: Crisis and Evasion in the Italian Renaissance*. Princeton: Princeton Univ. Press, 1987.

Bannach, Klaus. *Die Lehre von der doppelten Macht Gottes bei Wilhelm von Ockham: Problemgeschichtliche Voraussetzungen und Bedeutung*. Wiesbaden: Franz Steiner, 1975.

Bauschatz, Cathleen M. "Montaigne's Conception of Reading in the Context of Renaissance Poetics." In *The Reader in the Text*, ed. Susan R. Suleiman and Inge Crosman, 264–92. Princeton: Princeton Univ. Press, 1980.

Berry, Alice Fiola. *Rabelais: Homo Logos*. North Carolina Studies in the Romance Languages and Literatures 208. Chapel Hill: Dept. of Romance Languages of the Univ. of North Carolina, 1978.

Binswanger, Ludwig. *Melancholie und Manie: Phänomenologische Studien*. Pfullingen: Neske, 1960.

Blanchot, Maurice. *L'espace littéraire*. Paris: Gallimard, 1955.

Blum, Claude. "Les *Essais* de Montaigne: Les signes, la politique, la religion." In *Columbia Montaigne Conference Papers*, ed. Donald M. Frame and Mary B. McKinley. Lexington, Ky.: French Forum, 1981.

Blumenberg, Hans. *The Legitimacy of the Modern Age*. Trans. Robert M. Wallace. Cambridge, Mass.: MIT Press, 1983.

Böhm, Gottfried. *Studien zur Perspektivität: Philosophie und Kunst in der frühen Neuzeit*. Heidelberg: C. Winter, 1969.

Bonansea, B. M., O.F.M. *Man and His Approach to God in John Duns Scotus*. Lanham, Md.: Univ. Press of America, 1983.

Bossuat, André. "The Maxim 'The King Is Emperor in His Kingdom': Its Use in the Fifteenth Century before the Parlement of Paris." In *The Recovery of France in the Fifteenth Century*, ed. P. S. Lewis, 185–95. London: MacMillan, 1971.

Braden, Gordon. *Renaissance Tragedy and the Senecan Tradition: Anger's Privilege*. New Haven: Yale Univ. Press, 1985.

Breen, Quirinus. "Giovanni Pico della Mirandola on the Conflict of Philosophy and Rhetoric." *Journal of the History of Ideas* 13 (1952): 384–412.

Brockmeier, Peter. *Lust und Herrschaft: Studien über gesellschaftliche Aspekte der Novellistik: Boccaccio, Sacchetti, Margarete von Navarra, Cervantes*. Stuttgart: J. B. Metzler, 1972.

Burckhardt, Jacob. *The Civilization of the Renaissance in Italy*. Trans. S.G.C. Middlemore. 2 vols. New York: Harper and Row, 1958.

Burke, Kenneth. *The Rhetoric of Religion: Studies in Logology*. Boston: Beacon Press, 1961. Repr. Berkeley: Univ. of California Press, 1970.

Camporeale, Salvatore I. *Lorenzo Valla: Umanesimo e teologia*. Florence: Istituto nazionale di Studi sul Rinascimento, 1972.

Carré, Meyrick. *Nominalists and Realists*. Oxford: Oxford Univ. Press, 1946.

Cassirer, Ernst. *The Individual and the Cosmos in Renaissance Philosophy*. Trans. Mario Domandi. New York: Barnes and Noble, 1963.

Castor, Grahame. *Pléiade Poetics: A Study in Sixteenth-Century Thought and Terminology*. Cambridge: Cambridge Univ. Press, 1964.

Cave, Terence. *The Cornucopian Text: Problems of Writing in the French Renaissance.* Oxford: Clarendon, 1979.

———. "The Mimesis of Reading in the Renaissance." In *Mimesis: From Mirror to Method*, ed. John D. Lyons and Stephen G. Nichols, Jr., 149–65. Hanover, N.H.: Univ. Presses of New England, 1982.

Cave, Terence, Michel Jeanneret and François Rigolot. "Sur la prétendue transparence de Rabelais." *Revue d'histoire littéraire de la France* 86 (1986): 709–16.

Chenu, M.-D. "Auctor, actor, autor." *Bulletin Du Cange (ALMA)* 3 (1927): 81–86.

Compagnon, Antoine. *Nous, Michel de Montaigne.* Paris: Seuil, 1980.

———. "A Long Short Story: Montaigne's Brevity." *Yale French Studies* 64 (1983): 24–50.

Cornilliat, François. "L'autre géant. Les *Chroniques gargantuines* et leur intertexte." *Littérature* 55 (1984): 85–97.

Courtenay, William J. "John of Mirecourt and Gregory of Rimini on Whether God Can Undo the Past." *Recherches de théologie ancienne et médiévale* 39 (1972): 224–56 and 40 (1973): 147–74.

———. "The Critique on Natural Causality in the Mutakallimun and Nominalism." *Harvard Theological Review* 66 (1973): 77–94.

———. "Nominalism and Late Medieval Religion." In *The Pursuit of Holiness in Late Medieval and Renaissance Religion*, ed. Charles Trinkaus and Heiko A. Oberman, 26–59. Leiden: E. J. Brill, 1974.

———. "Late Medieval Nominalism Revisited: 1972–1982." *Journal of the History of Ideas* (1983): 159–64.

———. Review of Francis Oakley, *Omnipotence, Covenant, and Order.* In *Speculum* 60 (1985): 1006–9.

Curtius, Ernst Robert. *European Literature and the Latin Middle Ages.* Trans. Willard Trask. Bollingen Series 36. Princeton: Princeton Univ. Press, 1953.

Dal Pra, Mario. *Nicola di Autrecourt.* Milan: Bocca, 1951.

Daly, James. "The Idea of Absolute Monarchy in Seventeenth-Century England." *The Historical Journal* 21 (1978): 227–50.

D'Amico, John F. "Humanism and Pre-Reformation Theology." In *Renaissance Humanism: Foundations, Forms, and Legacy*, ed. Albert Rabil, Jr., 3:349–79. Philadelphia: Univ. of Pennsylvania Press, 1988.

Damisch, Hubert. *Théorie du nuage.* Paris: Seuil, 1972.

Defaux, Gérard. *Pantagruel et les sophistes: Contribution à l'histoire de l'humanisme chrétien au XVIe siècle.* The Hague: M. Nijhoff, 1973.

———. *Le curieux, le glorieux, et la sagesse du monde dans la première moitié du XVIe siècle: L'exemple de Panurge (Ulysse, Démosthène, Empédocle).* Lexington, Ky.: French Forum, 1982.

———. "Clément Marot: Une poétique du silence." In *Pre-Pléiade Poetry*, ed. Jerry C. Nash, 44–64. Lexington, Ky.: French Forum, 1985.

———. "Sur la prétendue pluralité du prologue de 'Gargantua': Réponse d'un positiviste naïf à trois 'illustres et treschevalereux champions.' " *Revue d'histoire littéraire de la France* 86 (1986): 716–22.

———. *Marot, Rabelais, Montaigne: L'écriture comme présence.* Paris: Champion-Slatkine, 1987.

Dettloff, Werner. *Die Entwicklung der Akzeptations-und Verdienstlehre von Duns Scotus bis Luther. Beiträge zur Geschichte der Philosophie und Theologie des Mittelalters.* Texte und Untersuchungen 40:2. Münster: Aschendorff, 1963.

Dictionnaire de théologie catholique. 15 vols. Paris: Letouzey et Ané, 1923–1950.

Di Napoli, Giovanni. "Libertà e fato in Pietro Pomponazzi." In *Studi in onore di Antonio Corsano*, 175–220. Manduria: Lacaita, 1970.

Donato, Eugenio. " 'Per selve e boscherecci labirinti': Desire and Narrative Structure in Ariosto's *Orlando furioso.*" In *Literary Theory/Renaissance Texts*, ed. Patricia Parker and David Quint, 33–62. Baltimore: Johns Hopkins Univ. Press, 1986.

Dragonetti, Roger. *La vie de la lettre au moyen âge (Le conte du Graal).* Paris: Seuil, 1980.

Dubois, Claude-Gilbert. *Mythe et langage au seizième siècle.* Bordeaux: Ducros, 1970.

Durling, Robert. *The Figure of the Poet in Renaissance Epic.* Cambridge, Mass.: Harvard Univ. Press, 1965.

Duval, Edwin M. "Montaigne's Conversions: Compositional Strategies in the *Essais.*" *French Forum* 7 (1982): 5–22.

———. "Interpretation and the 'Doctrine absconce' of Rabelais's Prologue to *Gargantua.*" *Etudes rabelaisiennes* 18 (1985): 1–17.

Eagleton, Terry. *Literary Theory: An Introduction.* Minneapolis: Univ. of Minnesota Press, 1983.

Edgerton, Samuel. *The Renaissance Rediscovery of Linear Perspective.* New York: Basic Books, 1975.

Effler, Roy R, O.F.M. *John Duns Scotus and the Principle 'Omne quod movetur ab alio movetur.'* Franciscan Institute Publications, Philosophy Series 15. St. Bonaventure, NY: Franciscan Institute, 1962.

Ehalt, Hubert C. *Ausdrucksformen absolutistischer Herrschaft: Der Wiener Hof im 17. und 18. Jahrhundert.* Munich: Oldenbourg, 1980.

Eisenstein, Elizabeth L. *The Printing Press as an Agent of Change: Communication and Cultural Transformations in Early-Modern Europe.* 2 vols. Cambridge: Cambridge Univ. Press, 1979.

Esmein, A. "La maxime *Princeps legibus solutus est* dans l'ancien droit public français." In *Essays in Legal History*, ed. Paul Vinogradoff, 201–14. London: Oxford Univ. Press, 1913.

Esposito, Roberto. *Ordine e conflitto: Machiavelli e la letteratura politica del rinascimento italiano.* Naples: Liguori, 1984.

Farge, James K. *Orthodoxy and Reform in Early Reformation France: The Faculty of Theology of Paris, 1500–1543.* Leiden: E. J. Brill, 1985.

Febvre, Lucien, and Henri-Jean Martin. *L'apparition du livre.* Paris: Albin Michel, 1958.

Foucault, Michel. "What Is an Author?" Trans. Josué Harari. In *The Foucault Reader*, ed. Paul Rabinow, 101–20. New York: Pantheon, 1984.

Franklin, Julian H. *Constitutionalism and Resistance in the Sixteenth Century: Three Treatises by Hotman, Beza, and Mornay.* New York: Pegasus, 1969.

————. *Jean Bodin and the Rise of Absolutist Theory*. Cambridge: Cambridge Univ. Press, 1973.

Friedrich, Hugo. *Montaigne*. Bern: Francke, 1949.

Fromm, Erich. *Escape from Freedom*. New York: Holt, Rinehart and Winston, 1941.

Fumaroli, Marc. "Blaise de Vigenère et les débuts de la prose d'art française: sa doctrine d'après ses Préfaces." In *L'automne de la Renaissance 1580–1630*, ed. Jean Lafond and André Stegmann, 31–51. Paris: Vrin, 1981.

Ganshof, F. L. *Feudalism*. Trans. P. Grierson. New York: Harper and Row, 1961.

Garin, Eugenio. *La cultura filosofica del rinascimento italiano*. 1961. Repr. Florence: Sansoni, 1979.

Gauna, Maxwell. "Fruitful Fields and Blessed Spirits, or Why the Thelemites Were Well Born." *Etudes rabelaisiennes* 15 (1980): 117–28.

Gilson, Etienne. *La philosophie au moyen âge: Des origines patristiques à la fin du XIVe siècle*. 2d ed. Paris: Payot, 1962.

————. "Notes médiévales au *Tiers livre* de Pantagruel." *Revue d'histoire franciscaine* 2 (1925): 72–88.

————. *Les idées et les lettres*. Paris: Vrin, 1932.

————. *L'être et l'essence*. Paris: Vrin, 1948.

Glauser, Alfred. *Rabelais créateur*. Paris: Nizet, 1964.

Goux, Jean-Joseph. "Descartes et la perspective." *L'esprit créateur* 25 (1985): 10–20.

Grafton, Anthony, and Lisa Jardine. *From Humanism to the Humanities: Education and the Liberal Arts in Fifteenth-and Sixteenth-Century Europe*. Cambridge, Mass.: Harvard Univ. Press, 1986.

Grane, Leif. *Contra Gabrielem: Luthers Auseinandersetzung mit Gabriel Biel in der 'Disputatio contra scholasticam theologiam.'* Acta theologica danica 4. Copenhagen: Gyldendal, 1962.

Gray, Floyd. "Structure and Meaning in the Prologue to the *Tiers livre*." *L'esprit créateur* 3 (1963): 57–62.

————. *La poétique de Du Bellay*. Paris: Nizet, 1978.

Greene, Thomas M. "*Il cortegiano* and the Choice of a Game." In *Castiglione: The Real and the Ideal in Renaissance Culture*, ed. Robert W. Hanning and David Rosand, 1–15. New Haven: Yale Univ. Press, 1983.

————. *The Vulnerable Text: Essays on Renaissance Literature*. New York: Columbia Univ. Press, 1986.

Greenfield, Concetta Carestia. *Humanist and Scholastic Poetics, 1250–1500*. Lewisburg, Pa.: Bucknell Univ. Press, 1981.

Griffin, Robert. "Cosmic Metaphor in *La concorde des deux langages*." In *Pre-Pléiade Poetry*, ed. Jerry C. Nash, 15–30. Lexington, Ky.: French Forum, 1985.

Guillory, John. *Poetic Authority: Spenser, Milton, and Literary History*. New York: Columbia Univ. Press, 1983.

Hamm, Berndt. *Promissio, Pactum, Ordinatio: Freiheit und Selbstbindung Gottes in der scholastischen Gnadenlehre*. Tübingen: Mohr, 1977.

Harwood, Britton J. "*Piers Plowman*: Fourteenth-Century Skepticism and the Theology of Suffering." *Bucknell Review* 19 (1971): 119–36.

Hollander, Robert. *Studies in Dante*. Ravenna: Longo, 1980.

Hubatsch, Walter, ed. *Absolutismus*. Wege der Forschung 314. Darmstadt: Wissenschaftliche Buchgesellschaft, 1973.

Jaeger, C. Stephen. "Der Schöpfer der Welt und das Schöpfungswerk als Prologmotiv in der mittelhochdeutschen Dichtung." *Zeitschrift für deutsches Altertum und deutsche Literatur* 171 (1978): 1–18.

Jakobson, Roman. *Essais de linguistique générale*. Trans. Nicolas Ruwet. Paris: Minuit, 1963.

Jauss, Hans Robert. "Poiesis." Trans. Michael Shaw. *Critical Inquiry* 8 (1982): 591–608.

Javitch, Daniel. *Poetry and Courtliness in Renaissance England*. Princeton: Princeton Univ. Press, 1978.

———. "*Il cortegiano* and the Constraints of Despotism." In *Castiglione: The Real and the Ideal in Renaissance Culture*, ed. Robert W. Hanning and David Rosand, 17–28. New Haven: Yale Univ. Press, 1983.

Kahn, Victoria. "The Figure of the Reader in Petrarch's *Secretum*." *PMLA* 100 (1985): 154–66.

———. "Humanism and the Resistance to Theory." In *Literary Theory/Renaissance Texts*, ed. Patricia Parker and David Quint, 373–96. Baltimore: Johns Hopkins Univ. Press, 1986.

Kantorowicz, Ernst H. *The King's Two Bodies: A Study in Medieval Political Theology*. Princeton: Princeton Univ. Press, 1957.

Keller, Luzius. *Palingène, Ronsard, Du Bartas: Trois études sur la poésie cosmologique de la Renaissance*. Bern: Francke, 1974.

Kelly, Douglas. "The Genius of the Patron: The Prince, the Poet, and Fourteenth-Century Invention." *Studies in the Literary Imagination* 20 (1987): 77-97.

———. "Le patron et l'auteur dans l'invention romanesque." In *Théories et pratiques de l'écriture au moyen âge*, ed. Emmanuèle Baumgartner and Christiane Marchello-Nizia, 25–39. Paris: Centre de recherches du Département de Français, Fontenay/Saint-Cloud, 1988.

Kennedy, William J. *Rhetorical Norms in Renaissance Literature*. New Haven: Yale Univ. Press, 1978.

Kermode, Frank. *The Sense of an Ending: Studies in the Theory of Fiction*. Oxford: Oxford Univ. Press, 1966.

Kerrigan, William, and Gordon Braden. *The Idea of the Renaissance*. Baltimore: Johns Hopkins Univ. Press, 1989.

King, Preston. *The Ideology of Order: A Comparative Analysis of Jean Bodin and Thomas Hobbes*. London: Barnes and Noble, 1974.

Kline, Michael B. *Rabelais and the Age of Printing*. Geneva: Droz, 1963.

Knecht, R. J. *Francis I*. Cambridge: Cambridge Univ. Press, 1982.

Krailsheimer, A. J. *Rabelais and the Franciscans*. Oxford: Clarendon, 1963.

Kristeller, Paul Oskar. *Studies in Renaissance Thought and Letters*. Rome: Edizioni di Storia e Letteratura, 1956.

Kristeva, Julia. "Narration et transformation." *Semiotica* 1 (1969): 422–48.

Krüdener, Jürgen Freiherr von. *Die Rolle des Hofes im Absolutismus*. Stuttgart: G. Fischer, 1973.

Landgraf, Artur Michael. *Dogmengeschichte der Frühscholastik*. Vol. 1, pt. 1. Regensburg: F. Pustet, 1952.

Langer, Ullrich. *Rhétorique et intersubjectivité: 'Les tragiques' d'Agrippa d'Aubigné*. Biblio 17, 7. Tübingen: Papers on French Seventeenth-Century Literature, 1983.

———. "A Courtier's Problematic Defense: Ronsard's 'Responce aux injures.' " *Bibliothèque d'Humanisme et Renaissance* 46 (1984): 343–55.

Leff, Gordon. *Gregory of Rimini: Tradition and Innovation in Fourteenth-Century Thought*. Manchester: Manchester Univ. Press, 1961.

———. *William of Ockham: The Metamorphosis of Scholastic Discourse*. Manchester: Manchester Univ. Press, 1975.

Lestringant, Frank. "L'ouverture des 'Tragiques': D'Aubigné, César, et Moïse." *Bulletin de la Société de l'histoire du protestantisme français* 133 (1987): 5–22.

Levao, Ronald. *Renaissance Minds and Their Fictions: Cusanus, Sidney, Shakespeare*. Berkeley: Univ. of California Press, 1985.

Lindberg, David C. *Theories of Vision from Al-Kindi to Kepler*. Chicago: Univ. of Chicago Press, 1976.

Mahoney, Edward P. "Duns Scotus and the School of Padua around 1500." In *Regnum hominis et regnum dei*, ed. Camille Bérubé, 215–27. Studia Scholastico-Scotistica 7. Rome: Societas Internationalis Scotistica, 1978.

Margolin, Jean-Claude. "Duns Scot et Erasme." In *Regnum hominis et regnum Dei*, ed. Camille Bérubé. Studia Scholastico-Scotistica 7. Rome: Societas Internationalis Scotistica, 1978.

Marin, Louis. *La critique du discours: Sur la "Logique de Port-Royal" et les "Pensées" de Pascal*. Paris: Minuit, 1975.

———. *Le portrait du roi*. Paris: Minuit, 1981.

Martin, Alfred von. *Soziologie der Renaissance*. 1932. Repr. Munich: C. H. Beck, 1974.

McCord Adams, Marilyn. *William Ockham*. Vol. 2. Notre Dame, Ind.: Univ. of Notre Dame Press, 1987.

McGrade, Arthur Stephen. "Ockham on Enjoyment: Towards an Understanding of Fourteenth-Century Philosophy and Psychology." *Review of Metaphysics* 34 (1981): 706–28.

———. "Enjoyment at Oxford after Ockham: Philosophy, Psychology, and the Love of God." In *From Ockham to Wyclif*, ed. Anne Hudson and Michael Wilks, 63–88. Oxford: Basil Blackwell, 1987.

McGrath, Alister E. *Iustitia Dei: A History of the Christian Doctrine of Justification*. 2 vols. Cambridge: Cambridge Univ. Press, 1986.

———. *The Intellectual Origins of the European Reformation*. London: Basil Blackwell, 1987.

Meller, Bernhard. *Studien zur Erkenntnislehre des Peter von Ailly*. Freiburger Theologische Studien 67. Freiburg: Verlag Herder, 1954.

Miel, Jan. *Pascal and Theology*. Baltimore: Johns Hopkins Univ. Press, 1969.

Miernowski, Jan. "L'accès aux vérités spirituelles: Continuités et ruptures des codes intertextuels dans *La sepmaine* de Du Bartas." In *Continuités et ruptures dans l'histoire de la littérature*, ed. Michèle Weil, Halina Suwala, and Dominique Triaire, 33–45. Geneva: Champion-Slatkine, 1988.

Miethke, Jürgen. *Ockhams Weg zur Sozialphilosophie*. Berlin: Walter de Gruyter, 1969.

Miller, Jacqueline T. *Poetic License: Authority and Authorship in Medieval and Renaissance Contexts*. New York: Oxford Univ. Press, 1986.

Minnis, Alistair J. *Medieval Theory of Authorship: Scholastic Literary Attitudes in the Later Middle Ages*. Philadelphia: Univ. of Pennsylvania Press, 1987.

Mitteis, Heinrich. *Lehnrecht und Staatsgewalt: Untersuchungen zur mittelalterlichen Verfassungsgeschichte*. Weimar: H. Böhlaus, 1933.

Mölk, Ulrich. *Literarästhetik des 12. und 13. Jahrhunderts: Prologe, Exkurse, Epiloge*. Tübingen: M. Niemeyer, 1969.

Nash, Jerry C. "Rabelais and Stoic Portrayal." *Studies in the Renaissance* 21 (1974): 63–82.

Norton, Glyn P. *Montaigne and the Introspective Mind*. The Hague: Mouton, 1975.

Nykrog, Per. "Thélème, Panurge et la Dive Bouteille." *Revue d'histoire littéraire de la France* 65 (1965): 385–97.

Oakley, Francis. *The Political Thought of Pierre d'Ailly: The Voluntarist Tradition*. New Haven: Yale Univ. Press, 1964.

―――. *Omnipotence, Covenant, and Order: An Excursion in the History of Ideas from Abelard to Leibniz*. Ithaca: Cornell Univ. Press, 1984.

Oberman, Heiko A. "Some Notes on the Theology of Nominalism with Attention to Its Relation to the Renaissance." *Harvard Theological Review* 53 (1960): 47–76.

―――. *The Harvest of Medieval Theology: Gabriel Biel and Late Medieval Nominalism*. Cambridge, Mass.: Harvard Univ. Press, 1963.

―――. "*Via antiqua* and *via moderna*: Late Medieval Prolegomena to Early Reformation Thought." In *From Ockham to Wyclif*, ed. Anne Hudson and Michael Wilks, 445–63. Oxford: Basil Blackwell, 1987.

Ozment, Steven. "Mysticism, Nominalism, and Dissent." In *The Pursuit of Holiness in Late Medieval and Renaissance Religion*, ed. Charles Trinkaus and Heiko A. Oberman, 67–92. Leiden: E. J. Brill, 1974.

―――. *The Age of Reform (1250–1550): An Intellectual and Religious History of Late Medieval and Reformation Europe*. New Haven: Yale Univ. Press, 1980.

Panofsky, Erwin. *Aufsätze zu Grundfragen der Kunstwissenschaft*. 2d ed. Berlin: B. Hessling, 1974.

Parente, Margherita Isnardi. "Le volontarisme de Jean Bodin: Maïmonide ou Duns Scot?" In *Jean Bodin: Verhandlungen der internationalen Bodin Tagung in München*, ed. Horst Denzer, 39–51. Munich: C. H. Beck, 1973.

Parker, Patricia A. *Inescapable Romance: Studies in the Poetics of a Mode*. Princeton: Princeton Univ. Press, 1979.

Pelikan, Jaroslav. *Reformation of Church and Dogma (1300–1700)*. Vol. 4 of *The Christian Tradition: A History of the Development of Doctrine*. Chicago: Univ. of Chicago Press, 1983.

Perreiah, Alan. "Humanistic Critiques of Scholastic Dialectic." *The Sixteenth Century Journal* 13 (1982): 3–22.

Pine, Martin L. "Pietro Pomponazzi and the Medieval Tradition of God's Foreknowledge." In *Philosophy and Humanism: Renaissance Essays in Honor of Paul*

Oskar Kristeller, ed. Edward P. Mahoney, 100–15. New York: Columbia Univ. Press, 1976. 100–115.

———. *Pietro Pomponazzi: Radical Philosopher of the Renaissance*. Padua: Antenore, 1986.

Polizzi, Gilles. "Thélème ou l'éloge du don: Le texte rabelaisien à la lumière de l'*Hypnerotomachia Poliphili*." *Réforme, Humanisme, Renaissance* 25 (1988): 39–59.

Prince, Gerald. "Introduction à l'étude du narrataire." *Poétique* 4 (1973): 178–96.

Quint, David. "Astolfo's Voyage to the Moon." *Yale Italian Studies* 1 (1977): 398–408.

———. *Origin and Originality in Renaissance Literature: Versions of the Source*. New Haven: Yale Univ. Press, 1983.

Rebhorn, Wayne A. "The Burdens and Joys of Freedom: An Interpretation of the Five Books of Rabelais." *Etudes rabelaisiennes* 9 (1971): 71–90.

———. *Courtly Performances: Masking and Festivity in Castiglione's Book of the Courtier*. Detroit: Wayne State Univ. Press, 1978.

Regosin, Richard L. *The Matter of My Book: Montaigne's 'Essais' as the Book of the Self*. Berkeley: Univ. of California Press, 1977.

Reiss, Timothy J. *The Discourse of Modernism*. Ithaca: Cornell Univ. Press, 1982.

Riesenhuber, Klaus. *Die Transzendenz der Freiheit zum Guten: Der Wille in der Anthropologie und Metaphysik des Thomas von Aquin*. Munich: Berchmannskolleg Verlag, 1971.

Rigolot, François. "Du Bellay et la poésie du refus." *Bibliothèque d'Humanisme et Renaissance* 36 (1974): 489–502.

———. *Le texte de la Renaissance: Des rhétoriqueurs à Montaigne*. Geneva: Droz, 1982.

Riley, Patrick. *The General Will before Rousseau: The Transformation of the Divine into the Civic*. Princeton: Princeton Univ. Press, 1986.

Rutner, Vinzenz. "*Homo secundus Deus*. Eine geistesgeschichtliche Studie zum menschlichen Schöpfertum." *Philosophisches Jahrbuch* 63 (1954): 248–91.

Saccone, Eduardo. "*Grazia, Sprezzatura, Affettazione* in the *Courtier*." In *Castiglione: The Ideal and the Real in Renaissance Culture*, ed. Robert W. Hanning and David Rosand, 45–67. New Haven: Yale Univ. Press, 1983.

Saffrey, H. D. " 'Cy n'entrez pas, hypocrites . . .': Thélème, une nouvelle académie? [Rabelais, *Gargantua*, chap. LII (LIV)]." *Revue des sciences philosophiques et théologiques* 55 (1971): 593–614.

Said, Edward. *Beginnings: Intention and Method*. New York: Basic Books, 1975.

Saulnier, Verdun-L. "L'utopie en France: Morus et Rabelais." In *Les utopies à la Renaissance*, 137–62. Paris: Presses univ. de France, 1963.

———. *Rabelais dans son enquête*. Vol. 1 of *Rabelais*. Paris: SEDES, 1983.

Schmitt, Charles B. *Studies in Renaissance Philosophy and Science*. London: Variorum Reprints, 1981.

Schramm, Hans-Peter. "Zur Geschichte des Wortes 'obligatio' von der Antike bis Thomas von Aquin." *Archiv für Begriffsgeschichte* 11 (1967): 119–47.

Screech, Michael Andrew. "Some Stoic Elements in Rabelais's Religious Thought (The Will-Destiny-Active Virtue)." *Etudes rabelaisiennes* 1 (1956): 73–97.

Screech, Michael Andrew. *The Rabelaisian Marriage. Aspects of Rabelais's Religion, Ethics and Comic Philosophy*. London: Arnold, 1958.

———. *L'évangélisme de Rabelais: Aspects de la satire religieuse au XVIe siècle*. Etudes rabelaisiennes 2. Geneva: Droz, 1959.

———. *Rabelais*. Ithaca: Cornell Univ. Press, 1979.

Seeberg, Reinhold. *Lehrbuch der Dogmengeschichte*. Vol. 3. Darmstadt: Wissenschaftliche Buchgesellschaft, 1959.

Silver, Isidore. "Pierre de Ronsard: Panegyrist, Pensioner, and Satirist of the French Court." *Romanic Review* 45 (1954): 89–108.

Smith, Pauline M. *The Anti-Courtier Trend in Sixteenth-Century French Literature*. Travaux d'Humanisme et Renaissance 84. Geneva: Droz, 1966.

Soulié, Marguerite. *L'inspiration biblique dans la poésie religieuse d'Agrippa d'Aubigné*. Paris: Klincksieck, 1977.

Steinmetz, David C. "Calvin and the Absolute Power of God." *Journal of Medieval and Renaissance Studies* 18 (1988): 65–79.

Tetel, Marcel. *Etude sur le comique de Rabelais*. Florence: L. S. Olschki, 1964.

Thompson, Craig R. "Better Teachers than Scotus Or Aquinas." In *Medieval and Renaissance Studies*, ed. John L. Lievsay, 2:114–45. Proceedings of the Institute of Medieval and Renaissance Studies, Summer 1966. Durham, N.C.: Duke Univ. Press, 1968.

Tierney, Brian. " 'The Prince Is Not Bound by the Laws.' Accursius and the Origins of the Modern State." *Comparative Studies in Society and History* 5 (1963): 378–400.

Todorov, Tzvetan. *Poétique*. Vol. 2 of *Qu'est-ce que le structuralisme?* Paris: Seuil, 1973.

Tournon, André. *Montaigne: La glose et l'essai*. Lyons: Presses univ. de Lyon, 1983.

Trinkaus, Charles. *In Our Image and Likeness: Humanity and Divinity in Italian Humanist Thought*. 2 vols. London: Constable, 1970.

———. *The Scope of Renaissance Humanism*. Ann Arbor: Univ. of Michigan Press, 1983.

———. "Italian Humanism and Scholastic Theology." In *Renaissance Humanism: Foundations, Forms, and Legacy*, ed. Albert Rabil, Jr., 3:327–48. Philadelphia: Univ. of Pennsylvania Press, 1988.

Uhlig, Claus. *Hofkritik im England des Mittelalters und der Renaissance: Studien zu einem Gemeinplatz der europäischen Moralistik*. Berlin: Walter de Gruyter, 1973.

Ullmann, Walter. *Law and Politics in the Middle Ages: An Introduction to the Sources of Medieval Political Ideas*. Ithaca: Cornell Univ. Press, 1975.

Urban, Linwood. "Was Luther a Thoroughgoing Determinist?" *Journal of Theological Studies*, n.s. 22 (1971): 117–33.

Vignaux, Paul. *Le nominalisme au XIVe siècle*. Montreal: Institut d'études médiévales, 1948.

Walker, D. P. *Spiritual and Demonic Magic from Ficino to Campanella*. Leiden: Warburg Institute, 1958.

Weinberg, Florence M. *The Wine and the Will: Rabelais's Bacchic Christianity*. Detroit: Wayne State Univ. Press, 1972.

Weinberg, Julius Rudolph. *Nicolaus of Autrecourt: A Study in 14th-Century Thought*. Princeton: Princeton Univ. Press, 1948.

Weller, Barry L. "The Rhetoric of Friendship in Montaigne's *Essais*." *New Literary History* 9 (1977–1978): 503–23.

Whigham, Frank. *Ambition and Privilege: The Social Tropes of Elizabethan Courtesy Theory*. Berkeley: Univ. of California Press, 1984.

White, John. *The Birth and Rebirth of Pictorial Space*. London: Faber and Faber, 1967.

Wilson, W. Daniel. "Readers in Texts." *PMLA* 96 (1981): 848–63.

Wolter, Allan B., o.f.m. *Duns Scotus on the Will and Morality*. Washington, D.C.: Catholic Univ. of America Press, 1986.

INDEX